THE EVOLUTION
OF AMERICAN SOCIETY,
1700–1815

CIVILIZATION AND SOCIETY

Studies in Social, Economic, and Cultural History

General Editor

Theodore K. Rabb, Princeton University

Consulting Editors

Thomas W. Africa, State University of New York, Binghamton
David J. Herlihy, University of Wisconsin, Madison
David S. Landes, Harvard University
Henry Rosovsky, Harvard University
Stanley J. Stein, Princeton University
Stephan A. Thernstrom, University of California, Los Angeles

THE EVOLUTION OF AMERICAN SOCIETY, 1700-1815

An Interdisciplinary Analysis

James A. Henretta
University of California, Los Angeles

D. C. HEATH AND COMPANY
Lexington, Massachusetts   Toronto   London

To Thomas and John Henretta

PREFACE

Most books about American history deal primarily with *public* events, with the activities of individuals as they are manifest in the formal institutions of economy, society, or polity. If it is included at all, historical data relating to family life, religious and cultural activities, or social life is relegated to a few separate and prosaic chapters. Thus segregated and subordinated, this rich and vital material lies inert and lifeless on the page; it does not exert leverage on the crucial questions of historical interpretation.

This dichotomy between private experience and public activity is artificial and misleading. The lives of men and women constitute an integrated and indivisible whole; and so also does the multi-dimensional social space in which they work out the possibilities of their existence. In all societies, both past and present, the personal and private is also the public and political.

This fundamental insight has long been obscured by the paucity of theoretical or conceptual models which would permit the historian to visualize the social system as a single interrelated whole. Only those writers who benefited from the analytical technique bequeathed to posterity by Karl Marx were able, in some measure, to escape this fragmented (and therefore distorted) view of historical reality.

With the utilization by growing numbers of historians of the methods and assumptions of the modern social sciences, the situation has been dramatically altered. Demographic analyses of past populations have begun to reveal the basic patterns of birth, marriage, and death and to hint at the psychological and cultural implications of particular forms of family life and household organization. At the same time anthropological studies of cultural units and sociological investigations of class, status, and power have revealed the intimate connection which exists between the family and the wider structure of community life. Other studies of political organization, of psychological maturation, and of economic change have disclosed the myriad threads of causation which link the various facets of social existence. In the end, the underlying unity of all aspects of human life has emerged with startling clarity.

With this conceptual advance, the elucidation of pattern, configuration, and direction has replaced the study of discrete acts, facts, and events as the major concern of historical and social analysis. It is no longer sufficient simply to describe what happened, or even to "explain" individual occurrences in terms of cause and effect. This approach is too limited, too static, too linear. The new vision of reality has created a new method and a new vocabulary; we speak of the political *process;* of economic *development;* of the *context* of social action; of ecological *relationships;* of the *direction* of social change. The emphasis is one of motion, not inertia; and the assumption is that the lives of individual historical actors can only be understood in terms of a larger dynamic whole. Thus the structure and the content of this book: the evolution (the growth and structural differentiation) of an entire social system through time.

Students and colleagues at the University of Sussex and at Princeton University helped me to formulate many of the concepts and interpretations in this book. The final draft was completed while I was teaching on a Fulbright Fellowship at the University of New England in Australia. The book was read in manuscript by Gary B. Nash, who offered a series of valuable suggestions; by Stanley Engerman, whose criticisms saved me from a number of errors and prompted me to restate some of my propositions; and by John Gillis, whose incisive critique forced me to make a number of specific arguments more precise and showed me the way to make my overall interpretation more coherent. My greatest debts, however, are to those scholars whose data and ideas I have used.

CONTENTS

PLATES

MAPS

CHARTS

AN OVERVIEW

To study the laws of history we must completely change the subject of our observation, must leave aside kings, ministers, and generals, and study the common infinitesimally small elements by which the masses are moved. No one can say in how far it is possible for man to advance in this way toward an understanding of the laws of history; but it is evident that only along that path does the possibility of discovering the laws of history lie.

Tolstoy, *War and Peace*

History is the study of change over time. Some of this change is cyclical in character, the reflection of certain basic regularities in nature. Day changes into night, winter into spring, one year into the next. In the past these natural rhythms exercised considerable influence over the lives of all men and women; indeed, they constituted the overarching framework within which all experience took place. Mankind slept when natural light failed, planted and reaped as the seasons dictated, and struggled against the rigors of the environment to maintain life itself.

These simple yet demanding regularities, characteristic of the lives of most humans both past and present, no longer constitute the basic ingredients of American existence. Millions of Americans still measure the passage of time and of events by the seasonal clock of agricultural life, but they are now in a distinct minority. Their habits, customs, and way of life do not reflect the experience of the nation as a whole.

It was not always so. Between 1700 and 1815

1

the overwhelming majority of Americans, black and white, rich and poor, lived on the land and received their daily sustenance from its produce. Their lives were different from ours; and yet their accomplishments are of the first importance to us. For it was the men and women of the eighteenth century who established the United States as a separate political entity and who initiated the long process which eventually transformed the new nation into an urban and industrial society.

In 1815 this era of development had barely begun. There were few cities and even fewer large manufacturing enterprises. And yet great changes had already taken place. The population had increased from 250,000 in 1700 to more than 8.5 million in 1815, and the number of people in Boston, New York, and Philadelphia exceeded the total continental population of a century before. An equally impressive economic alteration had also taken place. In little more than a hundred years the American settlements had emerged as the primary suppliers of wheat, tobacco, and cotton to the markets of Europe and had amassed one of the largest merchant fleets in the entire world.

This period of American history was marked therefore not only by the cyclical and essentially repetitive change of the agricultural year but also by a cumulative and irreversible modification of the character of American life. Small gains in population, in economic development, and in political maturity were compounded and amplified from decade to decade and from generation to generation. By 1815 American society was very different—much larger, more diverse, and with much greater structural differentiation—from what it had been at the end of the seventeenth century.

The organization of this book reflects this historical reality.* Its emphasis is on those events and processes which prompted this pattern of cumulative change. Between 1700 and 1775 this dynamic role was assumed by demographic growth and economic development. In more than a figurative sense the size and nature of the population and the extent and the complexity of the economy outgrew the institutional framework which had been inherited from the past. By the sixth decade of the century people's actions no longer conformed to accepted norms, and the extant principles of government could no longer encompass the divergent social reality.

*The British West Indies are included until 1775 both because their existence affected imperial policy with regard to the mainland and because neither southern slavery nor the economic development of the North can be understood without reference to the islands.

With the outbreak of the war for independence in 1775, this cultural lag—this sharp dichotomy between private behavior and public doctrine—was gradually redressed. Some of the implications of the preceding period of social change had already found fulfillment (during the decade of anti-imperial agitation) in the form of a revolutionary ideology, and the adumbration of a new system of values was underway. The subsequent process of incorporating these principles in new institutions of government and in new forms of social and economic organization constituted one of the most creative and propulsive elements in the formative years of the new nation. By 1815 the always-tenuous equilibrium between ideology and action had been at least partially restored.

Yet even as this congruence was being achieved, new lines of cleavage and new sources of tension were appearing in the United States. Some of these, such as the growth of an urban and a rural proletariat, had roots which extended far back into the economic and demographic history of the colonial period; others were the product of the war for independence and of the revolutionary ideology which it legitimized. For in a nation formally dedicated to the principles of liberty and equality, hundreds of thousands of blacks were still held in slavery; millions of women were denied a full legal identity and the rights of citizenship; and much of the population was refused a just access to the country's wealth. This disparity between the myths of the new republic and the actual social and economic structure was to be an acute source of conflict during the subsequent history of the new nation. One cycle of dialectical change had run its course and a new and different cycle was about to begin.

But what of the actors in this cumulative historical drama? Thousands of people acted in roughly congruent patterns during the years between 1700 and 1815: bearing large numbers of children, building a new type of economy, creating through their behavior a new set of ideological principles, offering their allegiance to new institutions of government. This mass participation in the development of American society will be analyzed here—not the lives of the famous statesmen, politicians, and merchants; for it was the experiences, strivings, and beliefs of the great multitude of men and women that determined the context within which the heroes lived and worked and prescribed the limits within which they could take effective action. Then, as now, this vital fact has too often gone unnoticed.

The poor man's conscience is clear [remarked John Adams]; yet he is ashamed. . . . He feels himself out of the sight of others, groping in the dark. Mankind takes no notice of him. He rambles and wanders unheeded. In the midst of a crowd, at church, in the market . . . he is in as much obscurity as he would be in a garret or a cellar. He is not disapproved, censured, or reproached; he is only not seen.

Before 1815 America was a preindustrial society. This was not unusual in the least. Before the industrial revolution in England during the second half of the eighteenth century created a new form of social and economic organization, all cultures had exhibited this one central characteristic. More interesting and more significant was the fact that two new and distinct *types* of preindustrial civilization had developed in the English colonies as early as 1700. The first, located geographically in the southern part of the mainland and in the islands of the West Indies, was based upon the exportation of staple crops to the European market and was defined by its central institution: the system of racial slavery. This "plantation" society, the product of the territorial and commercial expansion of early modern Europe, was an historically new creation; there had never been anything quite like it before.

The same was true (although to a lesser degree) of the settlements to the north of the Chesapeake Bay. The inhabitants of this area were mostly small freeholders—purposeful and resourceful tillers of the soil—who were joined together in self-governing communities. The extent of the self-sufficiency and the independence of these settlers and these communities clearly differentiated them from their European antecedents. No less than the racially divided culture to the south, the northern colonies had produced a unique type of social order.

POPULATION AND SOCIETY IN THE NORTH

Northern Agricultural Society

Until 1700 the small-scale agriculture of the northern colonies was directed primarily toward providing sustenance for the resident population. Some households might sell produce in the towns or even export it to the West Indies, but for most of the inhabitants farming was more a way of life than a way of making money. This pattern of subsistence rather than commercial production was not a

new phenomenon; it had been one of the basic characteristics of many European peasant societies in the centuries preceding the settlement of America. And yet these pioneers were not really "peasants," for they did not possess the settled culture of the traditional rural cultivators; nor were they burdened by the latter's restrictive world view and their subordination to outside social and political authorities.

There were several reasons for this. When Englishmen began to settle in the new world in 1607, the old legal restraints on the peasantry had already been abolished and the country was experiencing a period of rapid social and demographic transition. In the century after 1540 the English population doubled, setting in motion other changes in family structure and social behavior. At the same time extensive enclosures of old open-field communities created a considerable body of landless laborers and produced an extraordinary amount of geographical mobility. By 1641, one English historian has estimated, only 16% of the agricultural population had a hundred years in the same village behind them.

Those who migrated to New England (and later to New York and Pennsylvania) during the seventeenth century, therefore, did not bring with them the values and assumptions of a settled peasant society. The shared language and customs of the first migrants—even the rigorous principles of Puritan ideology which infused the minds and hearts of many—were only the bare ingredients of a unified and integrated culture. They would have to be blended and refined by the passage of time before they could take shape as a viable social entity. If there was to be an American peasantry, it would have to be created anew, from the slow organic growth of a coherent culture within the confines of the new environment.

And, in point of fact, the rudiments of an indigenous peasant society appeared during the second and third generation of settlement, among those American colonists who came to maturity between 1680 and 1740. Following the death of the first migrants, many of whom were highly educated and intellectually vigorous men and women, the new settlements were unable to generate or even to maintain an independent cultural life. Harvard College, founded in a burst of intellectual enthusiasm in 1636, soon regressed to the level of a provincial seminary for the New England ministry. Isolated in the wilderness, these agricultural communities had been transformed from autonomous offshoots of the civilization of the mother country into dependent "part-societies" with a "part-culture" that was no more than a pale, partial reflection of the English model. The life of the mind had atrophied in America: intellectual discourse and cultural conduct had lost its vitality and creativity. All that remained was a derivative rural "folk" version of the dynamic civilization of the urban centers of England.

There were other respects, however, in which these colonial settlements escaped the stultifying dependence characteristic of peasant life. After 1700 more and more of the migrants began to produce wheat, cattle, and horses for sale in the coastal cities and in the West Indies. One index of this growing involvement in a commercial economy was the appearance of paper currency in Massachusetts by the 1690's and in most of the other mainland colonies by 1715. This shift in the focus of agricultural activity brought with it changes in perception and in behavior. Land and labor came increasingly to be seen not as the source of livelihood but as commodities which could be bought and sold in the pursuit of wealth and status. Considerations of profit, of possessions, of economic calculation came to figure prominently in the lives of men, inhibiting the development of moribund farming communities with fixed social norms and precapitalistic values.

This newly found economic strength bolstered the long-standing political autonomy of these self-governing towns and villages. The system of exploitation characteristic of most peasant societies—the arbitrary demands and sanctions imposed by outside political, social, or religious elites—was absent here. The institutions of local government and of provincial representation were more than sufficient to offset the power of the imperial governor sent over from England and to ensure that the overwhelming preponderance of tax receipts were used for local purposes. Thus, one Scotch-Irish immigrant in New York wrote in 1737:

Read this letter, Rev. Baptist Boyd, and look and tell all the poor folk of ye place that God has opened a door for their deliverance . . . for here all that a man works for is his own; and there are no revenue hounds to take it from us here . . . no one to take away yer Corn, yer Potatoes, yer Lint or yer Eggs. . . .[1]

Culturally dependent, yet economically progressive and politically independent, northern agricultural society during the eighteenth century represented a strange blend of passivity and vitality, of traditional and modern elements. Taken together, however, it was clear that the forces of change outweighed those of stability. There was a certain disquietude, a certain dynamism, which infused the lives of these settlers and which pushed constantly (and naggingly) toward improvement, experimentation, and risk. "The desire of finding better," Brissot de Warville noted during his travels in the new United States, "embitters the enjoyment even of the inhabitants of Connecticut. . . ." [2]

It was this aggressive psychological outlook which most clearly differentiated the inhabitants of eighteenth century America from a traditional peasantry. Very little in their behavior suggested the existence of a mental world dominated by an "image of limited good," the cognitive orientation often produced in peasant societies by the paucity of uncultivated lands and by the general scarcity of material wealth and resources. Some of the ingredients of this restrictive world-view—this conception of social reality within which the increase of production was seen as a threat to the established way of life—had been imported by the first migrants as part of their cultural baggage. How else can one explain the initial insistence on a compact pattern of settlement and on the cautious allocation of tiny 20-acre plots of land in the midst of thousands of square miles of virtually unoccupied territory?

But these mental residues of the old life and of the old conditions were gradually erased by experience—by a fresh perception of the possibilities and alternatives afforded by the new environment. J. Hector St. John de Crevecoeur wrote from his farm in New York in the 1780's, that

A European, when he first arrives, seems limited in his intentions, as well as in his views; but he very suddenly alters his scale; two hundred miles formerly appeared a very great distance, it is now but a trifle; he no sooner breathes our air than he forms schemes, and embarks in designs he never would have thought of in his own country. There the plenitude of society confines many useful ideas and often extinguishes the most laudable schemes which here ripen into maturity.[3]

Even before the death of the first generation, the lands of the New England towns had begun to be distributed in royal fashion, and the nucleated villages had given way to widely dispersed holdings.

Here were the first tentative signs of a new cognitive orientation, an "image of unlimited good," a set of half-conscious, unverbalized assumptions that reflected a perception of the opportunities for accumulation of material possessions through purposeful action and risky entrepreneurial behavior. In time this intuitive reaction to the possibilities inherent in the natural and in the social environment would become a pervasive feature of the behavior of hundreds of thousands of Americans. "What most astonishes me in the United States," Tocqueville would comment in 1835, "is not so much the marvelous grandeur of some undertakings as the innumerable multitude of small ones." [4]

By the middle of the eighteenth century this expansive mentality had been buttressed by decades of political autonomy and of economic growth. These changes were now complemented by the first signs of cultural independence. No fewer than five new colleges were founded in the three decades beginning in 1745, impressive testimony to the resurgence of intellectual and religious vitality. Suffusing all of this varied activity was the confident state of mind which had come to distinguish the inhabitants of these rapidly growing colonies. "They are men and women whose features are not marked by poverty, by life-long deprivation of the necessities of life, or by a feeling that they are insignificant subjects and subservient members of society." [5] In this remark of yet another French observer we can detect that quality of personal autonomy and psychological independence among the broad masses of the people which constituted the unique and the historically new aspect of this preindustrial agricultural society.

Population Growth and the Disease Environment

The self-confident attitude of the colonists was at once a cause and a result of a high rate of population growth. During the first three-quarters of the eighteenth century the population of the northern settlements increased from 144,000 to 1,260,000 and that of the entire continent from 250,000 to 2,500,000. The American colonies were growing at the rate of 3% per annum, thus doubling their size every 25 years. Since English growth languished at the rate of 0.5% per annum until 1750 and about 0.8% thereafter, this sustained increase in the American population effected a dramatic shift in the balance of power within the British empire. There were 20 Englishmen for every American colonist in 1700; by 1775 this ratio had fallen to 3 to 1.

This remarkable alteration was the subject of considerable contemporary comment. As early as 1745 William Shirley, the royal governor of Massachusetts Bay, predicted that the colonies would soon have more inhabitants than France, then the most populous country in western Europe. Six years later Benjamin Franklin again called attention to this phenomenal growth in his influential *Essay on the Increase of Mankind*. And by 1770 Ezra Stiles, the circumspect future president of Yale College, could confidently observe in his diary that English would probably "become the vernacular Tongue of more people than any one Tongue on Earth, except the Chinese."

Immigration was one cause of this population explosion.

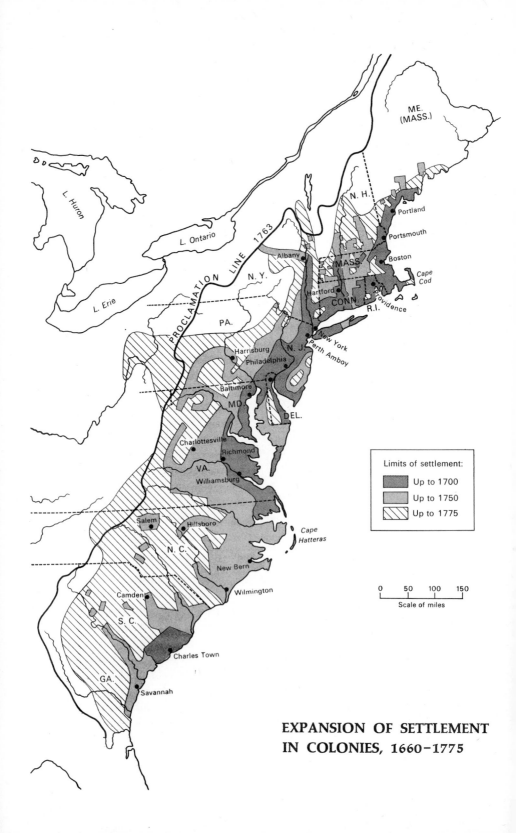

EXPANSION OF SETTLEMENT
IN COLONIES, 1660–1775

Table 1.1
Population of the British Empire in the Eighteenth Century

Year	Mainland America Population (millions)	Index No.	England and Wales Population (millions)	Index No.	Ireland Population (millions)	Index No.
1687	—	—	—	—	2.2	100
1700	0.25	100	5.2	100	—	—
1725	0.57	228	5.8	111	3.1	140
1750	1.17	448	6.5	125	—	—
1767	—	—	—	—	3.5	161
1775	2.5	1,000	7.8	150	—	—
1781	—	—	—	—	4.1	187
1800	5.3	2,120	9.6	185	5.3	241

SOURCE: Compiled from *Historical Statistics of the United States*, Ser. Z 1–19; and B. H. Van Bath, *The Agrarian History of Western Europe* (St. Martin, 1963), p. 91.

Between 1700 and 1775 nearly 400,000 white settlers and indentured servants, mostly of English, Scottish, Irish, or German origin, migrated to the American mainland. The great majority of these immigrants were young adults at the time of their arrival, and therefore eventually bore more children than a group of the same size with a less favorable age distribution. Still, large families were not unique to immigrant groups and the predominance of males among the new colonists was not conducive to rapid growth. In the end foreign migration accounted for only about one-quarter of the expansion in the size of the white population.

The greater part of the increment came, rather, from natural increase. As Franklin noted, the ready availability of land in the new world permitted sons and daughters to marry at an early age, while the acute shortage of labor prompted parents to have children at regular intervals. The possibilities inherent in the environment had induced hundreds and thousands of young people to decide—quite independently of one another—to marry early and to bear offspring in large numbers.

The question of "decision" in these matters was a very real one, for even before the appearance of modern methods of birth control, societies had devised a number of ways by which to keep the size of the population within the limits imposed by the exigencies of agricultural production. One of the most effective of these social customs, and one that was practiced in the European cultures from which the white settlers had come, was to control the incidence and the age of marriage. During the seventeenth and the eighteenth centuries many European women, of all classes, did not marry at all; those that did delayed marriage until their mid- or late 20's, and thus rarely bore more than eight children. This was partly the result of biology, since the woman's fertile period ended approximately at age 45; and partly the product of the cultural habit of breast feeding which, by inhibiting conception, resulted in a normal interval between births of 23 to 28 months. Then, too, the death of one or both parents often kept family size well below the biological and cultural maximum. In one French village during the first half of the eighteenth century, the average number of births per marriage was only four.

The transplantation of European society to the new world effected a marked change in this established demographic pattern. During the first wave of American settlement in the seventeenth century the average age-at-marriage for women dropped to 20 or 21 years. This dramatic decrease, sufficient in itself to produce two more births per marriage, was in part a result of the temporary scarcity of women in new-world communities. When natural increase raised the proportion of women in the total population, the average age-at-marriage began to revert to the traditional European norm. In Andover, Massachusetts, for example, this figure rose from a mere 19 years in the second half of the seventeenth century to 23 or 24 years a century later.

This alteration produced a corresponding decline in the number of births per marriage. The first generation of settlers in Andover produced an average of 8.3 children per completed marriage (one in which both parents survived to age 45), but this mean fell to 7.2 births when the third generation bore its children during the first three decades of the eighteenth century. By then the average for all marriages in the town was even lower— a mere 4.8 births per marriage—a brute reminder of the number of conjugal unions disrupted by death, increased migration to the frontier, and a deliberate policy of birth control. It was only in the first generation in a given community, therefore, that a low age-at-marriage for women was the reason for a significantly higher rate of reproduction; subsequently it was the much higher proportion of women who married which raised the American level of natural increase above the European norm.

A second (and perhaps more important) cause of the rapid growth of the American population was the low rate of mortality—what Governor Shirley referred to as the "Healthfulness of the Climates on this Continent." Here again there was a remarkable contrast to the European experience. Infant deaths accounted for nearly 25% of all burials in Sweden between 1751 and 1799, and child mortality (in this case deaths between the ages of 1 and 15) for an additional 25%. An identical pattern appeared in the French village of Crulai where 40% of all children born died by the age of 10, and 50% by age 21. In these European societies fully one-half of the children born never reached an age where they themselves would bear offspring. Those who did survive, therefore, had to have at least 4 births per marriage simply to keep the population at a constant level.

This slow and fitful pattern of population growth—hampered still further by war, limited supplies of new land, and the twin scourges of famine and disease—was broken in America by a startling decline in the rate of infant and child mortality. In both Andover and Plymouth, Massachusetts, nearly nine of ten children born before 1700 survived to age 20. When these youngsters grew to maturity, married, and began to bear offspring themselves, they set in motion an everwidening dynamic of population growth.

The healthfulness of the American environment was the result of both the low density of settlement and the character of economic activity. The small size of the agricultural communities, the great distance between them, and their isolation from the mainstreams of commerce made them pleasant and wholesome to live in. The land was bountiful in its produce, and any outbreak of an infectious disease affected only a very limited area. These benefits of geographical segregation were present in some areas of Europe as well: As late as the 1840's the Swedish county of Jointland, secluded on the Norwegian border, had a crude death rate of 13 per 1000 per year, just half that of the metropolitan area of Stockholm.

In America, as in Europe, the incidence of disease and death was not arbitrary and accidental, but conformed to a wider configuration of economic development and population density. The crude death rate in Boston, Massachusetts, averaged 37 per 1000 during most of the eighteenth century, a clear reflection of crowded living conditions and endemic disease in a port city. In 1722 a smallpox epidemic took the lives of 840 of the town's inhabitants, nearly 8% of the total population. Young children were particularly vulnerable in the biologically hazardous urban environment. Roughly one-half of all deaths in Philadelphia in the 1780's were youths under the age of 10. Given this high rate of infant and child mortality in the cities, it was the creation of a surplus population in the countryside and the immigration from abroad which permitted a steady increase in the size and the importance of the urban areas.

With the increase of travel, trade, and population during the eighteenth century, the harsh disease environment of the established maritime centers spread outward into the hinterland. There were severe outbreaks of infectious dysentery in New England in 1745, 1756, and 1775, as soldiers and militiamen carried the contagion out from their crowded barracks and camps. Many towns had one-half of their inhabitants stricken in these epidemics. The infection was so debilitating (especially to the very old and the very young) that epidemics normally took the lives of 5 to 10% of the population.

Even more serious, because they were intimately related to the rapid growth of the population itself, were the childhood diseases of measles and diphtheria. The increasing number of immigrants raised the possibility of contagion just at the time that the high birth rate was producing a more rapid renewal of nonimmune children. Between 1735 and 1737 a virulent diphtheria epidemic spread across the northern and middle colonies taking the lives of thousands, 95% of whom were age 20 or below. Once this outbreak had begun in New Hampshire, it spread inexorably from town to town and from colony to colony, because the high rate of natural increase had raised the proportion of nonimmune inhabitants above the point of safety. In the absence of preventive innoculations, there was nothing to do until the disease had burnt itself out.

The diphtheria epidemic of 1735–1737 provided clear proof, if any was needed, that the demographic characteristics of the heavily settled regions of the northern colonies had regressed to the European norm. Andover, Massachusetts, was a case in point. In 1760, after a century of uninterrupted growth which had raised the population of the town to 1,600 people, Andover entered a period of stagnation and actually decreased in size over the next 40 years. Part of this decline was the result of outmigration, as many inhabitants perceived the short supply of arable land within the town boundaries and moved elsewhere in search of better opportunities; while those that remained in town deliberately limited the size of their families (there was a steadily increasing interval between successive births). Finally, there was the restraint on population growth posed by the increasingly dangerous biological environment. Only half the children who were born and raised in the town survived to adulthood. This community, and many other "old" settlements, had reached the point of ecological balance; the forces working toward economic and demographic growth had been counteracted by those pushing toward decline and deterioration.

The situation was replete with irony. The momentous

achievements of the first century of settlement in the American wilderness had culminated not in utopia but in decline. The northern colonists had been too successful. Through their prosperity and their proliferation they had re-created the density of settlement and the intensity of disease they had left behind in Europe. Given the limits of their medical knowledge, they had reached the point of biological balance. Here then was a situation fraught with danger: all of the expansive values and psychological energies unleashed by a century of steady development in a bountiful environment and transmitted from one generation to the next would now be challenged by a new and a more restrictive set of material conditions.

Population Growth and Agricultural Change

Indeed, by 1750 many of the older regions of the American colonies were confronted by an agricultural as well as by an epidemiological crisis. During the first generations of settlement, the farms in the northern regions had been spacious; families commonly held title to 200 to 300 acres, of which at least 100 acres was prime arable land. These ample dimensions proved transitory in the face of rapid population growth. The average holding underwent a steady decline in size as farmers settled their sons on sections of the family property or sold portions to eager buyers at constantly rising prices. By the second half of the eighteenth century ordinary farms in New England and the middle colonies were rarely more than 100 acres, with a third in woodland and waste, a third in pasturage, and the final third in mowing lands and cultivated fields. The ratio between the proportions of the farm and the size of the household had steadily decreased. In fact, only one element had remained constant from the previous century: each year the farmer would plant crops on only 10 or 12 acres of his land.

The relatively small amount (and small percentage) of land under active cultivation at any one time was not the result of indolence but of technological restrictions. Plows of any sort were in short supply in the colonies and those that were available were extremely inefficient. The Carey plow, the most widely used instrument, generated so much friction because of its cumbersome construction that it needed two to three horses or four to six oxen to pull it. The more efficient Bull plow cultivated adequately with two to four oxen, but required the use of a second man. Even with such a large concentration of human labor and of animal power, a farmer could plow only an acre each day. Given the relatively short planting season in the spring,

Four contemporary woodcuts depicting farm activities. Note the heavy reliance on human labor and the gain in productivity following the substitution of the "cradle" for the ordinary sickle.

AGRICULTURAL CHANGE   **17**

particularly in New England, it was difficult to cultivate more than 12 acres in a given year, especially since draft animals often had to be borrowed from neighbors or relatives.

An equally stringent technological bottleneck appeared at the time of the fall harvest. Wheat began to sprout and oats started to rust unless they were gathered within ten days of maturity; and, using an ordinary hand sickle, a hard-working man could reap no more than half an acre a day. Even with the help of his wife (who was restricted by cultural practice to certain types of work) and his children, a farmer could not hope to harvest much more than ten or twelve acres unless he could stagger the ripening of his crops over an extended period of time.

The crucial problems posed by the short harvest season were alleviated somewhat during the 1760's and 1770's by the introduction of the "cradle," a long-handled scythe with a framework of long wooden fingers placed above the cutting blade. With this simple but ingenious implement the mower could cut the grain and, in the same motion, cradle it into a heap with the stalks perfectly aligned for gathering into a sheaf. This innovation more than tripled the output of a farm worker during harvest time, since an experienced mower could now cut nearly two acres of grain per day. However impressive this increase, it only hinted at the possibilities of technological development. By the 1840's a farmer using a horse-drawn self-raking reaper was able to cut ten to twelve acres in a single day, a twenty-fold increase in agricultural productivity.

Until these mechanical advances effected a major increase in the productivity of human labor, the farmers of the northern colonies could till only a small fraction of their total acreage each year. This did not mean, however, that the rest of the arable land was superfluous. On the contrary, this fallow land played a crucial role in the economic life of the farm. It was the hidden resource that differentiated colonial farming from that practiced in the more heavily populated and more finely subdivided lands of Europe.

On both sides of the Atlantic during the first half of the eighteenth century, a field was sown with grain until its fertility was considerably exhausted, usually in three years' time. The field would then be left fallow, perhaps for as long as a decade and a half, in order to restore its fertility. This system of extensive cultivation was possible only where land was abundant, since for a farmer to plant a new ten-acre field every three years and to provide for a fallow period of twelve years, he needed a full fifty acres of arable land. A reckless cultivator might choose to plant a new field every four years or to reduce the length of fallow, but either of these alternatives would result in a marked

Table 1.2
Planting Schedule for 50 Acres—with 12 Years of Fallow

Ten-Acre Field Number				
I	II	III	IV	V
1701–1703	1704–1706	1707–1709	1710–1712	1713–1715
1716–1718	1719–1721	1722–1724	1725–1727	1728–1730
1731–1733	1734–1736	1737–1739	1740–1742	1743–1745

Years Planted

decline in his annual yield and in the rapid exhaustion of his lands.

The rapid growth of the American population and the consequent decline in average farm size destroyed the advantage enjoyed by the early settlers over their European counterparts. By the 1770's the period of fallow in most of the northern colonies had been shortened drastically from 7 to 15 years to a mere 1 to 2 years. The colonists' once-prevalent pattern of extensive farming had given way to the European system of intensive land use and its annual cropping of all available arable land.

This transition, which had taken place very gradually in many countries of Europe during the previous two centuries (the result of a slow but steady increase in population), created two sorts of problems. The first, and most obvious, was preservation of the fertility of land under constant cultivation. It had to be plowed deeper, weeded more carefully, and fertilized more extensively. And this, of course, required more time and more labor. Even the greater availability of farm laborers to perform these tasks (for the appearance of a rural proletariat was another result of population growth) was small consolation to the farmer faced with the prospect of constantly declining yields.

The second difficulty was less apparent but no less real. This was to find ways of replacing the land which previously had been allowed to lie fallow. This land had been used as a pasture area for work animals, milk cows, and sheep; and now some other way had to be found to provide food for this livestock, for it was the presence of an ample number of farm animals which made a crucial difference in the economic fortunes of an agricultural household. Wool from the sheep was processed and made into clothing; cows supplied milk, cheese, and leather; and horses and oxen provided the bulk of the physical energy needed for cultivation. Finally, the manure of all these animals was the prime source of fertilizer, a factor of production which was needed even more now that the length of the fallow period had declined.

The shortage of adequate forage for livestock had been a problem in New England from the first years of settlement. The heavily wooded hillsides and the short growing season resulted in a chronic lack of hay or other suitable feed. Farmers would often overstock during the summer only to have large numbers of cattle and sheep die from lack of food during the long and harsh winters. The paucity of forage dictated the choice of work animals. Long after their importance had declined in the rest of the colonies, oxen continued as the primary draft animals in New England because they required only half the quantity of oats consumed by work horses.

In the more fertile and less hilly colonies of New York, New Jersey, and Pennsylvania the pressure of the animal population upon the available resources of feed reached a danger point only in the mid-eighteenth century. In 1748 the Swedish traveler Peter Kalm reported that the pasture lands in the older settlements in the middle colonies were failing because of "the great increase in cattle which devoured the annual grasses so rapidly that they had no opportunity to ripen and seed themselves." The continual subdivision of farm holdings and the consequent decline in the amount of fallow had made it impossible for most farms to support a great number of livestock.

This agricultural transformation had a direct effect upon the colonial diet. Traditionally the American settlers had been great consumers of meat. "That they eat larger quantities of Animal food [than at home] . . . is certain," reported one visitor to Virginia in the 1770's. "You can be contented with one joint of meat is a reproach frequently thrown into the teeth of an Englishman." [6] Such sentiments were voiced less frequently as the century progressed and meat gradually ceased to be the principal item in the diet of the more affluent classes. Dr. Benjamin Rush, the noted Philadelphia physician, observed that there had been a very beneficial "revolution in diet" between 1760 and 1810 because of the "profusion of winter and summer vegetables."

This was hardly the unqualified advance that Rush suggested. Green vegetables were certainly effective in preventing scurvy (which had been widespread among lower-class farmers and their families, who subsisted upon a monotonous diet of salt pork, Indian beans, and corn meal); but an increase in the consumption of potatoes and other vegetables also signaled a decline in the availability of low-priced meat. (Beef and pork prices were 1.7 times higher in Philadelphia in 1770 than they had been in 1725, while flour prices had risen by a factor of only 1.5.) The consequent substitution of vegetables and carbohydrates for protein-rich animal products proceeded directly from the disappearance of an extensive pattern of farming; since it took five to six times more land to produce the same amount of caloric energy in meat as in vegetables. The American diet was still clearly superior to that found in those European regions where annual cropping had been practiced for decades, but this advantage was steadily diminishing.

This shift in relative standards was the result not only of the declining ratio between arable land and population in America but also of the gradual improvement in European agriculture. By the first decades of the eighteenth century England and parts of the continent were on the threshold of an agricultural revolution. The stimulus for the experiments and innovations which eventually culminated in a marked increase in productivity came, in part, from the slowly increasing pressure of population upon resources. Faced with the growing scarcity of fallow land for pasture, progressive European farmers had begun to cultivate their lands intensively and to produce fodder crops in order to feed their farm animals.

Similar circumstances worked to bring about the same result in America. Forage crops—such as Timothy grass, cowpeas, and red clover—were now sown on uplands and artificial meadows, or planted during the short interval between grain crops on land previously left fallow. Gradually this rudimentary system of crop rotation took on a more coherent form. By the last decades of the century the gentlemen farmers of the James River region of Virginia had evolved a four-field schedule of rotation consisting of wheat planted over clover fallow, corn, wheat, and then clover turned in by deep plowing.

Although the introduction of fodder crops and field rotation in America owed something to the diffusion of English agricultural knowledge, of greater influence was the fact that hundreds of farmers were faced with new and trying conditions and were sufficiently astute and imaginative to experiment with new methods and new crops. If the gentry of Virginia were among the first to come to grips with the altered agricultural reality, it was partially because they had relatively few options. Tied to ancestral lands by an established status within their counties, the Virginians were literally forced to take remedial action.

The same conditions did not obtain in New England. The harsh climate and the rocky soil, along with deterioration in the ratio between resources and population, prompted many families to give up their small farms and to move southwestward to New York and Pennsylvania. Those who remained adapted as best they could to the new agricultural environment. The spread of rust in long-cultivated areas and the inroads made by the Hessian fly had banished the production of wheat from large areas. The declining fertility of the heavily used arable land constituted yet another reason for giving up the cultivation of grain crops (which could now be produced much more cheaply in the middle colonies) and for concentrating upon the production of cattle for market. This specialization of function was especially evident in areas with ready access to urban and West Indian markets. Fully two-thirds of all farm land in Essex County in Massachusetts was in pasture by 1801; and the land that was tilled (only 6% of the total) was mostly planted in Indian corn, a fine feed for livestock because of its high yields and luxuriant growth.

With this redeployment of resources, the pattern of agricultural activity in New England had come to approximate that found in much of England and in parts of northwestern Europe. This Atlantic-Celtic type of rural economy was dominated by the raising of sheep and cattle for sale (in the form of meat, wool, and hides) in the market. The extensive outfields of the farm were devoted to this purpose, while the small infields were intensively cultivated for domestic foodstuffs. This system of small-scale capitalistic enterprise had important social ramifications. Because it was convenient for each farmer to have direct access to his pasture lands, this mode of production discouraged settlement in the large nucleated villages favored by the first colonists. It acted instead like a centrifugal force, pushing individual families outward on to their own lands and making dispersed autonomous farmsteads the most common form of settlement.

The disappearance of compact village communities in New England tended to break down the attachment of individual farming families to a larger social unit. And it also placed the locus of authority and responsibility for the well-being of the next generation within the confines of the family unit. This, in turn, had its effect on the pattern of settlement, particularly through the creation of hundreds of small hamlets. In most cases these tiny settlements appeared over the course of two or three generations as neighboring farmers subdivided their lands among numerous progeny and as a number of these separate households congregated in a central area. The ties of community in these hamlets were almost indistinguishable from those of family and kinship.

A similar process of conglomeration also took place in the middle colonies as the pressure of rapid population growth gradually transformed the pattern of dispersed settlement which had been prevalent during the first decades of the eighteenth century. The craft and artisan industries which appeared in these small towns and villages absorbed some of the surplus agricultural population but, in the end, most of the population increase had to be accommodated by changes in the character of the rural economy. As the century progressed more and more of the total farm acreage was brought into annual or semiannual cultivation. By 1801 fully 40% of all farmland in the middle colonies was under the plow and many farmers, deprived of their pasture lands, concentrated on the production of wheat and flour for sale in the West Indies and in southern Europe.

By the beginning of the nineteenth century, then, American farming had become specialized along geographical lines. Under the pressure of population growth and the demands of a market economy the inhabitants of each region had adapted its system of production in order to exploit to the utmost the possibilities inherent in the agricultural environment. That this was not an automatic process—many peasant communities in various parts of the world have failed to respond creatively to these same pressures and have stagnated both economically and demographically—provides further testimony of the dynamic character of the agricultural sector of the American (and the English) economy. It was this type of change, this improvement of agricultural productivity through innovation and specialization, which was a prerequisite for the industrial revolution that would eventually occur in each of these societies.

Family and Community

In some societies at various times in world history, the need to create a system of authority and assistance exceeding that provided by the conjugal family unit has led to the formation of corporate or extended families. Neither of these alternatives developed in colonial America. Corporate families—patrilineal clans in which all of the male offspring are incorporated into the household of the father and, eventually, of the eldest brother—were not part of the English cultural heritage. Nor were extended families—those in which brothers and sisters or grandparents lived in the same household—very prevalent in seventeenth century England. Lacking the experience of these institutions, the individuals and families who migrated to the new world created nonfamilial organizations to provide the basic services of government and administration. Especially in New England, the colonists created strong and cohesive village communities to deal with the important questions of land distribution, taxation, public works, and the recruitment of specialist craftsmen.

This dependence on the community for the provision of the entire range of social, economic, and political services decreased steadily over time. Once the first hard years had passed, the settlers showed no desire to sacrifice familial autonomy to the demands of corporate existence. The early demise of cooperative farming, initially a necessity because of the lack of implements and the enormous task of land clearance, undermined the economic basis of village unity. The technical capabilities of each household had reached a point which maximized the effectiveness of the nuclear family settled on its own lands. The social existence of these families living in isolated homesteads gradually became distinct and separate from that of the community; the once pervasive interpenetration of family and society had come to an end.

The resulting pattern of social organization was based on conjugal family units living in separate households. A complete census of the residents of Bristol, Rhode Island, in 1689 disclosed a total population of 421, distributed among 70 families. Each of the 68 married couples in this small community occupied a separate dwelling. These households were rather large by modern standards—usually containing four, five, or six residents. This was both because of the large number of children (54% of the entire population) and because nearly every family had a servant. The latter were often young nephews and nieces of the householders, serving as apprentices or as laborers. In the education and the socialization of children, as in so many other spheres of life, the colonial family had begun to hold the wider society at a distance and to expand the zone of family life: The practice of sending children, during their formative years, into the homes of relatives confined primary emotional ties and affective bonds within the orbit of the kinship system.

There were very important economic forces pushing the pattern of social organization in this direction. In Massachusetts (and, after 1685, in Connecticut as well) the proprietors of a town divided the land granted them by the General Court among the heads of the households settling in the new community. This procedure, readily comprehensible in terms of the values and expectations brought by the majority of the migrants to America, placed the agricultural resources of these settlements in the hands of individual family units. Under this system, a potential inhabitant had to purchase an estate from a resident landowner or (increasingly during the eighteenth century) from an absentee speculator. Equally important, the children of each successive generation of settlers had to look to their parents rather than to the town meeting or the provincial government for a grant of land. In New England as in the middle colonies, the lack of economic and social power in the hands of the wider community had made the family the first refuge of the individual.

The transfer of land and the accumulated capital goods

from one generation to the next created a complex mosaic of kinship ties within each settlement. There were no fewer than 25 adult male members of the Abbot family resident in Andover, Massachusetts, in 1750, all of them patrilineal descendants of George Abbot I. Intermarried into a dozen different Andover families and related, in one way or another, to as many more, the Abbots inhabited a world in which the boundaries between family and community had once again become blurred. This family was not an "extended" one in the full sense of the term, for each conjugal unit continued to reside in a separate household, but the proliferation of related nuclear families had created a community based on the biological ties of family and kinship.

Here then was a complicated and even contradictory process of social evolution: by the middle of the eighteenth century in the northern American colonies there were thousands of small towns and villages in which the bonds of kinship helped to create a cohesive social unit and a strong sense of community. At the same time, however, the conjugal household had emerged as the primary economic and social unit, a fact which meant that the most important decisions were made with reference to the advantage of the nuclear family.

The considerable autonomy achieved by the various conjugal units shaped the character of family life during the first generations of colonization. In Andover, the sons of the original settlers married for the first time at an average age of 27, which was almost identical to the traditional European norm; while in Plymouth colony, only in the eighteenth century did the average age fall below 25 years. There were a number of reasons for this. The average age at death of the 30 men who settled in Andover before 1660 was 71 years, while that of the 138 men of the second generation was 65 years. The effect of the longevity of these settlers was accentuated by their determination to retain legal title to their lands until their deaths. With no other sources of livelihood available in these agricultural communities, the male children had little choice but to delay marriage, to work on the family farm, and to hope for the grant of economic independence in the paternal will.

The prospects were considerably wider for those colonists who came to maturity after 1700. Most of the inhabitants of Germantown, Pennsylvania, were "manufacturers," Peter Kalm noted in 1748; and thirty years later there were more than 100 master artisans in the town, engaged in 27 different trades. Similarly, at Lancaster, Pennsylvania, in 1786 there were 234 manufacturers among the 700 resident families. The expansion and diversification of economic life had created new types of employment, thus lessening the dependence of male children upon their fathers. Another set of developments was leading to the same result. Unable to settle all of their male offspring on the already subdivided family estate, fathers lost a vital measure of control over the lives of their children. The contours of family life, like those of the agricultural landscape, were being gradually altered by the rapid growth of population.

In these changed circumstances there were two broad sets of alternatives, each with many variations, open to those colonists who came to maturity and married during the eighteenth century. The first was to maintain the relatively high living standards of the preceding generations by limiting the number of their children. This, in fact, was the solution adopted in England itself during the seventeenth and eighteenth centuries. In the mother country thousands of parents maintained a low level of fertility by using preventive methods of birth control. As the marriage continued, the intervals between the births of children steadily lengthened. Determined to bear only the number of offspring for whom they could easily provide, these parents either practiced *coitus interruptus* or abstained from intercourse altogether.

The alternative was to ignore the difficulties posed by the pressure of population upon resources and to continue to have large numbers of children. This was the "choice" of thousands of Irish peasants during the century and a half following 1700 (as the population data in Table 1.1 clearly shows). This cultural decision was far-reaching in its ramifications: The eighteenth century saw a gradual transition in the Irish countryside, from an agricultural system based on animal husbandry to one heavily dependent on cultivation of the potato. There was a consequent shift from a meat to a cereal diet for the peasantry; and, in the nineteenth century, a massive migration of the surplus population to Australia, Canada, England, and the United States. By refusing to curb the size of their families, the Irish peasants had condemned their children to either a lower standard of living at home or exile in a foreign land.

The colonists in North America tended, on the whole, to follow the Irish rather than the English example. Before 1770, the average rate of population growth per decade was over 25% in New England and over 35% in the middle colonies, with much of the difference the result of trans-Atlantic migration. The growth rates of both regions declined noticably during the war for independence and increased sharply in the decade that followed (the result of delayed marriage and childbearing rather than fluctuations in immigration). Subsequently, however, there was a significant divergence. By the 1790's the middle Atlantic states were growing at twice the rate of their northeastern

Table 1.3
Percentage Increase, by Decade, of the White American Population

							Last Year of Decade					
	1710	1720	1730	1740	1750	1760	1770	1780	1790	1800	1810	1820
New England	24	48	27	33	24	25	29	23	42	21	20	13
Middle colonies	29	48	41	46	33	47	32	30	42	47	44	34
Connecticut	52	49	28	19	24	28	29	12	15	5	4	5
New York	13	71	32	31	20	53	39	29	61	73	62	43

SOURCE: Computed from *Historical Statistics*, Ser. Z 1–19.

counterparts. Indeed, New York was increasing the number of its inhabitants 8 to 14 times as fast as neighboring Connecticut.

This disparity was not so much the product of the restriction of fertility by the inhabitants of New England as of their massive migration to the southwest. When the pressure of population upon resources came to be felt in Kent, Connecticut, in the last decades of the eighteenth century, no fewer than ten different families—many of them descended from the original settlers of the colony—moved across the border to the fertile lands of Amenia, New York. By that time in Kent (which had been settled only in the 1740's), there were 209 adult males on 103 separate homesteads; the birth rate remained high, but these subdivided Connecticut farms would support only a single heir.

The "demographic transition," the shift in the schedule of fertility from the Irish to the English pattern, thus came very slowly in the agricultural society of North America. One reason may have been the increased autonomy of the nuclear family. The communal sanctions which had kept reproduction within acceptable limits in many parts of Europe were absent in the new world. It became necessary for individual families to develop their own internalized system of restraints and to develop their own priorities. Such a massive cultural transformation takes time.

Since, in Europe, an average of 5 births per marriage had been the usual prerequisite for even a slow rate of population growth, these families may have been misled by historical experience. There was no way the settlers could have known that high rates of marriage and low rates of child mortality in sparsely settled areas would completely discredit the traditional formula. Also, many may have been willing to bear large numbers of children because of their perception of the possibility of migration to the frontier. Their own experience (or that of their parents) had demonstrated the feasibility of such an enterprise; they could feel, with some justice, that their fecundity would not condemn their children to landless poverty. Such hopes, unfortunately, were not always justified. By 1730, 1 of every 10 adult males in the rural community of Dedham, Massachusetts, was without land of his own. And a similar proportion of permanent proletarians, men who would *never* own land during their entire lives, had appeared in Kent, Connecticut, within forty years of its founding in 1738.

The unwillingness of the members of this surplus population to leave the town of their birth in search of better opportunities was the result, in part, of the system of partible inheritance. Under cultural sanction to provide for all of their offspring, parents did not constantly warn their children that they would have to go elsewhere if they wished to prosper. Lacking such "anticipatory socialization"—the type of childhood training found in cultures practicing primogeniture—many younger sons waited upon the death of their fathers in the hope of succeeding to the family estate. Disappointed in the end, these men were often financially or psychologically unable to move; they eschewed the hope of a better life elsewhere for the security offered by their friends and by the familiarity of their childhood community.

Given the absence of corporate or extended families into which they might have been silently absorbed, these victims of cultural practice and rapid population growth formed the nucleus of the free labor force which appeared in northern America at the end of the eighteenth century. Some of these landless and familyless men worked as agricultural laborers; others took up a trade, serving as apprentices to local craftsmen in the industrially oriented villages which began to dot the New England countryside. During the first half of the nineteenth century, these men moved into small manufacturing enterprises begun by astute entrepreneurs who sought to take advantage of the abundant supply of labor. Thus, the existence of autonomous nuclear families and the cultural practice of partible inheritance are seen to be underlying factors in the emergence of New England as the first American industrial area.

And yet the inheritance system, like so many other institutions and customs in this rapidly developing society, was gradually altered by the very conditions it had helped to produce. The continuity was greatest among female children. When a bride left the parental household to live in the vicinity of the family of her husband, she was provided with a dowry, a gift of money or livestock or land, to aid in the establishment of a financially viable household. The creation of this dowry had been a major concern of the family since the day of her birth, for the provision of an adequate endowment was crucial if the young woman was to attract a respectable suitor. It was the duty of the father both to arrange a satisfactory marriage for his daughter and to accumulate a movable surplus to facilitate such a union.

It was also the culturally prescribed responsibility of the father to provide a landed estate for his sons as part of the marriage bargain. Fully 95% of the estates of the first generation of settlers at Andover were divided among *all* of the male heirs, but only 75% were so distributed by the second generation of fathers, and only 58% by the third generation. The result was that less than half of the male members of the fourth Andover generation—those who came to maturity at the middle of the eighteenth century—remained in the town for the rest of their lives. This did not mean, however, that these sons had been abandoned by their parents; for when further subdivision of the family estate had proved to be impossible, the type of economic calculation traditionally reserved to female offspring had been extended as well to the males. Some sons were apprenticed, at family expense, to relatives or to craftsmen; others were offered a more formal education to prepare them for nonagricultural work; the great majority were given either a gift of money or a deed to land in a newly opened settlement.

Underlying all of these expedients was a new conception of parental duty and authority. Fathers had begun to consider their role not as that of patriarchs grandly presiding over an ancestral estate and minutely controlling the lives of their sons and heirs, but rather as that of benefactors responsible for the future well-being and prosperity of their offspring. The delicate balance between the two traditional concerns of agrarian families —preservation of their holding and provision for their children —had been tipped decisively in favor of the latter. Once, the farm had been an end in itself; now it was the means to another and a more important end. This tendency for parents to find the fulfillment and justification of their own lives in the success of their children marked the appearance of a new and different type of family life, one characterized by solicitude and sentimentality toward children and by more intimate, personal, and equal relationships.

Viewing all of these fragments of social change as a whole, we can detect, in very rudimentary and blurred form, the picture of an emerging American family system. These colonial families were nuclear in structure and were distinguished by the isolation of the individual conjugal units; the lines of descent from one generation to the next were traced through all sons, with the eldest having little or no advantage; there was partible inheritance among all children, male and female; and upon marriage there was, for both sexes, emancipation from the ties of kinship established by birth.

This symmetrically multilineal family structure was only barely in evidence in 1700 and it was still in the process of formation in 1815. The process of American economic and social development in the eighteenth century had succeeded in separating the family from the wider society. But it had not, as yet, divorced the individual conjugal units from the ties of the wider kinship system. This would occur only later, in an urban environment that provided *nonfamilial* public or private institutions to cater to the social, educational, and medical needs of the nuclear family. And yet, in retrospect, it is clear that the changes which had already taken place in this rural, agricultural environment were of the greatest significance. The family structure which most of the colonists brought with them from Europe had been easily adapted to deal with the exigencies of the environment and with the problems created by rapid population growth (which itself was the result, in part, of the inherited family system). The existence of the conjugal household as the primary social unit facilitated geographical mobility to frontier settlements or to the growing urban centers. This structure was also conducive to the concepts of political equality and republicanism, for in these families children were treated with equality and were taught to relate to others in the same way. Finally, this organization of family life contributed to the emergence of a liberated individual, a person who was exempt from all except voluntary ties to the family of his birth and free to achieve his own goals. The amplification, in the American environment, of the dimensions of the autonomous nuclear family inherited from England was thus another factor underlying the distinctive psychological orientation of these settlements and an important cause of their eventual commitment to the ideology of liberty and equality.

Time: Annual, Familial, and Ecological

The alterations and mutations in family life were part of a larger process of social evolution. Indeed, the element of "change," of a continuing transformation of the conditions of life in the direction of greater complexity, was a defining feature of the American social landscape during the eighteenth century. Change was not the same as chaos or disorder, however; for behind the complex facade of social existence there were certain basic constants which provided the colonists with a sense of reassuring regularity and progressive development. Not one but many types of determinate change were taking place at the same time, each with its own inner logic and each with its own chronology.

The basic unit of time for eighteenth century man was not the hour, as it is for the inhabitant of an industrial society, but the period of daylight which stretched between the rising and the setting of the sun. With artificial illumination available only in the expensive form of candles or of lamps fueled by whale oil, the settlers planned their activities according to the availability of natural light. They rested in the dark and were active when it was bright; the day fell naturally into two sections, not twenty-four.

The duration of daylight varied with the seasons, and this

too was a fact of crucial importance. The chronological year ended on December 31, but the new year did not really begin until March 15 (and until then the date was written as 1734/ 1735). The reason was clear. The middle of March signaled the beginning of the agricultural cycle in the northern hemisphere. The sun was in the sky for a longer period each day, bringing the change in climate which was vital to the economic life of the society. The calendar could do no less than reflect this momentous fact.

With the passing of the long winter night, the hard work of the farm recommenced. Fields were drained, plowed, and planted. Sheep were washed and shorn of their thick winter's wool. In June the first crop of hay was cut, dried in the fields, and stored as winter feed. Haymaking increased human thirst, and this too had its effect. "My demand with my country customers is so large now in hay time," one Boston brewer complained to a friend, "that I cannot distill fast enough for them." [7]

The heat of summer brought an increase of disease as well as of thirst. The debilitating effects of infectious dysentry made August and September close rivals to the cold months of winter as the most dangerous of the year. And these months were crucial ones, for it was at the end of the summer that the most important work of the farm had to be done quickly and efficiently.

Only when the harvest was over did the level of activity slowly begin to subside. Fruit had still to be picked, stored, pressed, or distilled in October; and November was the traditional killing time when the year's supply of pork, beef, and lamb would be salted and smoked. These were more leisurely tasks, however, and gave thousands of farmers the opportunity to reflect on crucial marketing decisions. Depleted stocks of salt and of other purchased commodities had to be replenished, a consideration which dictated the immediate sale of the year's crop of grain or the slaughter of fattened livestock. Because of the ample supply, however, prices of meat and cereal were always lowest in October, November, and December. It was much more advantageous to sell in the late spring, but this often meant going into debt in order to satisfy creditors and to purchase supplies to carry the household through the winter months.

Nor was it only such tangible indices as prices and deaths which followed the cycle of the agricultural year: the very act of procreation itself conformed to the influence of the wider environment. From a low point in February and March, the number of successful conceptions (as measured by births nine months later) rose steadily until it reached a high point in June. This figure then declined gradually until September, after which it increased again during the autumn months before regressing yet again during the depths of winter. This cycle may have reflected the periodic increase and decrease of conception itself (the result of more frequent intercourse or of variations in female fertility) or the seasonal alteration in the incidence of miscarriage (the product of monthly change in nutrition and disease). Although the precise cause is not yet known, the existence of this rhythmic pattern is not in doubt. Year after year, in village after village, the conception cycle followed the same regular schedule. It stands as pervasive and profound testimony to the influence of the annual cycle of nature on these agricultural communities.

Chart 1.1
Monthly Frequency of Conceptions and Births

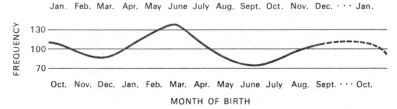

MONTH OF CONCEPTION

NOTE: If successful conceptions occurred with equal frequence in each month, there would be a horizontal line at 100.

SOURCE: This chart and the conclusions in the text are from a paper by Kenneth A. Lockridge, "The Conception Cycle as a Tool for Historical Analysis," presented to the Stony Brook Conference on Social History, 1969.

The inhabitants of colonial America were thus enmeshed in a pattern of existence which affected their behavior in ways they could only dimly comprehend. The more literate members of the community certainly understood that the religious calendar was carefully synchronized with that of the agricultural year. The great majority of Christian holy days fell during the cold months, when the burden of work was light. Then there was the coincidence of Easter and Thanksgiving with the period of planting and harvest, Christian rituals which had their genesis in more primitive and pagan agricultural festivals.

On a more mundane level, the ordinary farmer realized intuitively that the pronounced seasonality of labor was the most important factor limiting his output. The most productive work —ploughing, sowing, haying, harvesting—could only be done for seventy or eighty days of the year. It was the less fruitful tasks of threshing, repairing implements, and making clothes which occupied the greater part of the farm family's time.

What no one clearly realized at the time was that the mode

of economic activity shaped the very definition of "work" itself. In this agricultural society there was no compulsion to work constantly, for work was not constantly available. Unlike the modern factory or business, which is geared to produce at a steady rate throughout the year, the farm offered full employment only during restricted seasons. Thus the natural cycle of the year combined with relatively primitive technology to place severe constraints on the amount that could be produced. This meant, in the last analysis, that most men could not hope for great prosperity.

The improvements in agricultural productivity during the eighteenth century represented an initial attempt to overcome

(The New York Public Library)
Woodcuts suggesting the impact of culturally-determined sex roles and of climatic conditions on social life and agricultural productivity.

the problem of limited output. But the industrial revolution—the provision of year-round work and the maintenance of constant production—was the key factor in raising the general standard of living. With this alteration in the basis of economic enterprise came new conceptions of the nature and the value of work. High status in society had always been the prerogative of those whose wealth or occupation enabled them to escape from the rigors of hard manual labor. But farmers who worked for themselves could derive a good deal of pleasure from their achievements; for them, work was an end in itself, not a necessary evil to be endured for so many hours a day as the employee of another. In a society of freeholders there was no distinction between one's private time (one's leisure) and the time due to the employer. Nor was there such a thing as overtime; there was simply the task to be done. Time was not something to be lost or gained. Time was life, and life was the completion of the tasks vital to its own preservation.

Thus rural existence went on from year to year, one annual cycle succeeding another with a monotony punctuated only by a hard winter, a drought-ridden summer, or a severe outbreak of disease. This predictable pattern, however, was overlayed by another chronological schema, one which was both more uncertain and more indeterminate. This was the life history of a given family. Formed at a given moment by the marriage of a man and a woman, each family traced a unique path through time and space. The children of the union would grow to maturity, either as laborers on the farmstead or as servant-apprentices in the homes of relatives. Some would inherit the family property; others would settle elsewhere in the community or migrate to new settlements. By the time of the third generation each family had acquired a substantial history of its own. The house, lands, and livestock stood forth as the accumulated product of a half-century of labor, encapsulating in themselves the accomplishments of the first generations. In the vivid associations they evoked, these artifacts assumed a profound importance: they constituted no less than a source of the collective consciousness of the family itself.

This cycle of family life was as natural as that of the seasons, but it had greater vitality and variability. Couples would marry but not bear offspring; brothers would quarrel over the division of the paternal lands or become envious of another's success and move away; an estranged branch of the family would take root in distant soil and soon supplant its source as the main stem and support of the family's aggregate existence. Whatever the actual course of events, the great majority of settlers derived much of their psychological identity from the biological ties of kinship. The family was a breeding ground for tension and conflict (especially during the winter when its members were forced into close and constant contact with each other in small, cramped houses); but it was also an institution with a living past, a point of departure from which individuals could begin to define the future with a modicum of confidence and certainty. Here, then, was a separate dimension of experience, one which imparted a sense of cumulative and progressive change.

The orbits transcribed by the cycles of family life and of agricultural production intersected at innumerable points and exercised a determinative effect upon each other. The initial expansion in the size of a family, for example, would result in a higher output because of a larger labor force; subsequently, this proliferation presented the spectre of infinite subdivision. In these circumstances farmers might shift to more intensive cultivation; sons and daughters might be urged to leave home in search of better opportunities; or parents might limit their offspring. Whatever the ultimate choice, the conjunction of the two cycles had produced changes in both; each system was in a state of flux, constantly adjusting itself so as to remain in a state of equilibrium with the conditions extant in the larger environment.

Some of the developments which impinged upon these two natural cycles of life were accidental in effect and arbitrary in occurrence. Others were more predictable and disclosed yet another pattern of change—the life-experience of an entire community, its social morphology. Three distinct phases, corresponding roughly to the passage of generations, appeared in the histories of many northern communities. The first, which in some respects constituted a reversion to a more traditional society, was inaugurated by the first settlers in a given region and persisted, to some extent, during the lifetimes of their sons and daughters. Its distinctive features were an elitist political system in which effective authority resided in the hands of long-serving Selectmen; patriarchal control over the disposition of family lands; and low rates of geographical mobility. The inhabitants of these communities were content to farm their ample lands and to take directions from their ministers and leaders. Their lives were circumscribed, but secure.

There was a dynamic element to these settlements as well, and it was this characteristic which became predominant in the second—the expansive—phase in their histories. The epidemiology of these immigrant communities, coupled with the prevailing age of their inhabitants, was conducive to a high rate of demographic growth. This increase in population, in turn, helped to engender new forms of economic activity: the specialization of business enterprise, the appearance of artisans and merchants, and the emergence of capitalistic values. The gravitation of wealth into new hands subverted the power and the status of the traditional leaders of the community. A similar shift in authority took place within the conjugal unit. The diminished agricultural resources of the family and the increased number of alternative employments decreased the extent of patriarchal authority within the household.

These were just a few of the conflicts, most of them created by the process of growth itself, which confronted the inhabitants of a town during its expansive period. The increasing number of out-livers, those resident in hamlets or farmsteads outside of the nucleated villages of New England, prompted demands for the establishment of separate churches or for political autonomy as a new town. However logical in terms of geographical reality, these requests kindled hot political fires, since the creation of new administrative and religious entities lowered the prestige and increased the tax burden of the original settlements. Tension rose to such a level in Dedham, Massachusetts, in 1724 that a petition to divide the community resulted in a violent disruption of the town meeting.

The situation was much the same elsewhere in New England and in the middle colonies. Everywhere the increase in population had created new administrative problems and had destroyed the solid oligarchic stability of the old politics. Communities that had once had ten or twelve men with sufficient psychological resources to make them obvious candidates for office now boasted thirty or forty such men; yet the number of political posts to be filled had expanded hardly at all. In Dedham this surplus of potential political leaders brought a decline in the average length of service for Selectmen from 7.6 to 4.8 years, an increase in the number and in the length of town meetings, and the creation of ad hoc committees to deal with important problems. Superimposed upon a polity in which representative government was the accepted norm, the pressure of population had fragmented the power of the traditional leadership and had helped to create a more open, more responsive, and more democratic political order. Like many other aspects of life in these towns, this middle-class democracy was the manifestation of a discrete and transient stage of expansive social development.

As settlements entered the third, the static, phase of their social morphology, there was a reversion to a more coherent and more authoritarian political structure. In this "organized social system," Henry Adams pointed out in his compelling portrait of New England in 1800, community life was controlled by "the cordial union between the clergy, the magistracy, the bench and the bar." The exhaustion of the region's agricultural resources had halted the process of economic and demographic growth. The population of Connecticut had grown by 105% in the thirty years between 1740 and 1770, but in the three decades beginning in 1790 the number of inhabitants increased by only 20%. In this less dynamic and less expansive social milieu, established families had the opportunity to consolidate their power and status.

Given the continuity of agrarian technology and cultural practice, an ecological balance had been reached between the density of settlement in these older regions and the resources of the environment. Just as the opportunities for economic gain and social mobility had been abundant in previous decades, so now these possibilities were severely limited. Those families who did not respond creatively to these changed circumstances were doomed to a lower standard of living. The history of the individual family was inextricably intertwined with that of the settlement in which its members lived.

The three cycles of time and change—annual, familial, ecological—were mutually interdependent. Small alterations in one pattern inexorably produced subtle mutations in the others. In this dynamic equilibrium there was a continuous interaction among the constituent variables: individual propensities, family traditions, and environmental potentialities. The resulting social process was bewildering in its complexity. In the life of each family there was a multitude of possible outcomes, since each was enmeshed in a series of cycles which intersected at innumerable points. However perceptive the observer, this multiplicity cannot be reduced to unity.

And yet the historical development of American society was not completely adventitious. There was *not* an infinity of possible outcomes here. Looking closely at the variegated pattern of social development in the northern settlements during the eighteenth century, it is apparent that the changes took place within a multidimensional social "space," the boundaries of which were set by the biological and hereditary capabilities of the colonists; the nature of their culture, economic technology, and social organization; and the inherent possibilities of the natural environment. The borders defined by these fundamental social elements were wide, but they were not limitless. This was not to be a totally new society, but a variant of the English civilization from which most of the white settlers had come.

Within the definite historical and cultural bounds of this particular social system, there was no typical community, no average family, no characteristic individual. The history of each unit within this social space was different, and each revealed something new and unique about its intrinsic possibilities. In the last analysis, the history of this social space—the society which developed in America—was no less than the sum of the experiences of all those who lived within its bounds.

Notes to Chapter One

1. C. Ironside, *The Family in Colonial New York* (Ph.D. dissertation, Columbia University, 1942), p. 40.
2. John C. Miller, *The First Frontier* (New York: Delacorte Press, 1968), p. 13.
3. James Willard Hurst, *Law and Social Process in United States History*, (New York: DaCapo Press, 1971 reprint), pp. 112–113.
4. Ibid., p. 186.
5. Durand Echeverria, ed. and trans., "The American Character: A Frenchman Views the New Republic from Philadelphia, 1777," *WMQ* 16 (1959): 412–413. (See the list of abbreviations on p. 227.)
6. "Professor Gwatkin . . . on the Manners of the Virginians, c. 1770," *WMQ* 10 (1953) : 84.
7. Richard Pares, *Yankees and Creoles* (Hamden, Conn.: Shoe String Press, 1968), p. 131.

The population explosion in the preindustrial societies of the twentieth century has caused a general deterioration in the lives of their inhabitants and has engendered an increase in the amount of social conflict. Because of their rapid growth in numbers, the white settlers of the American colonies were faced with a similar series of problems. Precise measurements of colonial welfare are not available, but if living standards are measured by the per capita consumption of imported goods, then there was a significant decline in the American standard of living in the period between 1718 and 1748. (See Table 2.1 and also Chart 4.2, page 140.) A strong revival of business activity during the late 1740's raised the per capita consumption of British goods to a higher level by the middle of the eighteenth century, but it was only in the twenty years prior to the outbreak of the war for independence in 1775 that the colonists enjoyed an impressive increase in their standard of living.

There were a number of causes for the three-decade slump which began shortly before 1720 in American economic activity and prosperity. The first was a decline in the international demand for sugar produced in the British West Indies. The falling prices of sugar curtailed the rate of expansion in the market for fish, livestock, and breadstuffs from the northern mainland; and this, in turn, reduced the ability of the New Englanders to import English goods. A similar set of circumstances affected the middle colonies where, because of a series of good harvests in Europe, wheat prices rose only moderately between 1720 and 1740, thus limiting the purchasing power of the region. Finally, there was a slow but steady decline in the per capita value of tobacco exports from the Chesapeake between 1700 and 1740, a development which led eventually to a lower per capita consumption of imported British goods.

Nevertheless, by 1750 Americans were

THE PROCESS OF ECONOMIC DEVELOPMENT

Table 2.1

Per Capita Consumption of British Imports by American Colonies, 1700–1775

Year	Total Population	Value of British Imports in £ Sterling in Current Prices (5-yr. average)	Per Capita Consumption in Shillings and Pence in Current Prices
1700	250,800	£ 347,000	27s 8d
1710	331,700	294,000	17s 8d
1720	466,200	345,000	14s 10d
1730	629,400	491,000	15s 7d
1740	905,600	713,000	15s 8d
1750	1,170,800	1,110,000	18s 11d
1760	1,593,600	2,121,000	26s 7d
1770	2,148,100	2,788,000	25s 11d

SOURCE: *Historical Statistics*, Ser. Z 1; and John J. McCusker, "The Current Value of English Exports, 1697 to 1800," *WMQ* 28 (1971), Table III.

NOTE: The use of the constant price (1700–1702 prices) series in *Historical Statistics* Z 21–34 would have yielded a very similar curve, but current prices were used since it was at these prices that the colonists purchased imported commodities. McCusker's series also includes Scottish imports between 1755 and 1775 (when they amounted to 15% of the yearly total from Great Britain) and this was an additional reason for using current prices. In order to provide continuity with respect to Scottish imports, I have raised the value of English imports by 5% between 1720 and 1744 and by 10% between 1745 and 1754 (these dates relate to changes in the volume of the Chesapeake/Glasgow tobacco trade). The value of imports for the five years centering on 1700 is so high as to be suspect. There was probably an explosion of imports beginning in 1697 (when the statistical data also begins) because of pent-up demand during the preceding years of war. A similar depressive/expansive trade cycle occurred between 1741 and 1753 during another period of war. (See Chart 4.2, page 140.)

importing, in absolute terms, three times as many goods as fifty years before; and this substantial increase had been defrayed by a proportionate increase in colonial exports. Indeed, the determination of Americans to pay for imported goods only out of the returns of current production (and not to go into debt) was yet another reason for the low level of consumption during this period. Beginning in the 1750's the colonists would abandon this cautious practice of financing consumption through current exports and begin to use the credit advanced by British merchants to effect a rapid increase in their standard of living. This alteration in financial behavior would prove to be of immense importance both in the political history of the American colonies and in the development of the British economy.

The Pattern of Trade and the Balance of Payments

There had been a price revolution in England between 1500 and 1620, and there was to be an industrial revolution in the century beginning in 1750. Of equal significance in British economic history was the intervening age of mercantilism and commercial capitalism. It was during this period that England established a large overseas empire and began the exploitation of its sector of the South Atlantic System—that vast network of trade based on the production, processing, and sale of the historically "new" commodities of sugar and tobacco. The commercial revolution which proceeded from these new business activities generated a new financial and industrial infrastructure in England and thus facilitated the emergence of a new type of economic system by the beginning of the nineteenth century.

The West Indian islands and the Chesapeake region of southern America were the crucial sectors in this pattern of trans-Atlantic trade. As early as the 1650's these areas had concentrated on the production of the staple crops of sugar and tobacco for sale in the European market. The advantages of this specialization were twofold. By reducing the number and variety of agricultural activities, monoculture raised output by encouraging the development of special skills, equipment, and procedures. Secondly, this interregional division of labor insured the optimum pattern of land use. "Men are so intent upon planting sugar," a West Indian told the Governor of Massachusetts Bay in 1647, "that they had rather buy food from you at very deare rates than produce it by labour, so infinite is the profit of sugar. . . ."[1] As Bryan Edwards wrote in his History of Jamaica over a century later: "It is true economy in the planter . . . to buy provision from others . . . [for the] product of a single acre of his cane fields will purchase more Indian corn than can be raised in five times that extent of land, and pay besides the freight."[2]

This specialization of agricultural production in the colonies was dependent upon a strong market demand in Europe—a prerequisite gradually fulfilled during the second half of the seventeenth century. Sugar and tobacco, once luxury items consumed only by the wealthy, came into common usage among the members of the lower strata of the European class structure. As consumption spread in an almost compulsive fashion, demand for these commodities steadily increased. The rapid expansion of colonial production to meet this demand hinged on the ability of the more developed parts of the British empire to provide needed

NORTH ATLANTIC TRADE, 1770

transportation and financial services. By 1700 much of the social capital—the institutional framework and business enterprises required to bring the factors of production together—had been accumulated. The growth of the shipbuilding industry and the presence of a group of enterprising and ambitious merchants in England and in the northern colonies insured the reliable and inexpensive transportation of goods. And, with the capital advanced by investors and joint-stock companies in England, it was possible to purchase a laboring force from Africa. Between 1671 and 1712 the Royal African Company alone dispatched 500 ships to Africa and delivered more than 100,000 slaves to the plantations. Land, labor, and capital were being combined, more than three thousand miles away from home, in the commercial production of staple crops by slave labor. And, by the opening decades of the eighteenth century, the English sector of this great South Atlantic System had assumed a relatively coherent form.

Between 1698 and 1717 England received £12.7 million worth of produce from its West Indian colonies. During these same years it sent back manufactured goods—agricultural equipment, sugar mills, clothes, household items—valued at £5.9 million. The difference (£6.8 million) between these figures represented, in economic terms, the commodity balance of trade in favor of the planters of the West Indies.

This advantage accruing to the sugar islands through the exchange of goods was offset by other items on the imperial balance of payments account. In the first place, much of the credit accumulated by the islands from the exportation of sugar was used to purchase marketing services from abroad. During these two decades the cost of freight, insurance, and commission charges paid to English merchants amounted to £1.2 million. When this sum was deducted, the balance on current account in favor of the West Indian planters stood at £5.6 million. Two other interregional financial exchanges still had to be taken into consideration before the final balance of payments account could be rendered. The first was capital expenditure on new slaves imported into the islands; during these years, this cost totaled £2.4 million. Second, was the drain of £1.2 million from the islands by absentee planters resident in the mother country. This latter deficit on the bullion account was, in a sense, the most damaging to the economic future of the region. For these dividends from the lucrative sugar industry were not invested in the West Indies but diverted into the economy of the mother country.

The relatively high standard of living in the northern colonies was the result, at least in part, of the production of sugar in the West Indies. Over £2 million of the surplus accumulated by the planters in their commodity trade with the mother country flowed to the North American continent in exchange for lumber, livestock, and foodstuffs. These funds, mostly in the form of bills of credit drawn on English merchant houses, were used by the American settlers to purchase needed imports. Indeed, the substantial income from the West Indian trade permitted New England and the middle colonies to run a huge deficit on their commodity account with the mother country (with imports of £2.4 million between 1698 and 1717 and exports of only £0.7 million) without falling hopelessly into debt. John Adams would write without exaggeration, more than fifty years later:

The commerce of the West Indies is a part of the American system of commerce. They can neither do without us, nor we

Table 2.2
Imperial Balance of Payments Account, 1698–1717

(in millions of £ sterling)

Region	Commodity Exports	Imports from England	Imports from Colonial Regions	Shipping and Marketing Fees	Capital Costs: Slaves	Bullion or Credit Flow	Final Balance (Must be Zero)
West Indies	12.7	−5.9	−2.0	−1.2	−2.4	−1.2	0
Southern mainland	4.4	−2.8	0	−1.3	−0.3	0	0
Northern mainland	2.7	−2.4	0	−0.3	0	0	0
England and Wales	11.1	—	−17.8	2.8	2.7	1.2	0

SOURCE: Calculated from data in Curtis Nettels, *The Money Supply of the American Colonies Before 1720*, (Kelley, 1934), 49–85.
NOTE: This table gives only a very approximate description of the balance of payments account, for two reasons. First, Nettels' figures are in constant (1700–1702) prices and not current prices. Second, this table is simplified for ease of presentation; it is assumed, for example, that all shipping costs and fees borne by the West Indies were earned by English merchants whereas a fair percentage went to traders from the northern colonies. This table, therefore, suggests the direction of the flows of goods, services, and money, not the actual values of the specific items.

without them. The Creator has placed us upon the globe in such a situation that we have occasion for each other.[3]

There was an equally vital relationship between the economy of the Chesapeake region and that of Great Britain. Between 1698 and 1717 Maryland and Virginia exported an average of thirty million pounds of tobacco per year to the mother country. The £4.4 million earned by these shipments was partially offset by imports valued at £2.8 million. The remaining surplus of £1.6 million on the commodity account was much less than that achieved by the West Indian planters during the same years, but it was just as quickly eroded by the ubiquitous charges (£1.3 million) for shipping, insuring, and marketing this produce.

Although tobacco was a less lucrative crop than sugar, the American planters enjoyed certain advantages over their counterparts on the islands. Since they produced most of their own food, the total import costs of the Chesapeake planters (as a percentage of exports) were much smaller. More important still was the greater availability of white indentured servants and the positive rate of natural increase among the black population of the mainland. Fewer new slaves were needed each year to increase the level of production and this had an important effect on the balance of payments. Finally, the paucity of absentee planters meant that most of the funds accumulated by trade were not continually drained off to England (the exceptions being interest payments on borrowed capital) but were kept within the economic life of the Chesapeake region.

Nevertheless, the inhabitants of the mother country benefited handsomely from this trade with the southern mainland. Half of the tobacco imported into England during these two decades was subsequently reexported to Europe. These reexports bolstered the balance of payments position of the mother country with the Continent, thus permitting the importation of greater amounts of needed foreign goods and facilitating the accumulation of sizeable reserves of gold and silver (which were eventually diverted into the lucrative trade with the East Indies). In fact, between 1700 and 1740 the reexport trade played a crucial role in maintaining England's international financial position, for it increased at twice the rate of domestic exports. In certain sectors of the British economy the effect was even more dramatic. By 1775, when it had become the entrepôt for the tobacco trade, Scotland received 43% of its total imports from America and sent nearly 60% of its exports to the colonies.

The effects of colonial trade were not limited to improvement of the balance of payments account of the mother country. There were at least three other important ways in which the

Table 2.3
Average Annual Value of English Exports and Reexports
(Excluding Specie)
(in millions of £ sterling)

Period	Exports	Re-exports
1706–1710	4.75	1.54
1711–1720	4.76	2.19
1721–1730	5.00	2.91
1731–1740	5.84	3.20
1741–1750	6.99	3.59
1751–1760	8.90	3.55

SOURCE: Compiled from data in A. H. John, "Aspects of English Economic Growth in the Eighteenth Century," in E. M. Carus-Wilson, ed., *Essays in Economic History* (St. Martin, 1954–1962), II, 363.

British economy profited from commercial connection with its American dependencies. The first such "linkage" extended backward from the metropolis to the colonies. The high rates of return from the production of staple crops had prompted large-scale investment in the plantation economies; in 1775 the assessed valuation of the sugar plantations owned by British merchants or by West Indians permanently resident in England was at least £15 million. The income from these investments was more than £1 million per year. Considerable profits had also been made from the transportation of goods to and from the colonies. During the period from 1670 to 1730 the net returns to capital invested in the rapidly expanding shipping industry were at least 5 to 10% per annum.

There was a second tie between the two economies, a forward linkage between the production of staple crops in America and the development of new industries in the mother country. Sugar refineries, tobacco processing and marketing agencies, and (later) cotton-weaving plants were all lucrative English enterprises based on the importation of colonial crops. These new businesses raised the general level of economic activity and, by giving employment to thousands, they increased the size of the domestic market for manufactured goods.

Finally, the internal growth of the American settlements provided yet another stimulus to the expansion of the English manufacturing industry. This was through a final-demand linkage, the production in the mother country of goods such as woolens and metalwares for sale in the colonial market. English industries oriented primarily to the export market increased their output by 76% between 1700 and 1750 and by another 80% in the following two decades; while home-oriented industries expanded their production by a mere 7% in each of these periods. The demand generated by the expanding North American market accounted for much of this increase in the export-oriented sector of the economy. By 1750 North America was taking 11% of all domestically produced British exports, and by 1797/98 the proportion had risen to 32% of a trade that was twice the size it had been half a century before.

There was no single overriding cause of the industrial revolution in England during the eighteenth century, but the role played by the colonial economies cannot be overestimated. The exploitation of the English sector of the South Atlantic System had stimulated both domestic and colonial investment, created new types of financial institutions and expansion in the level of business activity, and stimulated industrial growth. That Britain (unlike Spain) was able to convert the advantages bestowed by a colonial empire into a process of cumulative growth and industrialization was the result of domestic achievements and potentialities, but this fact should not disguise the extent of the colonial contribution.

Sugar and Slavery

Each of the American regions that contributed to the growth of the British economy was rich in land and poor in capital and labor. In the Chesapeake and in the West Indies the shortage of workers was solved by the forced importation of black slaves; capital requirements were met by the resources of English and Scottish mercantile houses. These two developments were closely related: from one-third to one-half of all the capital imported from the mother country was used in the purchase of African labor. In these preindustrial economies slaves constituted a capital expense.

Indeed, the cost of entry into the sugar industry was so great that the expansion of production required the creation of a great international structure of credit. In order to take advantage of the economies of scale, a new sugar estate had to be at least 300 acres in size; and the initial cost of such a property—complete with buildings, milling equipment, and slaves—was in excess of £6,000. The yearly operating expenses of these establishments were high as well—usually about £1,200. On most estates it took the sale of all of the rum produced on the plantation and about one-third of the sugar crop simply to meet current expenses.

The economic realities of sugar production were reflected in the marked social divisions among the white population of the islands. A sharp line of wealth and status separated the great majority of secondary whites, mostly male and of Scottish or Scotch-Irish extraction, from the small number of principal families for whom they worked as overseers, agents, accountants, or storekeepers. There was a similar, if less acute, distinction between the great sugar planters and the rest of the white land-owning population. In St. Andrew's Parish in Jamaica in 1753 only 26 (or 17%) of the 154 estates produced sugar; the rest—generally one-half the size and with one-sixth the number of slaves—raised foodstuffs and livestock for sale to the great plantations and perhaps some coffee and ginger for export to England. These small producers were relatively well-off, but they were little more than economic dependents of the large sugar planters who dominated the political and social life of the island. In 1754 more than 75% of the 1.6 million acres of land patented in 19 Jamaica parishes was owned by 467 individuals. This small group of men constituted less than one-third of the total number of property owners and a tiny proportion (3–4%) of the total adult white male population of 15,000.

It was these few families who reaped the handsome profits of the sugar trade. Edward Long, a leading Jamaican planter, realized a net return of 9.5% per annum on his plantation investments between 1771 and 1781. Even those planters who were forced to rely on borrowed capital (at rates of 4 to 6%) for part of their financing showed consistent profits. In 1764 the 300 sugar estates on the island of Antigua produced a crop of sugar worth more than £160,000, 8% of their assessed capital value. Even when all charges had been deducted, these estates yielded an annual profit of 4 or 5%. As Adam Smith noted in *The Wealth of Nations*, "The profits of a sugar plantation in any of our West Indian colonies are generally much greater than those of any other cultivation that is known either in Europe or America."

These high rates of return, combined with extravagant living styles, tempted planters to go further and further into debt in order to increase the output of their estates. By the 1770's West Indian producers owed at least £10 million to English creditors. The debt was a large one, but it could be supported as long as the returns from production exceeded the interest payments on the old liabilities. Financial disaster threatened only when the American war for independence disrupted the normal market pattern and destroyed the lucrative trade in rum and molasses with the American colonies. By 1780 sugar exports had been cut by almost 20% and those of rum by over 50%. By 1792 nearly half of the

775 sugar estates that had been operating in Jamaica twenty years before had been sold for debt, placed in receivership, or simply abandoned.

The rapid collapse of the West Indian sugar industry after 1775 was the result, in part, of the artificial nature of its prosperity during much of the eighteenth century. Before 1700 the industry had been a healthy one; 40% of the sugar produced in the islands was reexported from Britain to the Continent and the entire crop had commanded the high price of 41 shillings per hundredweight (112 lbs). During the next thirty years, however, there was an unmitigated decline in foreign demand and in price. By the early 1730's the wholesale price of sugar had dropped to 18 shillings per hundredweight (the lowest level of the entire century) and England was exporting only 4% of its West Indian crop to the European market.

Table 2.4
English Sugar Imports, Consumption, Reexports, and Prices
(annual averages, selected years, 1698–1757)

Years	Total Imports (Cwt.)[a]	Domestic Consumption (Cwt.)[a]	Percentage Reexported	Price in Shillings (Per Cwt.)[b]
1698–1700	471,000	295,000	37.5%	41s
1716–1720	653,000	493,000	24.5	33s
1728–1732	926,000	797,000	14.0	
1733–1737	806,000	772,000	4.2	18s
1748–1752	896,000	857,000	4.4	
1753–1757	1,092,000	1,043,000	4.5	37s

SOURCE: Richard B. Sheridan, "The Molasses Act and the Market Strategy of the British Sugar Planters," *JEH* 17 (1957).
a Short hundred weight = 100 lbs.
b Long hundred weight = 112 lbs.

Underlying this dramatic deterioration was a sustained increase in the sugar output of the French West Indian colonies. As the supply of sugar on the international market began to grow more rapidly than the demand, there was a sharp decline in price. This, in turn, effectively excluded high-priced British sugars from the European market. The greater fertility of their islands provided the French with an initial competitive advantage, for it permitted higher yields with a lower input of slave labor and scarce fertilizer. This advantage was then compounded by the taxation policy of the English government. In 1734 British planters were paying duties and charges amounting to 19% of the value of their product, while their French counterparts were taxed at the rate of 5%. The result was inevitable; after the 1720's British sugar could only be sold in markets protected by the high walls of mercantilist legislation.

Faced with falling prices and a contracting international demand for their product, the West Indian planters and their merchant allies sought a political cure for their economic ills. The first parliamentary result of the pressure brought to bear by the West India interests was the Molasses Act of 1733. By prohibiting the legal importation of French sugar into North America and Ireland, this legislation expanded the area monopolized by British producers. In Ireland the effect was immediate and overwhelming. By the 1740's this closely governed dependency was taking over 65% of all the sugar exported from England.

The results were rather different in North America. The island planters had hoped that the high duties placed upon foreign molasses would effectively stifle the rapidly expanding American distilling industry, and thus maintain a market for the rum produced on the plantations of Barbados and Antigua. These dreams were crushed by a combination of merchant guile and administrative incompetence. The terms of the Molasses Act permitted the colonists to continue to provide the French islands with provisions, and northern merchants used this opportunity to import the lower-priced French molasses. At the same time they connived—by bribery, evasion, and sheer intimidation—to evade payment of virtually all of the prescribed duties.

This wholesale repudiation of the Molasses Act by hundreds of American merchants and distillers was tolerated by the home government because of a lack of agitation by the West India interests. The steady increase in the domestic consumption of sugar in England after 1737 raised wholesale prices to a high level by the 1750's, diverting attention from the recalcitrant colonials. By this time the island planters had won two more political victories which strengthened their position in the domestic market. The Sugar Act of 1739 allowed planters to ship their goods directly to Europe, thus eliminating the burdensome handling charges and duties for reexported goods. More importantly, by providing the possibility of an alternative market, this act forced English refiners and grocers to pay high prices for sugar. Then, in the 1740's, the sugar lobby successfully thwarted attempts of the Treasury to impose even higher taxes on sugar. Thus, faced by near disaster in the 1730's, the West Indian planters and their merchant friends had used their political influence in England to protect and to expand their domestic and colonial monopoly.

The depression of the sugar market during the 1720's and 1730's brought about a consolidation of the smaller units of production in the West Indies into large estates. This oligopolistic structure gave the planters greater control over price levels and shipping costs. The large planters now sold their produce through agents in London, and thus weakened the bargaining position of the independent West Indian sugar merchants. The emergence of this commission system also affected the slave traders, who found it difficult to get return cargoes of sugar except at very high prices. By mid-century the balance of power within the sugar industry had shifted from middlemen to producers. In 1753 English refiners and grocers entered a formal protest against the high prices they were forced to pay for sugar, but to no avail; by 1770 the wholesale cost of sugar had risen again, to 42 shillings per hundredweight. With prices once again at 1700 levels and with production doubled, the planters were enjoying a (brief and tenuous but) golden age of prosperity.

The same could not be said for the vast majority of the inhabitants of the British West Indies—i.e., the slaves who actually planted, harvested, and milled the sugar cane. Blacks constituted 82% of the total population of the islands in 1700, and nearly 90% seven decades later. This numerical preponderance of Africans and of those of African descent was one distinguishing demographic characteristic of the West Indies.

Table 2.5
Blacks as a Percentage of Total Population, 1700–1780

Region	1710	1730	1750	1780
West Indies	82%	82%	86%	87%
Carolinas	19	43	42	41
Chesapeake	25	22	36	36

Another was the failure of the black population to reproduce itself by natural increase. At least 750,000 slaves were imported into Barbados, Jamaica, and the Leeward Islands between 1710 and 1780, but the total black population of these colonies at the end of the period was only half that number. The murderous conditions of slavery had killed hundreds of thousands during these seven decades and had stifled the reproductive drive of those who survived.

Table 2.6
Black Population and Slave Imports into Barbados, Jamaica, and the Leeward Islands

Years	1703–1712	1720–1734	1745–1748	1756–1762	1773–1778
Black population	122,000	158,300	218,900	286,800	335,277
Numerical increase		36,000	60,600	67,900	48,400
Importation during interval		151,300	189,900	245,400	266,800
Excess of imports over numerical increase		115,300	129,300	177,500	218,400

SOURCE: Compiled from Philip Curtin, *The Atlantic Slave Trade* (University of Wisconsin Press, 1969) Tables 39 and 40; and Frank W. Pitman, *The Development of the British West Indies, 1700–1763*, (Shoe String, 1967), pp. 372–383.
NOTE: The paucity of census returns makes the compilation of a table showing the population of all of the islands at any one time an impossible task; therefore the returns falling within a limited period of time have been grouped together. For this reason the above figures should be considered as approximations only.

The high rate of attrition was the result of a number of factors. There was the brute force of slavery itself: "I have lost in one year a dozen new Negroes by dirt eating though I fed them well," William Fitzmaurice, a Jamaican planter reported in the 1770's, "when I remonstrated with them, they constantly told me, that they preferred dying to living. . . ." [4] "A new Negro is not very tractable," another white observer commented, "he languishes for some time, then dies, and his death is ascribed to the climate, which has been but little to blame." [5]

Over the long centuries when mankind was multiplying to cover the face of the earth, the process of natural selection had eliminated those without an intense desire to live. Now a force had arisen which was so unnatural as to undermine that passionate will for survival. Even the basic biological urge for reproduction was extinguished by this particular system of racial slavery. Testifying at the trial of Sabina Park, a black woman accused of the murder of her 3-month old child, a white witness reported that the mother "felt she had worked enough for buckra already and that she would not be plagued to raise the child . . . to work for white people." [6] For every woman who took the life of her newly born child rather than condemn it to spiritual death under slavery, there were two or three others who aborted the fetus before birth. These personal acts of protest constituted a direct attack upon the institution of slavery by those imprisoned within its walls.

This unorganized campaign of infanticide and abortion was aided and abetted by the white planters. Slaves could be purchased so inexpensively in Africa that it was not economically advantageous for the planters to support black children until they had reached working age. Black women were therefore kept working in the cane fields, discouraged from bearing offspring, and imported in very small numbers. At the middle of the eighteenth century males constituted at least two-thirds of the black adult population of the West Indies, and this severely imbalanced sex ratio further inhibited black population growth.

A third factor underlying the peculiar demographic situation in the West Indies was the high incidence of infectious disease. Fierce epidemics swept across the islands at regular intervals, carrying off large numbers of whites and blacks. This great loss of life was not the result of climatic conditions but rather of the continued importation of highly contagious European and African diseases that struck with devastating effect against new groups unprotected by immunities derived from previous exposure.

This epidemiological crisis was intensified by the diverse origins of the slaves brought from Africa. Forty percent of the blacks imported by four Jamaican brokerage firms between 1764 and 1788 came from the Gold Coast, 35% came from the Niger and Cross Deltas, 12% from the Slave Coast, and the remaining 13% from the southern coast of Angola. With points of origin stretching along 2,000 miles of coastline and inland for hundreds of miles, these slaves came from a wide variety of disease environments. Forced together on a slave ship or on an overcrowded plantation, these transplanted blacks could not avoid infecting each other with diseases for which many had no natural immunity.

Just as the introduction of European diseases into Mexico by the Spanish in the sixteenth century had reduced the Indian population from 20 million to 6 million within a hundred years, so the importation of African and European diseases produced a similar catastrophe in the West Indies. Hundreds of thousands of blacks and thousands of whites were caught up in this wholesale microbial slaughter. One of every five European sailors died while on route to America in a slave ship, and the African diseases of yellow fever and malaria nearly wiped out two regiments of British troops sent to Jamaica in the 1730's.

Sixty years later the story was much the same. Of 19,676 white soldiers sent to the West Indies in 1797, 17,173 had died within five years. The survival rate among blacks was considerably higher, primarily because many were immune to those diseases indigenous to their natural environment. During the early decades of the nineteenth century, for example, African troops serving with British forces in the West Indies outlived their white counterparts by a ratio of 3.2 to 1. And yet there was no period, on any of the islands, when the resident black slave population increased (or even maintained) its numbers.

This immense wastage of human life was smugly accepted by most Europeans. For the mercantilist Nathaniel Postlethwayt, writing in 1745, the slave trade was the Great Pillar of the British empire, that "magnificent superstructure of American commerce and naval power on an African foundation." [7] Merchants and planters as well as nations grew wealthy and powerful from the profits of the South Atlantic System while the mass of the European population delighted in its new addiction to sugar. Although only a few men and women perceived, at the time, the social and moral cost of this gross exploitation of African labor, their reaction has proved the most just and the most satisfying to posterity. "Without this labor these lands . . . would remain uncultivated," the Abbé Raynal, a distinguished *philosophe*, noted rhetorically in his *Histoire des deux Indes*, published in 1781. "Well, then," he replied in a magisterial verdict which has survived the test of time and of experience,

let them lie fallow, if it means that to make these lands
productive, man must be reduced to brutishness, whether he be
the man who buys, or he who sells, or he who is sold.[8]

The Economy of Rice and Tobacco

The system of racial slavery that developed in North America
had very different demographic characteristics from that of the
West Indies. The black inhabitants of America showed a remarkable ability to survive and to increase. Over 250,000 new
slaves were introduced into the mainland during the first eight
decades of the eighteenth century, but the black population increased by twice that amount during the same period (from
28,000 to 567,000). This disparate demographic history of the
various sugar colonies in the islands and the American colonies
has had a permanent effect on the racial composition of North
America. In 1950 one-third of the total Afro-American population in the Western Hemisphere was resident in the United
States despite the fact that it had originally received less than
5% of the total number of slaves.

The high rate of natural increase in the slave population of
North America became amply clear between 1775 and 1790.
During this period of war and of minimal slave imports, the
black population registered a gain of 21%, as compared to an
increase of 34% among the more-favored whites. This wartime
difference was very close to that which had prevailed during
much of the eighteenth century. The growth rate of the total
white population in the southern mainland colonies ranged between 16% and 44% per decade during this period. Most of
this variation was the result of fluctuations in immigration. With
the exception of the war decades of the 1710's and the 1740's,
the rate of natural increase among whites was remarkably stable
at about 27% per decade. When allowances are made for slave
importations, the rate of natural increase among blacks assumed
a similar regularity of 17–20% per decade, two-thirds of the
white average. The disparity provided a very rough indication
of effect of the slave system on family life and reproduction.

Given the low survival rates of the slaves in the West
Indies and in Portuguese Brazil, the natural increase of the North
American black population was remarkable. Certainly the
nature of the master-slave relationship in the American colonies
was not its main cause, for the records are replete with the same
reports of spiritual death, suicide, and simple sadism. "My wife
caused Prue to be whipped violently," William Byrd II noted in
his diary, "notwithstanding I desired not; which provoked me to
have Anaka whipped likewise who had deserved it much

Table 2.7
White and Black Population Growth in the Southern American Colonies
(in thousands)

	1700	1710	1720	1730	1740	1750	1760	1770	1780	Total
White population	84	114	143	201	289	337	464	621	822	
Decennial increase		30	29	58	88	48	127	157	201	738
Estimated immigration		10	10	20	20	5	30	30	20	145
Natural increase		20	19	38	68	43	97	127	181	593
Natural increase		24%	17%	27%	34%	15%	28%	27%	29%	
Total increase		35%	25%	40%	44%	16%	38%	34%	32%	
Black population	23	37	54	74	126	206	285	409	513	
Decennial increase		14	17	20	52	80	79	124	104	490
Slave imports		9	10.8	10	40.5	59	42	69.5	20	260.8
Natural increase		5	6.2	10	11.5	21	37	54.5	84	229.2
Natural increase		22%	16%	18%	16%	17%	18%	19%	21%	
Total increase		62%	49%	35%	70%	64%	39%	43%	26%	

SOURCE: Compiled from *Historical Statistics*, Ser. Z 1–19; and Philip Curtin, *The Atlantic Slave Trade* (University of Wisconsin Press, 1969), Tables 39 and 40.

more."[9] Nor did such pettiness measure the extent of the violence institutionalized in this system of human relations. One English visitor to Virginia noted:

A new Negro if he must be broke, either from Obstinacy, or, which I am more apt to suppose, from Greatness of Soul, will require more hard Discipline than a young Spaniel . . . and they will often die before they can be conquer'd.[10]

If the brutality of the slave system worked constantly to decrease the size of the black population, then the character of American economic life had the opposite effect. Because tobacco was a less lucrative crop than sugar, there was not the same determined concentration on the marketing of a single crop. The greater diversity of agricultural production, in turn, gave American blacks a more varied and a more reliable food supply. The lower profitability of tobacco had another effect as well. American planters lacked both the high rates of return and the easy access to large amounts of English capital enjoyed by their counterparts on the islands. Unable to afford slaves on the same lavish scale, they imported a higher proportion of female blacks and this had an important effect on the character of plantation life. There was less polygamy and a greater number of bilateral unions than in the West Indies, and there were fewer abortions. Moreover, many southern planters sought to encourage childbirth among their slaves. One Virginian wrote to his agent in 1759:

The breeding wenches particularly you must instruct the overseers to be kind and indulgent to, and not to force them when with child upon any service or hardship that will be injurious to them . . . and the children to be well looked after.[11]

However callous and self-interested the planter's attitude, the more equal ratio between men and women was conducive to a more satisfying emotional and sexual existence among the black population and was an important cause of the high rate of natural increase in America.

A third positive factor affecting the demography of North American slavery was the absence of an extremely dangerous disease environment. Because of the relatively small market for slaves, few slave ships sailed directly to the continent. This meant that many slaves were imported from the West Indies, from among those Africans who had survived the initial exposure to new diseases. Between 1710 and 1718, for example, over 40% of all new mainland slaves came from the islands. A similar pattern appeared in Georgia during its first period of slavery, when the demand for black labor was small. The extant lists for

Table 2.8

Rice Production, Prices, and Value of Per Capita Exports in Georgia and South Carolina

Year	Millions of Pounds Exported (5-yr. average)	Price Per Pound Using Philadelphia Prices	Market Value in £ Sterling	Population of Georgia and South Carolina	Rice Exports Per Capita in £ Sterling
1730	16.8	1.07 pence	£ 74,400	30,000	50 shillings
1740	30.6	1.07 ''	136,400	47,000	58 ''
1750	30.3	1.13 ''	142,600	69,200	41 ''
1760	41.9	1.04 ''	181,500	103,500	35 ''
1770	76.9	1.17 ''	374,900	147,500	51 ''

SOURCE: *Historical Statistics*, Ser. Z 262–266 and 340.
NOTE: The fluctuations in the value of per capita exports are reflected in the import figures plotted in Chart 2.1. Philadelphia wholesale prices were used to determine the price of rice and a conversion made into £ sterling.

the decade beginning in 1755 do not register a single arrival from Africa.

The situation was rather different during the boom periods in the production of Virginia tobacco and Carolina rice. Only 14% of the slaves imported into the Chesapeake in the fifty years preceding the American war for independence were purchased in the West Indies. But even then the Chesapeake was saved from the virulent epidemics of the islands by the decentralized character of agricultural production. Unlike sugar or rice, tobacco was not inherently a plantation crop. There were no mills or elaborate drainage systems required for its production; no great capital expenditures which required a large output to offset the costs of fixed equipment. All that was needed was the diligent cultivation of the crop itself; and this could be done as well, if not better, on a small scale. For the most part the black population was not concentrated on a few large estates, but was spread out among hundreds of small slaveholders.

The production of tobacco required, on an average, only one laborer for every five acres—far less than the 1 to 2 ratio in the sugar industry. This led to a low population density which was accentuated by the extensive methods of cultivation employed.

New land is taken up . . . tobacco is grown on it for three or four years, and then Indian corn as long as it will come. And in the end, if the soil is thoroughly impoverished, they begin again with a new piece and go through the rotation.[12]

This pattern of farming, as reported by a Dutch traveler to Virginia in 1783, required large holdings (40 acres per worker under optimum conditions) so as to permit a long period of fallow. Eventually this consideration combined with the growth in population to prompt migration to new lands farther to the west. As Thomas Jefferson informed the English agronomist Arthur Young, "manure does not enter into this because we can buy an acre of new land cheaper than we can manure an old one." [13]

Virulent outbreaks of disease in North America were reserved to those areas where the mode of economic activity resulted in a high density of population. Such an area was the lowlands of South Carolina and Georgia where the white inhab-

Chart 2.1

Population Growth and English Imports into Georgia and North and South Carolina, 1700–1775

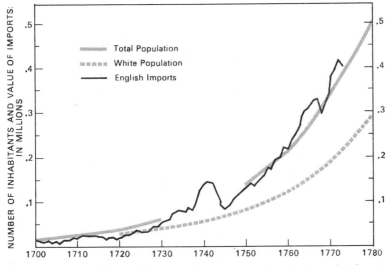

SOURCE: Compiled from *Historical Statistics*, Ser. Z 15–17; and John J. McCusker, "The Current Value of English Exports," *WMQ* 28 (1971), Table III.

NOTE: Imports from Scotland are not included, even for the period between 1762 and 1775 when they are available, because they would disrupt the continuity of the chart and because during these years they amounted to only 4.3% of total imports from Great Britain. Imports are expressed as 5-year moving averages in £ sterling at current prices.

itants experienced a sudden economic prosperity created by the rapidly expanding cultivation of rice. This region exported 18 million pounds of rice in 1730; 40 years later the total had risen to 76 million pounds and the price per pound had risen by nearly 10%. Indeed, by 1770, the value of rice exported from these colonies constituted one-tenth of the total value of all North American exports. The profits from this cultivation enabled these planters to effect a rapid increase in their own standard of living and also to import thousands of new slaves from Africa. By the middle of the eighteenth century blacks constituted more than 60% of the total population of South Carolina. Concentrated on the rice-producing estates of the lowlands, these slaves found themselves at the mercy of a disease environment nearly as deadly as that in the West Indies. The pattern was clear: when-

Table 2.9
Exports, Prices, and Per Capita Value of Chesapeake Tobacco Exports, 1700–1770

Year	Exports in Millions of Pounds (5-yr. Average)	Price Per Pound in English Pence (5-yr. Average)	Value in £ Sterling	Total Population Virginia Maryland & Delaware	Tobacco Exports Per Capita in English Shillings and Pence
1700	32	2.3d	£306,000	90,600	67s 7d
1710	30.4	—	—	124,700	—
1720	35.6	1.02	151,300	159,200	19s 0d
1730	43.8	1.1	200,700	214,300	18s 7d
1740	52	1.2	255,800	316,400	16s 2d
1750	66.2	1.4	330,700	400,800	16s 7d
1760	69.8	1.5	436,250	535,200	16s 5d
1770	83.8	2.0	700,000	685,100	20s 3d

SOURCE: *Historical Statistics*, Ser. Z 12–14, 230–237, 339.
NOTE: The value of tobacco was derived from wholesale Philadelphia prices converted into £ sterling, except for the figure for 1700 which was calculated by comparing the official and current prices and values for later years. The extraordinary per capita figure for 1700 was probably the result of heavy shipments and high prices in the years between 1697 and 1702 following a period of war, and thus does not represent a long-term average. It is, however, quite consistent with the high level of imports during these years, as depicted on Chart 2.2.

ever the high rate of return to be obtained from the sale of plantation produce on the international commodity market brought about a high density of newly imported slave labor, epidemics appeared to decimate the population. In 1849 the highest death rate in the entire United States was recorded by the sugar-producing state of Louisiana. Tobacco was not a killer crop both because of the character of its cultivation and because of the low rates of return which its production brought during much of the eighteenth century.

As early as 1670, at a time when the laboring force was still overwhelmingly white, the Chesapeake region was exporting 15 million pounds of tobacco a year. This tremendous supply, which had grown far faster than the increase in demand, had brought a precipitous fall in price to less than a penny per pound. A gradual growth in demand during the last decades of the century raised annual production to 30–35 million pounds by 1700 and, for a short time, the value per pound rose to the impressive level of 2.3 pence. The earnings from this expansionary surge financed the first large importations of blacks. The slave population of the Chesapeake rose from 11,600 in 1690 to 31,500 in 1710, an increase of 163% in 20 years. These profits also guaranteed a high standard of living for the white population—which grew by only 33% during this period—and imports per capita during the first years of the eighteenth century reached a level not surpassed for more than fifty years.

This boom period was ended by a stagnation in demand and a rapid fall in tobacco prices. For the next quarter of a century there was no appreciable increase in output or return, with the result that the value of imports barely kept pace with the expansion of the population. Only after 1725 was there a marked improvement in market conditions, with a concomitant rapid growth in the number of blacks. At least 50,000 slaves were imported into the Chesapeake between 1730 and 1750 (as against 15,000 during the previous two decades), and the proportion of blacks in the total population rose from 25% in 1730 to 36% by the middle of the century.

Underlying this expansion in the output and the size of the tobacco economy during the middle decades of the eighteenth century was a successful penetration of the European market. Just at the time that English sugars were being effectively excluded from Europe, Chesapeake tobacco made a triumphal entry. Reexports of tobacco from Great Britain rose from 50% of the 15 million pounds imported in 1670 to 85% of the 100 million pounds shipped from the colonies a century later. British domestic consumption of American tobacco had doubled over this period; foreign demand had increased tenfold. Working

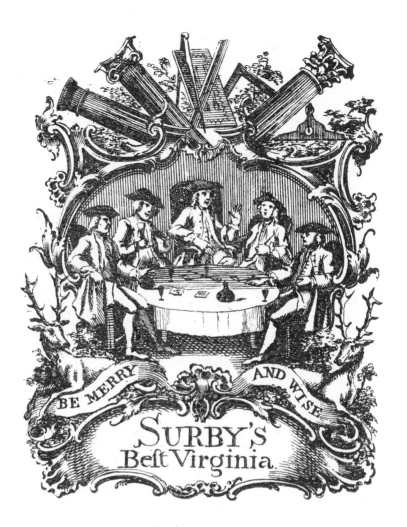

(George Arents Collection, New York Public Library)
An English trade card of about 1750, advertising Virginia tobacco. The great expansion in the production of colonial tobacco encouraged the appearance of brand advertising, as merchants were forced to create a demand to absorb the ever-increasing supply.

through Scottish merchant houses, the French government began to import Chesapeake tobacco in the 1720's, and within twenty years France had surpassed Holland as the prime recipient of British reexports. By the 1760's the French monarchy was receiving 22 million livres per year from the duties levied on the domestic consumption of tobacco.

The entire economy of the Chesapeake was stimulated by this sustained increase in international demand. The districts along the York and Rappahannock rivers, the traditional centers of the tobacco industry, increased their production from 18 to 30 million pounds between 1714 and 1774; and yet their share of the total output dropped from 59% to 31%. Their place as the leading tobacco regions was taken by the Piedmont area and the Potomac and James river valleys. By the 1770's the shipments from the customs districts on the James River alone amounted to 52% of the total.

This expansion into the interior was supported by an elaborate framework of international credit. The foundation of this financial edifice was the guaranteed demand of the French tobacco monopoly, while its superstructure consisted of the credit facilities of Scottish merchant houses. Confident that there would be a continuing European market for low-priced Virginia tobacco, Scottish merchants were only too willing to provide the capital resources needed to increase output. Dozens of subsidiary stores and shipping outlets were established in newly settled regions. The agents who managed these establishments granted credit to planters for their purchases, and took tobacco in payment. When the coming of war in 1775 disrupted the payment mechanism, 37 Glasgow firms with 112 stores in Virginia had more than 32,000 separate debts due to them. Although most of these were small (3,500 debts to two of these firms averaged only £29), the total indebtedness of the Chesapeake region, including that in longer established areas, was over £2 million. The continued expansion of European demand had prompted thousands of poor white farmers to continue the production of tobacco and had whetted the acquisitive appetites of wealthy planting families; each group had gone deeply into debt.

The financial plight of the Chesapeake stemmed as much from the structure of the industry and of the international market as from the cupidity of the planters. As producers in a market economy in which demand was not unlimited, the cultivators of tobacco had only two options in their quest for economic prosperity. The first—the West Indian solution—was to sell a limited supply of goods at high prices in a protected market. Because of the oligopolistic nature of the sugar industry the West Indian planters could control their output within certain broad limits and thus regulate prices and profits within their trading area. But the internal structure of the tobacco industry made it impossible for the Chesapeake planters to pursue this strategy. With tens of thousands of independent producers competing against one another, it was impossible to control output. The gradual increase in population and in production created a situation in which supply constantly grew more quickly than demand, thus continually forcing prices down. And when thousands of individual planters sought, in an eminently rational fashion,

Chart 2.2
Population Growth, Estimated Commodity Exports, and
Estimated Commodity Imports from Great Britain: Virginia,
Maryland, and Delaware, 1700–1775.

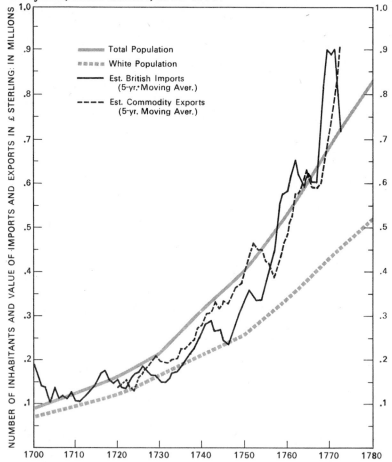

SOURCE: The population figures are from *Historical Statistics*, Ser. Z 12–14.
Import values are taken from John J. McCusker, "The Current Value of
English Exports," *WMQ* 28 (1971), Table III.
NOTE: The value of the tobacco exports in Z 230–237 has been calculated
by using wholesale prices from Philadelphia and converting this sum into
£ sterling. From 1740 to 1759 the value of tobacco exports has been increased by 5% (and from 1760 to 1775 by 10%) in order to secure a value
for total commodity exports by taking into account the diversion of resources into the production of wheat and corn for export. As noted in the
text, Virginia wheat exports amounted to more than one-tenth the value of
Chesapeake tobacco exports to Britain during the 1770's.

Import values are in current money values. Because of the growing importance of Scotland as a source of Chesapeake imports after 1720, I have
raised the value of English imports into the region by 10% from 1720 to
1739, by 15% from 1740 to 1749, and by 20% from 1750 to 1762. This
procedure seems defensible because between 1762 and 1775, when the full

to maintain their income at the old level by producing more tobacco, the result was a further decline in prices.

This inherent contradiction of a free-enterprise system of capitalistic agriculture in a limited market (partially remedied in the twentieth century by legislatively imposed quotas) forced American planters to seek the second solution: an international market for their product. Penetration of the European market did not, however, prove to be a panacea. Competition from the Mediterranean kept prices low, and so also did the entry of thousands of new producers into the industry. With prices rising only slowly and with few economies of scale, even tobacco planters with large estates were unable to accumulate fortunes to rival those of the rice-growers of the Carolinas. The economy of the Chesapeake as a whole benefited from this expansion of production, but many individual planters did not.

This was particularly the case in the longer-settled regions. With the fertility of their soil depleted by decades of cultivation and with their subdivided plantations now too small to permit long periods of fallow, the planters in these districts suddenly found that their yields were too low to compete successfully with the tobacco grown on the more fertile lands of the interior. More intensive cultivation and fertilization were futile in these circumstances, since the resulting capital costs would be too great to enable them to produce competitively. There was no alternative but to shift resources away from tobacco cultivation and into the production of crops that commanded higher prices—and an increased rate of return. By the 1770's Virginia was exporting 400,000 bushels of wheat per year, one-fourth of the total of the bread-basket colonies of New York and Pennsylvania; the value of this wheat—approximately £75,000 sterling—was over one-tenth of the current market value of the Chesapeake tobacco exported to Great Britain during these same years.

Problems of indebtedness and unprofitability affected large sectors of the Chesapeake economy by the middle of the eighteenth century but, in a sense, this was only to be expected. The rapid expansion of production into new regions involved high capital costs which had to be met through borrowing; in older areas the inertia of an established system inhibited a smooth and rapid transition from one type of agricultural production to another. There were real difficulties—soil exhaustion; the increasing

data is available, 26.5% of all British imports into the Chesapeake came from Scotland (which by that time was taking 45% of tobacco exports). Thus the graph provides a very rough approximation of the commodity balance of trade for the Chesapeake. No notice is taken of the coastal trade, invisible items, slave-purchase costs, or movements on the capital and bullion accounts.

cost of slaves; the rapacity of English, Scottish, or northern merchants; even the wealthy planters' extravagant habits of consumption. But it is clear in retrospect that these factors assumed importance only because they operated within the wider economic context created by low prices on the international market and by unrestrained domestic competition. In a less precarious economy, such as that of the West Indies or the Carolinas, these costs would have been easily absorbed by the producers or passed on to consumers in the form of higher prices.

Even so, the accomplishments of the tobacco industry were significant. In the first place, it financed the growth of the population of the Chesapeake region from 90,000 in 1700 to 685,000 in 1770, and thus preserved the primacy of this area as the numerically largest and the wealthiest in the American colonies. The proportion of the total North American population resident in the Chesapeake dropped from 36% to 32% over these seven decades, but this was a much more moderate decline than that experienced in New England (37% to 27%), its traditional rival. One legacy of this demographic growth was to be the political domination of the national government of the United States by the Virginia aristocracy between 1790 and 1820.

A second accomplishment was no less important: Per capita exports remained relatively steady despite the rapid growth in population, and the tobacco industry supplied the bulk of the overseas exports needed to maintain a high level of trade with Great Britain. Aggregate figures do not measure the true significance of this trade. For, in the years after 1725, the value of commodity exports increased at a far faster rate than the size of the *white* population. And it was this racially defined section of the community which received the overwhelming share of the total benefits from this overseas trade. The earnings derived from the sale of tobacco were used to pay for marketing services, to defray the cost of needed tools and clothing (and luxury items) manufactured in Great Britain, and to purchase still more slaves from Africa. In the southern American colonies, as in the West Indies, it was the white master race which appropriated the wealth produced by the South Atlantic System. The black population could only endure; ignore the insolence of white skins; and wait until, in the fullness of time, their descendents might extract a meager reward for their vital contribution.

Growth Versus Development

The failure of the economy and the society of the Chesapeake lay not only in its inequitable distribution of wealth but also—and more importantly—in its inability to generate new forms of economic enterprise and a general increase in the standard of living. There was a great multiplication of the number of producers raising tobacco and other crops, but this *growth* did not initiate a self-sustaining process of economic *development*. Quantitative output increased steadily, but the qualitative nature of business activity did not; there were no innovations in social organization, in financial institutions, or in agricultural technology. These settlements remained, at the end of this period, what they had been at the beginning: economic colonies heavily dependent on the capital, managerial skills, industrial output, and technology of more highly developed regions. They had been caught in the low-level equilibrium characteristic of many economies based on the exportation of primary commodities. By 1840, the per capita income of the south Atlantic states was only 70% of the national norm, while that of New England and the middle Atlantic region was 132% and 136% respectively.

The achievement of the northern settlements was as spectacular as the southern failure, for both economies were initially dependent on the exportation of agricultural products. "The main bent of our farmers is to raise wheat," Governor Cosby of New York noted in 1734, and this preference increased during the following decades. Wheat, flour, and bread constituted approximately 19% of the total value of all exports from North

Table 2.10
Value of Exports from the American Colonies, 1770

Products	Value in Official Prices	Percentage of Total Official Value	Current Market Value (Where Known)
Tobacco	£ 907,000	27.0%	£700,000
Wheat, bread, flour	636,000	18.9	
Fish and whales	502,000	14.9	
Rice	341,000	10.1	374,000
Timber and wood	242,000	7.2	
Furs, deerskins	155,000	4.6	
Meat, livestock	145,000	4.3	
Indigo	132,000	3.9	
Miscellaneous	296,000	8.8	
	£3,356,000	100.0%	

SOURCE: *Historical Statistics*, Ser. Z 76.

America in 1770, and were the chief items in the foreign exchange of the middle colonies.

The price of wheat, like that of sugar and tobacco, was subject to the laws of supply and demand and to the vagaries of the international market. Grain had been short in Europe, "yet," a Philadelphia merchant wrote to an Irish correspondent in 1710, "North America has so increased it, and overstocked the Plantations in the West Indies, that we have sold to excessive loss last year."[14] This was a temporary aberration. A series of poor harvests (along with an inefficient distribution system) produced a number of "subsistence crises" in various parts of Europe in the 1690's, and the general shortage of grain kept the price of colonial wheat high until the 1720's. For thirty years the prices of basic agricultural commodities rose in relation to those of other goods and services, reversing the long downward trend of farm prices between 1620 and 1690, and increasing the purchasing power of the primary producers. The declining price of sugar and molasses after 1700 also worked to the benefit of the North American farmer who, with the terms of trade in his favor, had to exchange relatively less wheat in return for a gallon of molasses.

These favorable market conditions for the northern grain producers vanished during the succeeding two decades. The increase in sugar prices in the mid-1730's reversed the terms of trade with the islands; more importantly, a series of good harvests in Europe kept the price of grain at a stable level and made it difficult for colonial farmers to dispose of their crops abroad. The results were first apparent in New England, where the increasingly high cost of agricultural production steadily cut away at the farmers' profit margins. From 1725 to 1745 the economy of New England underwent a steady decline, with population increasing much faster than the value of imports from England.

This period of economic stagnation was followed by an era of agricultural prosperity. By 1750 the price of wheat in the Philadelphia market was 50% above its level in 1720; and this upward trend continued until, in 1770, the value of wheat was double what it had been half a century before. The immediate cause of this dramatic increase was a succession of poor harvests in Europe but more fundamental forces were also at work. The growing use of horses for transportation (and war) in Europe was diverting more land into the production of fodder crops. While this agricultural transition began to curtail the supply of grain, the gradual acceleration in the rate of growth of the European population intensified the demand. For more than a century grain prices remained high, bringing substantial profits to the farmers of colonial America and, eventually, helping to subsidize

Chart 2.3
Population Growth and English Imports into New England, 1700–1775

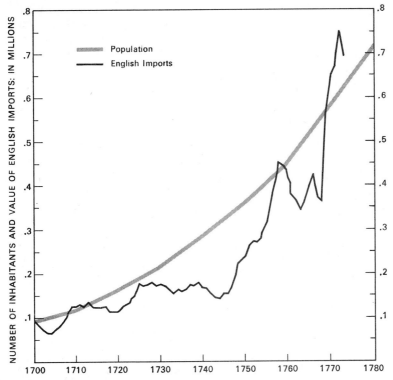

SOURCE: *Historical Statistics*, Ser. Z 3–8; and John J. McCusker, "The Current Value of English Exports," *WMQ* 28 (1971), Table III.

NOTE: Imports from Scotland are not included; between 1762 and 1775, when the data is available, Scottish exports to New England amounted to only 3.3% of the total value of British exports to the region.

Imports are 5-year moving averages in £ sterling at current prices.

the settlement of the wheat lands of the middle west of the United States.

Without the ever-increasing supply of grain from American producers, the price of wheat in Europe would have been higher still. Only large landowners, the French economist Quesnay noted as early as 1757, "could grow cereals cheaply enough to compete with the grain from Pennsylvania." Because of their comparatively low costs of production on fertile land, colonial farmers could easily undersell the European peasantry against whom they were competing, while still maintaining a high margin of profit.

Even relatively inefficient American producers—such as those employing slave labor on the depleted lands of tidewater

Table 2.11
Index of Prices, 1720–1770

Date	Wheat Prices in Philadelphia	All Prices in the American Colonies
1720	100	100
1730	105	114
1740	116	100
1750	158	124
1760	162	137
1770	213	136

SOURCE: *Historical Statistics*, Ser. Z 336 and 338.
NOTE: European wheat prices rose by 100% between 1721–1745 and 1791–1820. See B. H. Van Bath, *The Agrarian History of Western Europe* (St. Martin, 1963), pp. 221–228.

Virginia—could compete successfully in this market. And the rewards for efficient grain producers in the middle colonies were even greater. Given the returns from the wheat sold to colonial millers and merchants (who processed it into bread and flour for shipment to the West Indies and southern Europe), farmers could subdivide their property among the children of the family while maintaining its economic viability. This meant that many long-settled agricultural regions, such as Chester County in Pennsylvania, could maintain their prosperity even with a high density of population. Moreover, part of these earnings could be diverted into consumption. The value of English imports into the middle colonies increased by 400% between 1745 and 1760, far outstripping the rate of population growth.

The dynamic performance of the agricultural sector was a crucial factor in initiating a process of self-sustaining economic development in this preindustrial society. The high prices paid to thousands of independent farmers not only increased the demand for processed goods from England but also stimulated the growth of a rural-based manufacturing industry in America. By the last decades of the eighteenth century 30–40% of the taxable population of the farming areas of Lancaster County, Pennsylvania, was engaged primarily in nonagricultural occupations. This expansion in the framework of economic production and exchange generated new types of business activity and brought a rapid increase in the numbers of certain social groups: storekeepers, merchants, financiers, and ambitious entrepreneurs of all trades and descriptions. Finally, the high rate of return enjoyed by the rural sector and by the new enterprises

Chart 2.4
Population Growth and English Imports into the Middle Colonies, 1700–1775

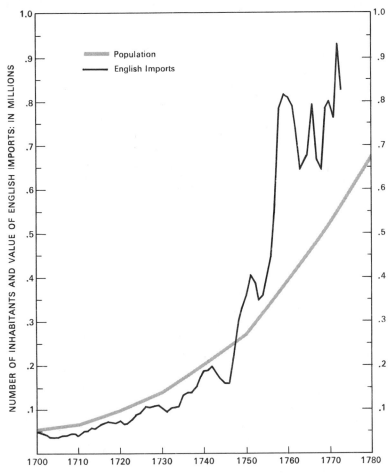

SOURCE: *Historical Statistics,* Ser. Z 9–11; and John J. McCusker, "Current Value of English Exports," *WMQ* 28 (1971), Table III.
NOTE: Imports from Scotland are not included; between 1762 and 1775, when the data is available, Scottish exports to the middle colonies amounted to only 2.3% of the total value of British exports to the region.
Imports are 5-yr. moving averages in £ sterling at current prices.

it supported helped to create the relatively high level of savings and investment (from 7 to 10% of annual income) required to escape from the low-level equilibrium of a traditional agricultural economy. By the eve of the war for independence a qualitatively different type of economic system had begun to emerge in the northern settlements.

This process of diversification and of capital accumulation

is apparent from a close analysis of the components of wealth —as revealed by probated wills—held by the (deceased) inhabitants of five counties in Pennsylvania, New Jersey, and Delaware in 1774. Because each of these counties was at a different stage of its economic evolution at this moment in time, this cross-sectional view of American business life has a dynamic element as well. The differential holdings of land, producer durables, and other forms of portable wealth reflect successive phases of the same process of capitalist development in a pre-industrial agricultural setting.

The key ingredient in this evolution was the accumulation of portable wealth, especially in the form of liquid financial assets (column C, Table 2.12). The opportunity to amass this capital varied with the nature of the agricultural economy. The county of Westmoreland in Pennsylvania had just been opened to settlement in 1774. Thus, 61% of its *total* wealth (column 2) was still in land and two-thirds of the remaining wealth was invested in farm machinery and livestock (column A). The preponderance of consumer items over financial assets as a proportion of gross portable wealth (16.9% versus 10.7%) was yet another indication of a primitive stage of economic development. Ordinary needs consumed a high proportion of the little wealth that was produced, leaving few resources to be saved for future investment.

The situation was rather different in counties whose economies were tied into the international grain market. Livestock and other producer durables constituted a rather minor proportion of gross portable wealth in Northampton and Burlington, especially when compared to the large percentage in cash, bills of credit, mortgages, and other liquid financial assets (compare column C with column A). By 1774 nearly 50% and 60% of the portable wealth of Northampton and Burlington respectively, was held in such financial assets. Here was a clear sign of the considerable income received from the sale of agricultural commodities and of the determination of property-owners in these counties to invest their profits in economic activities not directly related to their own businesses.

Such investment was not achieved at the cost of consumption: the higher general level of wealth and income in these counties—as compared to that in Westmoreland—permitted the *absolute* level of expenditure on consumer items to increase even as the *relative* importance of this component of wealth decreased. Hence the 8.9% of portable wealth spent on consumer items by the inhabitants of Burlington county purchased goods worth £45, three times the value of consumer expenditures in Westmoreland. In these economically advanced counties

Table 2.12
Components of Wealth: Five Counties, 1774
(*in local currency*)

County	(1) Mean Net Worth of Decedents (Includes Land)	(2) Percent of Net Worth in Land	(3) Mean Gross Portable Wealth (Excludes Land)	Percentage of Gross Portable Wealth (Col. 3) in:				
				(A) total producer durables (includes col. B)	(B) livestock (a producer durable)	(C) financial assets	(D) slaves	(E) consumer items
Philadelphia, Pa.	£949	34%	£602	7.2%	4.4%	57.7%	1.9%	11.6%
Burlington, N.J.	£652	17%	£542	14.0%	11.2%	58.4%	1.4%	8.9%
Kent, Del.	£531	51%	£257	29.7%	20.8%	19.8%	16.9%	15.0%
Northampton, Pa.	£420	60%	£168	32.3%	21.5%	46.3%	1.1%	10.2%
Westmoreland, Pa.	£250	61%	£98	66.3%	51.0%	10.7%	0.0%	16.9%

SOURCE: Compiled from Alice Hanson Jones, "Wealth Estimates for the American Middle Colonies, 1774," *EDCC* 18, no. 4, pt. ii, (1970), Tables 10 and 18.

the prosperity engendered by the grain trade had resulted in both increased consumption and high rates of investment in diverse economic activities.

This propensity to accumulate liquid financial assets differentiated northern agricultural development from that in the South. There was a high mean level of wealth among the white population of Kent county in Delaware in 1774, but 51% of the total assets of the decedents in the county was still invested in land. Of the remainder, 30% was invested in producer durables, 17% in slaves, and 15% in consumer items. This meant that only 19.8% of portable wealth (which was 10% of *total* wealth) among Kent county decedents was in the form of moveable financial assets. The profits from tobacco production had been reinvested in more land and more slaves, or frittered away in consumption, not diverted into new and more lucrative forms of business enterprise. Although the net worth of its white population was relatively high, the prevailing disinclination to save or to invest in nonagricultural activities meant that the potential for development was much less in Kent, Delaware, than in the region to the north. The demand for processed goods and mercantile services constantly increased, but the ability of the local economy to produce them did not.

The same was true of much of southern society by the middle of the eighteenth century. By this date the profits of tobacco production and the immense personal abilities of the planters and their sons were being channelled primarily into expansion of their landed estates. But this had not always been so. Buried in the history of each of the great white families of the colonial south was an ancestor with considerable commercial talent who had established the fortunes of the clan. It was his entrepreneurial skill and his political connections— not the sale of low-priced tobacco—that had produced a fortune far in excess of that of ordinary planters and guaranteed the predominance of his descendants. These planter-merchants lent money at 8 to 10%; charged commissions for the storage and shipment of tobacco; extracted high profits from the sale of imported commodities; and amassed great sums through the engrossment and sale of fertile lands to the west. Most of those who achieved great success were not "small planters writ large," [15] but entrepreneurs who began as petty merchants and tobacco factors and graduated to the status of exchange bankers and creative capitalists. Edward Dixon, a small trader of Hanover County in Virginia, represented one end of the spectrum. In the 1740's Dixon was selling goods worth £3,000 in Virginia currency each year, and his gross profit of £1,000 per annum on these sales raised him far above the great mass of planters with annual incomes of £100 or less. With time, good health, and luck Dixon might hope to rise to the position occupied by Charles Carroll of Maryland (at the other end of the spectrum) who, at his death in 1764, owned unoccupied lands worth £40,000, had loans of £24,000 out at interest, and held a £10,000 share in an iron works. Both Dixon and Carroll owned slaves and plantations but it was the "intangible" income and assets of the latter which differentiated him and most other members of the established gentry from socially mobile entrepreneurs like Dixon and—even more sharply—from the mass of poor tobacco-growing white planters.

As these successful planter-merchants established their sons on large estates and taught them to emulate the lives and values of the English gentry, the imperatives of capitalistic enterprise slowly atrophied. This development was accelerated, after 1730, by the presence of Scottish factors with their well-equipped stores, ready supplies of credit, and prime market connections. The commercial profits engendered by the great expansion of the tobacco industry during the middle decades of the eighteenth century were largely appropriated by Glasgow merchant houses; they did not underwrite the creation of a new group of entrepreneurs in the Chesapeake.

Lack of urban centers to encourage mercantile activity; a large slave population with little purchasing power; and firm control of the tobacco industry in the hands of outside capitalists were not conditions conducive to a process of economic diversification and development. In these circumstances many Chesapeake planters gradually turned in upon themselves, concentrating their energies on the management of their own estates or the creation of new ones for their sons. As one generation passed into the next, these planters developed a disdain for the commercial activities that had made their fortunes. Gone was the goal of maximization of profit through reinvestment of earnings in a wide variety of economic endeavors. In its place came the diversion of more and more capital resources into the profitable, but ultimately stultifying, ownership of land and slaves. Concurrently, there was the accentuation of an ethic which elevated the aristocratic penchant for consumption above the bourgeois compulsion to save. As these new values and patterns of behavior gained in importance, the intellectual and psychological as well as the economic foundations were laid for the next century of historical change: the *growth* of the agricultural economy of the south, dependent first on tobacco and rice and later on cotton, and the *development* of commercial and then industrial capitalism in the cities of the north.

The appearance of major centers of population and of business enterprise in the northern colonies was the result of two factors. The first was the existence of a dynamic agricultural economy which provided both a steadily increasing amount of exports and surplus capital for investment in nonagricultural activities. Secondly, there were the innovative entrepreneurial achievements of the New England merchants during the seventeenth century: the opening up of an American-managed trade with the Caribbean and the gradual appropriation of many of the commercial activities theretofore reserved for inhabitants of the mother country. The successful conjunction of these two (mutually dependent) forces was clearly apparent by the first decades of the eighteenth century. "Our trade to Surinam," Thomas Bannister noted in his *Essay on the Trade of New England* (circa 1714),

> . . . *imploys a great number of Ships and sailors. The Tradesmen feel the Benefit by the Merchandise of Soap, Candles, Beer, building of Ships and the great Number of Casks this Trade imploys. The landed Interest Shares with them in the Export of very much Hay, Oates, Onjons, Apples, Pork, Beef, Staves, board, butter, and Flower. The Fishery by a great Export of Macheril and refuse cod. . . .*
> *The return for these is Molassus, which we brew and distill, and thereby raise many good Liveings; And the Merchant finds it one of the most profitable Trade he drives upon.*[16]

As Bannister's prose reveals, the northern trade with the West Indies was creating the same types of linkages that were of so much importance in the development of the British economy. The creation of a strong colonial-owned shipping industry is a case in point. At the end of the seventeenth century one of every ten adult males in the small port city of Boston described himself as a "merchant" on the shipping records; and one of every six adult males had a share in a maritime venture. Most of these men were small traders, shopkeepers, millers, or farmers who had combined their scarce capital resources in order to enter into the West Indian trade. Soon they had exploited their prime geographic position and the resources of the agricultural hinterland to capture this trade from British firms (and Irish producers of food and livestock) and to undermine completely the nascent mercantile activity in the West Indies.

The victory of the merchants of Boston, Newport, Philadelphia, and New York was complete. By the seventh decade of the century 95% of the ships trading between the islands and New England and 82% of those serving the middle colonies were owned by the residents of those areas. By this time as well all of the American coastal trade was in colonial hands, as was 75% of all direct trade between northern ports and the mother country; only the direct trade with the sugar and tobacco colonies remained primarily under British control. The shipping industry had emerged as one of the most important of all colonial enterprises. In the five years between 1768 and 1772, American merchants earned an average of £600,000 per year through the provision of various shipping services. These "invisible" exports, especially important in the economy of New England, amounted to no less than one-fifth of the annual value of all North American commodity exports. Simply in the addition of substantial receipts on the balance of payments account, the mercantile interest served the colonies well.

The influence of the shipping industry was felt by the entire economy. The demand for vessels to transport continental produce to the West Indies sparked the appearance of dozens of small shipbuilding yards, which gave work to hundreds of carpenters, rope and sail makers, caulkers, and ordinary laborers. The large amount of wood required by this industry greatly expanded the number of lumbermen, sawmill operators, and wood merchants. Indeed, the ready supply of low-priced timber gave American shipyards a competitive advantage of 50% over their European counterparts and created a strong demand from English merchants. By 1775 one-third of the entire British-owned merchant fleet was composed of colonial-built ships.

The trend was clear. In one field after another the northern settlers of America were achieving economic self-sufficiency through the creation of import-substituting industries. The appearance of colonial refineries obviated the need for importation of English loaf sugar after 1750. And two decades later Boston was distilling 1.1 million gallons of molasses per year and exporting it to markets once served by the rum producers of the West Indies. By this time as well the merchants of Lynn, Massachusetts, had begun to organize a colonial shoe industry, furnishing artisans with raw materials and arranging for distribution of these market-shoes throughout the colonies. The dependence of the Americans on the more highly developed British economy for the provision of manufactured goods would remain for decades; but by 1775 the commercial expertise, artisan skills, and capital resources for domestic industrial development had been generated in the northern cities and in the surrounding rural areas.

The flow of commerce was the prime factor underlying this diversification of economic endeavor and an urban concentration of population. "The size of all towns in America," an English traveler reported in 1795, "has hitherto been proportionate to their trade." [17] There was no mystery in this. As entrepreneurs invested their profits from trade in new enterprises, the results—in terms of additional employment, new products, and greater spending power—were gradually diffused throughout the community. And the wages paid to sailors, dockhands, and clerks had a further positive economic effect in the creation of a demand for additional goods and services: housing, food, and clothing. Injected into the life of the port cities, the money generated by commerce had a "multiplier" effect on the level of business activity; it was "used" two, three, or four times as it passed from hand to hand and from business to business.

Yet another economic consideration encouraged the growth of these commercial centers. The productivity of the work force was higher in urban areas, both because it was actively employed for a greater part of the year and because its density permitted an extensive specialization of business activity. Then, too, these established trading and processing centers offered considerable "external economies" to new firms: with a ready supply of labor and services, a network of credit facilities, and an accessible market, the amount of capital resources needed to found a new business was greatly reduced and its chances for success were greatly increased.

Boston was the first American city to experience the leavening effects of trade. By 1700 40% of the carrying capacity of all colonial-owned shipping was controlled by merchants and traders in the town, and the lucrative commerce with the West Indies had raised the population to 6,000. By 1740 the number of inhabitants had grown to 16,000, but even this impressive increase was not sufficient to maintain Boston in its traditional position of primacy. The locus of agricultural prosperity had shifted to the middle colonies and this was immediately reflected in the growth of its port cities. Per capita exports of primary produce from Philadelphia increased from 17 shillings in 1731 to more than 50 shillings in 1771, and the value of imports increased accordingly. This increase in trade brought an expansion in the number of insurance clerks, storekeepers, and dockhands; while the rapid rise in the standard of living attracted a wide variety of artisans and craftsmen to the growing metropolis. By the time of the American war for independence, the commercial activity of Philadelphia was sufficient to support 25,000 people; and there were an additional 21,000 urban dwellers in New York and another 10,000 in Baltimore.

In 1770 7% of the American population was resident in cities of 2,500 or more inhabitants. This fact gives little indication of the full size and significance of the urban sector of the economy. There were scores of smaller ports and inland towns serving political functions as county seats in addition to their crucial economic role as nodal points in the vast network of commercial activity. Twenty percent of the population living within a thirty-mile radius of Philadelphia was resident in a small town in 1765, and three decades later there were no fewer than fourteen communities with 300 to 500 inhabitants in the backcountry that stretched out beyond the densely settled area toward the center of Pennsylvania. The existence of these settlements, in such numbers, was testimony to the fact that the returns received from the sale of primary products had been translated into an expansion of the nonagricultural sector of the economy; that a more modern commercial and financial super-structure had been built upon the traditional base of agricul-tural production; and that—by a process which partakes of wonder if not of alchemy—growth had been transmuted into development.

Notes to Chapter Two

1. Eric Williams, *Capitalism and Slavery* (New York: Russell and Russell, 1944), p. 110.
2. Joseph Ragatz, *The Fall of the Planter Class in the British Caribbean, 1763–1833* (New York: Random House, 1968), p. 88.
3. Williams, op. cit., p. 121.
4. H. Orlando Patterson, *The Sociology of Slavery* (Cranbury, N.J.: Fairleigh Dickinson University Press, 1970), pp. 264–265.
5. Ibid., p. 100.
6. Ibid., p. 106.
7. Williams, op. cit., p. 52.
8. David B. Davis, *The Problem of Slavery in Western Culture* (Ithaca: Cornell University Press, 1966) p. 16.
9. Edmund Morgan, *Virginians at Home: Family Life in the Eighteenth Century* (Charlottesville: University Press of Virginia, 1963), p. 59.
10. Ibid., p. 60.
11. E. Franklin Frazier, ed., *The Negro Family in the United States*, abridg. rev. ed. (Chicago: University of Chicago Press, 1966), p. 36.
12. Avery O. Craven, *Soil Exhaustion as a Factor in the Agricultural History of Virginia and Maryland, 1606–1860* (Magnolia, Mass.: Peter Smith, 1926), p. 56.
13. Ibid., p. 34.
14. Anne Bezanson et al., *Prices in Colonial Pennsylvania* (East Orange, N.J.: Kelley, 1935), p. 9.
15. The phrase is that of Aubrey C. Land; see his "Economic Behavior in a Planting Society," *JSH* 33 (1967): 475.
16. Frank W. Pitman, *The Development of the British West Indies, 1700–1763* (Hamden, Conn.: Shoe String, 1967), pp. 200–201.
17. James Lemon, "Urbanization and the Development of Pennsylvania," *WMQ* 24 (1967): 502–503.

The economic activities and demographic characteristics of each of the regions of early America were intimately related to a central framework of values, beliefs, and expectations which constituted the cultural identity of each of the subsocieties. This interdependence among economy, society, and culture reflected the basic fact that the mode of behavior demanded of each colonist in one sphere of life had to be broadly congruent with that required in other aspects of his daily existence. The integration and coherence visible in the life of the population of each region stemmed primarily from the existence of culturally prescribed and inherently coercive behavior patterns to which each individual was expected to conform.

This strain toward consistency within each of these subsocieties (and within each class in each subculture) may also have reflected the existence of similar personality structures among many of its members. There was, to be sure, no one-to-one correspondence between behavior patterns and character structure (for it was culture which was shared and not personality); but it is more than likely that in each of these regions and classes there was a "modal" personality. That is, a similar configuration of character traits appeared among many members of the same subsociety because it was encouraged by the child-training practices, or embodied in the role-expectations of the adult members of the society, or induced by the values passed from generation to generation. Consciously or not, each of these subsocieties had devised methods which influenced, persuaded, or coerced its members to behave in a culturally prescribed way and perhaps even to

THE SOCIAL SYNTHESIS: WEALTH, AUTHORITY, AND POWER

acquire the kind of character which makes them want to act in the way they have to act as members of the society or of a special class within it . . . to desire what objectively it is necessary for them to do.[1]

The relative success of each of these systems

of social organization lay in the degree to which they accomplished this task and in the cost in human suffering exacted in the quest. Some societies, like some men and women, were more humane and more just than others.

The Routinization of Mainland Slavery

The European peoples—Spanish, Portuguese, and British—have been the most successful in stamping their image on societies in the Western Hemisphere during the last four hundred years. But in Brazil and in the West Indies during the eighteenth and nineteenth centuries there was also a partial re-creation of African society. The effective ownership and control of these two areas were vested in Europeans, but the overwhelming numerical superiority of the slave population which inhabited them prompted the appearance of an indigenous African culture. This development was facilitated, ironically enough, by the murderous conditions of the plantation societies; the high rate of mortality brought a constant influx of new slaves and a continuous reinforcement of African practices and beliefs.

The transplantation of African society to the West Indies and the American colonies was severely circumscribed by the diverse geographic, linguistic, and cultural origins of the black population and by the forced conditions of its immigration and settlement. Most African political institutions and practices were rendered irrelevant by the condition of slavery or were superceded by those of the white masters, and other customs persisted only in a simplified form. As in all colonial societies composed of heterogeneous peoples, there was a drastic foreshortening of cultural and aesthetic experience: the rich store of homeland institutions and mores was lost or diluted in the search for a new common denominator of social life.

One such area of convergence in the West Indies was religion. Here the otherwise diverse practices of the various African tribes yielded a single basic perception of the nature of the world and of man's place within it. On many plantations an "obeah," a priest-like figure with a knowledge of "witchcraft," emerged as the spiritual (and political) leader of the black population. His status in the community, like that of the minister among the whites, stemmed from his ability to summon the forces of the supernatural world and to bring them to bear on earthly concerns. Indeed, the prestige of these leaders and the strength of these beliefs were so great that it was only after the American war for independence that the religious ideology of their European masters had any influence on the black population of the islands. Then the doctrines of English

Protestant Christianity underwent a strange metamorphosis.

One example of the result was the creed propagated by George Lewis, an African-born slave who had been taught the rudiments of Christianity in Virginia. A preacher of true genius, Lewis deliberately repudiated many European forms and ideas and substituted African practices in their place. His teachings stressed the authoritarian power of the leader of the sect and the great power of "the spirit" to work changes in the natural world. Here was a syncretic religion which assimilated certain tenets of Christianity, such as the belief in a Holy Ghost, into the larger spiritual configuration of the African cosmogony.

Lewis might never have attained such creative heights had he remained in Virginia. Because of the preponderantly white population, the dispersed pattern of black settlement, and the large proportion of American-born slaves, the American colonies lacked the invigorating African cultural environment found in the West Indies. There was little possibility—except perhaps in South Carolina—for re-creating the richness and vitality of African civilization or even of preserving a distinct cultural identity. Thus, as time went on, African Gods were replaced by a pale European substitute, and traditional patterns of family life were vitiated by the condition of servitude.

Even the thoughts and emotions of the black population soon came to be expressed in the language of their white masters. In their speech, as in other areas of life, the blacks had to work within borrowed cultural forms, adapting them as best they could to their own needs. English was spoken, but it assumed a new and different character in the mouths and expressions of African slaves. Certain features of external reality were accorded special prominence or symbolic meaning in the black vocabulary, or pulled to the forefront by the peculiarities of grammatical construction. Trained from infancy to decipher these subtle intonations and veiled references, blacks took them for granted, while whites groped, as in a foreign language, for the correct translation. The difference in dialect expressed, in concrete and tangible form, the cultural and social gulf separating black from white and hinted at their very different perceptions of the world.

Some of these disparities increased over time. The children born to slave parents never personally experienced freedom and could never fully comprehend its meaning. From the time they acquired the rudiments of language, they were made conscious of the limited social roles open to them; for certain types of options and aspirations were clearly categorized as belonging only to whites. These impressions were strengthened when children sought to explore and to fit into the world around

them; for the very act of emulating the behavior of those who had nurtured them unconsciously influenced black children to accept their subordinate place in the social order. More ambitious parents might encourage an appetite for achievement in their offspring, directing them toward domestic service or craftsmanship; but the black occupational hierarchy was a severely truncated version of its white counterpart, since even the highest positions brought only a limited degree of independence and offered few possibilities for the full development of the human personality.

Like the inmates of a prison or a mental hospital, both black children and black adults were systematically denied the full range of human experience. They had no opportunity to consider an alternative scheme of values or to contemplate a diverse range of social activity. Indeed, much of their energy and most of their ingenuity was expended in attempting to evade the more onerous aspects of the system in which they lived. The social vacuum created by the total-institution of slavery was all the more damaging because of its silent and

These prison-like slave quarters on a Virginia plantation contrast vividly
with the Georgian elegance of Westover Mansion, shown on p. 93. Note
the central fireplace around which the slaves slept.

insidious character. It existed as a given feature of the social
environment, shaping the lives and aspirations of entire generations without their full conscious knowledge.

In its effect on the character structure of the slave population, this system of social deprivation was complemented by the
regimentation enforced by white overseers and by the discipline
instilled by black parents. Anxious to insure the survival of
their offspring, many slaves taught their children to accept a
subordinate place in American society and to placate their
masters rather than to repudiate them. This historically necessary instruction in survival led inevitably to the creation, among
a part of the black population, of an ingrained feeling of inferiority. For these slaves, artful dissimulation had slowly slipped
into genuine deference.

Those slaves with more aggressive or less malleable personalities rejected both the advice offered by their elders and the

authority assumed by their owners. Deprived of the possibility of massive revolt by the dispersed character of agricultural production in most of the American south, these blacks waged a determined, if futile, individual struggle against the regime that oppressed them. Between 1783 and 1814 the state of Virginia paid compensation to no fewer than 434 owners whose slaves had been killed by other planters in the preservation of white law and white order.

A selective process was at work here which eliminated those blacks who dared to carry their instinctual and intellectual rejection of slavery into overt action. Year by year those who were psychologically unable to accept the discipline of the slave regime were systematically eliminated from the black population. Those who survived did so in part because they were temperamentally inclined or pragmatically prepared to accept their lowly position. This passive acquiescence was encouraged by the religious propaganda disseminated by the white majority. The conversion of the black population to Christianity, one South Carolina missionary pointed out as early as 1710, "would teach them obedience of their masters out of a Principle of Conscience and render them much more true and faithful to their interests." [2]

The successful routinization of mainland slavery through the inculcation of a submissive ideology, the application of overwhelming physical force, and the childhood socialization of American-born blacks took more than a hundred years. It could not be accomplished as long as the importation of new African slaves introduced a hostile element into the resident population, reinforced their cultural heritage, and presented them with a different model of black existence. Few whites claimed that slaves were satisfied with their condition during the eighteenth century, for their experience constantly belied the claim. Only in the decades following the partial suppression of the slave trade in 1807 would the results of a century of indoctrination, repression, and socialization become apparent; only then would a black population emerge which was, at least in comparison with past generations, relatively submissive and content with its lot.

The Evolution of the Southern Aristocracy

The presence of black slaves at the bottom of the social scale had a large, perhaps even a determinative, effect on the nature of white society. Before 1670 there had been relatively few blacks resident in the Chesapeake region, certainly not more than 5% of the total population, and not all of them were bound to hereditary lifetime service. From the very first, Africans had been perceived by whites as racially distinct and culturally different; but initially they had been treated in law in much the same manner as indentured servants from Europe. Then, rather suddenly, their status was completely undermined. A series of laws passed between 1667 and 1671 stated that conversion to Christianity did not relieve a black of his bondage. At the same time it became clear that Africans, and their children, served for life rather than for a specific period of years; and that color was the single defining feature of their status as slaves. By the end of the seventeenth century all of the southern American colonies had outlawed miscegenation: to be black or brown was to be a chattel slave, the personal property of one who was white and free.

Just at the time that this general debasement of blacks was taking place, the lines of class and status in white society were taking on a more coherent and a more permanent form. The high prices paid for Chesapeake tobacco during the first half-century of settlement had brought quick fortunes to those privileged colonists, many of them the younger sons of London merchants and bureaucrats, with large land grants and many indentured servants. The growing economic cleavages in Chesapeake society were accentuated by the falling price of tobacco after 1660, which struck particularly hard at the small yeoman farmers with limited capital resources, and by the attempts of certain leading families to appropriate control of government on the local and provincial levels.

In 1675 social discontent helped to precipitate an armed uprising led by Nathaniel Bacon, an ambitious planter of good connections and considerable means. The laws passed by Bacon's Assembly sought to limit the political power of important families on the county level by broadening the suffrage to include tenants and by creating elective posts to offset the power of appointed magistrates. Other laws, conceived and supported by the very families whose local predominance was under attack from below, attempted to combat the growing influence of the provincial council and its domination by a few families favored by the royal governor. The appointive powers of the governor were drastically limited while provincial councillors were excluded from the county courts and their tax exemptions were revoked.

Bacon's Assembly was ousted within a year, and the reform programs (especially on the local level) were as abortive as the revolt itself. Within a few decades it became generally accepted that certain established families were destined to be preeminent in wealth and power. During these same years the once-prevalent fear among the landed classes that white and black servants would rise together in rebellion gradually vanished; the fastening of a subordinate status on Africans had ensured that all white men would stand together. Subsequently, the social distance between black and white was to appear far greater than the social or economic inequalities among the classes of the white population.

The reasons for the simultaneous emergence of a caste and a class society in the Chesapeake are not completely clear, but this much is certain: In 1700, as throughout southern history, the extensive ownership of slaves and the expropriation of the produce of their labor was the prerogative of a privileged minority. There were about 3,000 slaves in Maryland at the beginning of the eighteenth century, but they were owned by only about 1,000 to 1,250 whites—less than one-fourth of the 5,000–6,000 white households in the province. The probate records in Maryland during the 1690's reveal that 75% of the planters whose wills were probated held property assessed at less than £100 sterling. Not only were these men too poor to own a slave or an indentured servant, but over one-third of them were landless and had to lease the very soil they worked. Shipping 1,200 to 3,000 pounds of tobacco each year (worth £6 to £15 sterling), this tarnished residue of the once-proud yeoman class scraped along at a subsistence level, often deeply in debt to the local storekeeper or moneylender.

A second distinct group in the white population was that 20% whose estates at probate were valued at £100 to £500 sterling. During their lifetimes most of these men had owned slaves —usually from one to five—and so had a vested interest in the perpetuation of the system. The labor of their black workers or, less often, investment in land or in a store had lifted these families above the majority of poor white planters. But social prestige and political power eluded these men as well. These honors were reserved, in the main, for the wealthiest 5% of the white population, the members of the 250 households who owned from a quarter to a third of all the slaves and who controlled the bulk of the wealth of the society.

During the first half of the eighteenth century the proportion of slaves in the total population increased dramatically (from 20 to 40% in Virginia and from 11 to 30% in Maryland). This development, the result of high rates of natural increase and of a significant increase in slave importation, had an important effect on the social structure of the white community. A greater proportion of whites employed slave labor. By the 1730's only 55% of the probated estates were assessed at less than £100 sterling, as compared to 75% a generation before. Nearly half of the white planters now had sufficient resources to own a slave (although not this many actually did). Even taking into account the rise in prices—which meant that £100 sterling was worth less in actual purchasing power—there had been a significant increase in the prosperity of the white population, but (interestingly enough) this general improvement had not resulted in greater equality within the white community.

Indeed, just the opposite, for the dimensions of the upper class expanded—in numbers and in wealth. In the 1690's the Great Planters of Maryland, those who at their deaths had estates worth £1,000 or more, constituted only 1.5% of those whose wills were probated. This proportion rose steadily: to 2.2% during the 1720's; to 3.6% during the 1730's; and to 3.9% of the total sample during the 1750's. The white population of Maryland had increased four-fold during these six decades, but the number of Great Planters had grown by a factor of ten. The wealth generated by the use of more slaves and the expansion of the tobacco industry had not been diffused equally among the members of the white community but had helped to create a relatively large class of wealthy planters.

Many of the members of this elite group were related by blood or marriage to those Great Planters who had established their predominance during the last quarter of the seventeenth century. The unique feature of the landed aristocracy of the Chesapeake was its ability to perpetuate its control over a society that was rapidly expanding, both in numbers and in geographic area. The total number of white households in Virginia increased from about 6,000 in 1700 to 80,000 in 1790, but economic wealth and political power resided in the hands of the same family clans at the end of this period as at the beginning. In the decades preceding the war for independence no less than 70% of the 110 leaders of the Virginia House of Burgesses were drawn from families resident in Virginia before 1690.

The remarkable success of the Great Planters of Virginia in preserving and extending the power of their families was the result of high rates of reproduction (which provided an ample supply of sons to take over family lands and of daughters to marry into established or rapidly rising families) and also of the system by which the resources of the family were transmitted from one generation to the next. The estate of the father did not pass to the eldest son (as among the aristocracy of eighteenth century England) leaving younger sons to find their fortunes in law, government, or the church. It was, instead, distributed among all of his male and female offspring. Thus, in his will of 1686, Robert Beverley, Sr.,

bequeathed to his eldest son Peter, all of his lands in Gloucester County lying between "Chiescake" and "Hoccadey's" creeks (an unspecified acreage); to Robert, the second son, another portion of the Gloucester lands amounting to 920 acres; to Harry, 1,600 acres in Rappahannock County; to John, 3,000 acres in the same county; to William, two plantations in Middlesex County; to Thomas, 3,000 acres in Rappahannock and New Kent counties; to his wife, three plantations including those "whereon I now live" for use during her lifetime, after which they were to descend to his daughter[s] Catherine . . . [and] Mary. . . .[3]

As these sons and daughters took up residence on the lands accumulated for them by the economic success and political acumen of their father, the family extended its influence into new localities. And this expansion more than matched the numerical and geographical growth of the colony as a whole. In the end, the weight of these established families came to press, like the atmosphere itself, evenly over the whole face of Virginia. (A similar proliferation of the upper classes had taken place in England during the sixteenth century, also during a period of rapid population growth.)[4] Of the 100 wealthiest men in the state in 1787, all except four owned lands in at least two counties, and more than half had estates in at least four counties. There was a certain irony in this development; for the practice of partible inheritance had produced both a greater equality within the ranks of the wealthy families and a greater disparity between the resources of these clans and the rest of the population. Seven members of the Carter family, the richest of all of the clans, owned a total of 170,000 acres of land and 2,300 slaves scattered over 7 different counties. They were joined, as members of the privileged one hundred, by nine members of Cocke family, eight Fitzhughs, seven Harrisons, eight Lees, seven Randolphs, and eight Washingtons.

It was this small homogeneous elite—English by descent, Anglican in religion, and linked to one another by ties of kinship and bonds of economic interest—which monopolized the political life of Virginia during the eighteenth century. There were seven members of the Lee family, all of the same generation, sitting in the Virginia assembly in the 1750's and representing five different counties. And the majority of all of the leaders of the House of Burgesses between 1720 and 1775, the men who sat on the important committees and dominated the debates, were related by blood or marriage to one or another of the dozen or so great family clans. That 60% of the white adult males had sufficient property to vote and that 45% of them regularly exercised the franchise was irrelevant given this concentration of hereditary power. In this deferential society the mass of poor

Westover, the home of the Byrd family and a fine example of the conscious emulation of English cultural models by the Virginia gentry.

white planters acquiesced in the decisions of their betters and submitted meekly to their rule.

The integration of economic wealth, social status, and political power in the families of the landed gentry gave them a degree of control over the white population almost equal to that they could exercise over their slaves. Indeed, the ever more elaborate and rigorous slave codes written by the assemblies were not designed in the first instance to coerce blacks but rather to remind whites of the duties imposed upon them by the type of society in which they lived:

It was the white man who was required *to punish his runaways, prevent assemblages of slaves, enforce the curfews, sit on the special courts, and ride the patrols [in order] to enforce slave-discipline. . . .*[5]

The principles of authority, discipline, and hierarchy embodied in these formulations were, in fact, pervasive throughout southern society. The children of the poor white planter sensed what their parents knew all too well: that they occupied an inferior place in the social hierarchy and should act accordingly. "We were accustomed to look upon, what were called *gentle folks*, as beings of a superior order," recalled the Reverend Devereux Jaratt, the son of a carpenter who eventually rose to a position of authority within the Church of England.

For my part, I was quite shy of them, and kept off at a humble distance. A periwig, in those days, was a distinguishing badge of gentle folk—and when I saw a man riding the road, near out my house, with a wig on, it would so alarm my fears, and give me such a disagreeable feeling, that, I dare say, I would run off, as for my life.[6]

The consciousness of social inferiority, inculcated in childhood to such an extent that it induced physical fear, became an enduring part of the behavior patterns (and perhaps even the personalities) of thousands of poor whites. Wherever they went, in the town or in the fields, in public or private, these men and women carried the stigma of subordinate rank with them: in their halting speech, gnarled hands, and emaciated faces. They were deferential to those above them and—especially when emboldened by drink or by numbers—harshly demanded respect from slaves and servants, whom they could consider as their social inferiors.

A hierarchical and authoritarian pattern of personal relationships had come to characterize southern colonial society by 1700, and it persisted for more than a century and a half because the conduct it sanctioned corresponded to the actual distribution of power and influence in the community. The existence of these established role expectations, these shared experiences and assumptions, also helped to perpetuate that system. The "difference between gentle and simple" which Jaratt testified was "universal among all of my age and rank," had become part of the social environment, accepted by the inhabitants as immutable and correct. Anchored in the child-training and· socialization process and solidified by the institutionalized roles of adult life, this pattern of relationships came to form an integral part of the sense of identity of thousands of adult individuals. The congruence between the social structure and the personalities of those who composed it was not exact; in this, as in any society, there was a great deal of "slippage," as the mobility achieved by Jaratt himself clearly demonstrated. And, yet, the strength and pervasiveness of these role expectations and values worked constantly to inhibit any widespread intellectual or personal challenge to the existing system. They became, in a very real sense, the social chains which bound this stratified society together. The shackles of psychological dependence and subordination had come to bind the minds of poor whites as tightly as iron chains bound the limbs of blacks.

Entrepreneurial Capitalism and Social Differentiation

It is not inequality itself, but its extent and the mode of its institutionalization, that differentiates one society from another. In the northern colonies women were placed in a position legally, socially, and economically inferior to men. The male population itself was divided by age, abilities, and accomplishments. Yet the spectrum of wealth and power in the agricultural sector of the North was much narrower than in the South and the hierarchy of social prestige was not based on the ownership of other men and women. The relative parity among the rural inhabitants of Pennsylvania, Benjamin Franklin suggested in 1759, arose

first from a more equal distribution of land by the assemblies . . . and secondly, from the nature of their occupation; husbandmen with small tracts of land, though they may by industry maintain themselves and families in mediocrity, [have] few means of acquiring great wealth. . . .

"The hopes of having land of their own and becoming independent of Landlords," observed another writer, "is what chiefly induces people into America." [7]

This commitment to independence as a prime social value had an important effect on the political life of the local community. Only those who were not dependent on others—in practical terms, those who controlled property—could hope to have a voice in the affairs of the town. This sharp line of demarcation excluded all married women, whose real and personal possessions belonged to their husbands. It also severely restricted the rights of children and of servants, who were the dependents of the male parent in the household in which they lived and worked.

During the seventeenth century the institution of bonded servitude had functioned as a means of introducing children into adult society, training them for their life's work on the farms or in the shops of others, or exposing them to good manners (and a steady diet) in the homes of the well-to-do. The system of indenture also served as a means of providing employment for adult immigrants who did not have resources sufficient to support themselves. In either case, bonded servitude was a step on the bottom of the social or agricultural ladder; as noted by one colonial official in 1767,

There can be no stronger instance of this than in the servants imported from Europe of different trades; as soon as the time stipulated in their indentures is expired, they immediately quit their Masters, and get a small tract of land.[8]

By the time these words were written the nature and the extent of the dependency relationship in northern society had undergone several significant changes. The proportion of servants in the population of Bristol, Rhode Island, remained relatively constant at 13% between 1689 and 1774 (while the total number of inhabitants increased from 421 to 1,209), but the racial composition of the group was dramatically altered as Negro or Indian "servants-for-life" replaced the indentured white sons and daughters of neighbors and kin. The same pattern prevailed in most of the port cities of the North. Less than 3% of the population of Boston was black in 1690, but this percentage rose to 8.4% in 1730 and to 9.7% in 1752. The proportions were even higher in New York; censuses taken in 1723 and in 1749 revealed that black servants-for-life constituted 18% of the total population.

The family unit, the institutional structure traditionally used to control the dependent population, was unable to cope with the problems created by this large, racially distinct, and enslaved group. Two dozen slaves revolted in New York City in 1712, killing nine whites, injuring numerous others, and setting a great many buildings on fire. White fears of a similar plot in 1740 resulted in a bloody inquisition: eighteen blacks and four whites—alleged accomplices—were hanged, thirteen Negroes were burned to death; and seventy slaves were transported to other colonies. In rural areas of the North the disturbances were less violent, usually involving unruly behavior or running away, but they were no less frequent. There was twice as much of this type of illegal protest by servants in the colony of Massachusetts Bay between 1720 and 1750 as there had been between 1629 and 1659 (while the number of cases of legal protest through court actions against masters remained the same).

By the middle of the eighteenth century the system of indentured servitude was breaking down as a method of social control. The family unit was unable to assimilate or control the culturally distinct groups which now composed the servant class. Moreover, in the large colonial cities, the majority of the dependent white population was no longer encompassed within the bounds of family government. In Boston in 1771, 29% of the adult male population were neither property owners nor the dependents of taxpaying members of the community.

These propertyless men, mostly laborers, seamen, or journeymen artisans who bargained their services for wages, introduced an element of instability into the bottom of the urban social order. Apart from the economic sanctions exercised by employers during the hours of work, there was no institutional method for controlling the activities of these men and their families, many of whom moved from town to town in search of economic subsistence. Of the 188 propertyless men resident in Boston in 1687, only 64 (or 35%) were resident in the town eight years later. This rate of persistence was less than half of that of the wealthiest portion of the population, those who were tied to the community by bonds of kinship and of economic investment. A century later the relationship between occupational status and permanence of residence was much the same; of the 546 proletarians in Boston in 1780 only 228 (or 42%) remained a decade later.

Given the differing material condition and life style of this floating population of workers, an increase in social disorder was only to be expected. Until the agitation against British rule gave an ideological edge to the antiauthoritarian and unruly activities of this lumpenproletariat, most of its violent energies were directed at other members of the class or against the black population. The scene at the Boston ferry dock following the Harvard commencement of 1755 was typical.

Notwithstanding the two Constables that placed themselves there, *two Gentlemen's Servants were thrown over, and not less than 20 of our poor Slaves (Male and Female) were thus injuriously served that Evening—The most astonishing Cursing and Swearing was continually sounding in my Ears—Women as they left the Boat, were indecently talked to, and some of them most immodestly handled—That part of the Town in the utmost Disorder and this effected by a Rabble that consisted of at least 200.*[9]

The members of this turbulent section of the population were not, as a rule, master mechanics or master craftsmen with established businesses or even the less affluent but stable and respected workingmen who were members of the dozens of private clubs and societies which had appeared among the urban lower classes. They were, rather, the drifters, the undesirables, the part-time workers, the unfortunate men who lacked the family background or class advantages or individual psychological resources to compete successfully in the harsh and impersonal world of a market economy. To survive, prosper, and thrive in a system based on commercial exchange demanded a very different set of moral and mental attitudes from those required in a culture founded on personal dependence. Life in a contractual society necessitated more calculating behavior than that in a community divided along the lines of inherited or ascribed status; sociability was suddenly less important than self-reliance. The way was open here for a man of great ambition and exceptional abilities to rise in his own lifetime to a position of great wealth. And yet, both individual initiative and the opportunity to exploit it were socially determined; the same opportunities were simply not open to all men.

The career of Thomas Hancock was a prime example of the cumulative advantages bestowed by social class and childhood training. Born in Lexington, Massachusetts, in 1703, Hancock was the third son of a Congregationalist minister. Although his two older brothers had been sent to Harvard, Thomas was apprenticed at the age of 14 to a bookseller. This was a relatively humble, but not an insignificant, beginning. His father's status and educational background had given the young man expectations and aspirations which went far beyond those of most children in the community. The accident of birth gave him greater opportunities as well. Those of less-favored backgrounds took their first job on the family farm or as an unskilled assistant to a mason, shipwright, or ropemaker; the pattern of their lives—the acquisition of a farm of their own, or the slow progression from apprentice to journeyman to master craftsman—had already been sketched in their minds by parents or employers. Beginning on a higher rung of the social ladder, Hancock had a few more options, a wider perspective, a better chance for success. After setting up his own business at the end of his seven-year indenture, he made a "good" marriage to the daughter of an established dealer in books and general merchandise.

The solid advantages bestowed by his class background explain only a part of Hancock's subsequent career. The traits of character fashioned during his childhood and young adult years also played a crucial role. He did not—indeed could not—rest content as an ordinary shopkeeper; his ambition was too strong, always prompting him to expand and to diversify his activities. Within a few years he was trading molasses for fish in Newfoundland; importing Dutch tea through St. Eustatius in the West Indies; working on a commission basis for English merchants with interests in Boston; investing in trading ventures; and accumulating his own fleet of merchant ships. Only in 1737, when his fortune was well established, did Hancock pause to erect a testimonial to his success in the form of a mansion on Beacon Hill.

The acquisitive mentality and the capitalistic activities

which raised Hancock far above his already substantial origins were, to some extent, merely the latest manifestation of an ethos characteristic of the commercial classes in European society for hundreds of years. The only unique feature of the appearance of these values in America was in the extent of their influence and in the relative absence of a countervailing (if not predominant) ethic of aristocratic leisure and gentility. "The only principle of life propagated among the young people is to get money," Cadwallader Colden reported from New York in 1748, "and men are only esteemed according to what they are worth—that is, the money they are possessed of." [10] This analysis was echoed by an English observer writing from Philadelphia in 1799: "It is a nation of Merchants, always alive to their interests; & therefore almost wholly engrossed with the thoughts of it; keen in the pursuit of wealth in all the various modes of acquiring it." [11]

The existence of these values and these patterns of behavior had a profound meaning. They hinted at the existence, on an extensive scale, of a new type of modal personality in the northern areas of colonial America. This was the dynamic character structure of the rational entrepreneur, an individual who is at once intensely ambitious, compulsively motivated, and yet cautious and calculating in his business activities.

The roots of this personality structure extended backward to an earlier phase of American (and English) history, to the religious upheavals in the mother country which, during the seventeenth century, led to the migration of dissenting Protestants to the new world. There was, in the communities formed in the American wilderness, a strange blend of old and new ideas, values, and institutions—an accurate reflection of the fact that Puritanism itself represented a key transitional phase in the long and slow evolution from a traditional to a modern conception of life, authority, and personality.

Initially, the transplantation of Puritanism to American soil accentuated the more traditional and conservative elements of this complex and contradictory social movement. In the small isolated agricultural settlements of seventeenth century New England, the father stood at the head of the family, exacting obedience from all those dependent on him; the village leaders, men dignified by age and experience, filled the offices of government and dominated political affairs; the minister directed the spiritual lives of his congregation, arranging their seating in church to reflect before God their standing among men. The pattern of authority and the institutions that gave it expression were one and the same. The key to the Puritan character as it developed in this environment "can be found in the responses of individuals to the series of stern fathers who stood over them in the homes of their childhood, in the church, in society, and in the state." [12]

The typical reaction was a peculiar blend of timidity and assertiveness, the product of a system of childhood training and social control which attempted to secure external behavioral conformity through the control and direction of all autonomous impulses. "Surely there is in all children . . . a stubbornness, and stoutness of mind arising from natural pride, which must be broken and beaten down. . . ," argued John Robinson—the pastor of the original Plymouth settlement—in an essay on "Children and Their Education,"

Children should not know, if it could be kept from them, that they have a will of their own: neither should these words be heard from them, save by way of consent, "I will" or "I will not." [13]

This attempt to mold the child's ego through education; to prevent the creation of a sharp dichotomy between the self and the society; to encourage the individual to incorporate into his own being the moral code of his culture was a very new and a very modern development. But here, in the closed, authoritarian environment of early New England, its full implications could not be realized.

This psychological evolution had a legal dimension, and it was in law that the nature of this change was first clearly articulated. In the more traditional society "law" had assumed the character of a positive prescription, the command laid down by an outside authority, "the carefully circumscribed areas where men could rightfully expend their energies";[14] it was not yet an abstract set of rules to which one freely subscribed. The two meanings of the term were caught together, at the point of historical transition, in an English dictionary of law published in 1729. Freedom was here defined, first, in the traditional sense of a "liberty" or a "privilege held by grant or prescription by which men enjoy some benefit beyond the ordinary subject,"[15] and, then, in the more modern sense as the right to do as one pleased unless restrained by law. The dimensions of authority were shifting; prescription had given way to proscription.

The locus of authority was changing as well. The ultimate effect of the Puritan emphasis on self-examination, self-knowledge, and self-mastery was to replace institutions external to the individual by an inner conscience as the arbiter of moral decisions. This internalization of social norms through the creation of a moral stabilizer within the individual was an exciting historical development. It represented, in the terms of Freudian psychology, the development in man of a more effective superego to control the basic human drives and to channel them into socially acceptable forms.

This cultural advance was possible because of the plasticity of the human organism and because of its long period of biological growth. The process of becoming a complete man or woman extends beyond the circumscribed confines of the womb into the more demanding and more varied environment of the world of childhood. Within the limits imposed by the parameters of human nature itself, the young developing individual can be shaped and molded as the culture demands. As the pattern of childrearing in the northern settlements of colonial America continued to emphasize self-control but became less concerned with the vigilant suppression of autonomy and aggression, there was a perceptible shift in the character structure of certain social groups.

This transformation can be traced, with some assurance, to the beginning of the eighteenth century. In his *Bonifacius: Or Essays to Do Good* (published in 1710 and heavily dependent, in some parts, on John Locke's *Some Thoughts Concerning Education* [1693]) Cotton Mather, the eminent Puritan divine, expressed his determination "to avoid that fierce, harsh, crabbed usage of children, that would make them dislike and tremble to come in my presence." "I would treat them," he continued, "so that they shall fear to offend me, and yet heartily love to see me." [16] In the place of the punishments of physical coercion and humiliation previously used to control children, Mather substituted anxiety; he would withhold or bestow affection as a conscious instrument of childtraining. As he explained in another essay,

I first beget in them a high opinion of their father's love to them, and of his being best able to judge, what shall be good for them. Then I make them sensible, tis a folly for them to pretend unto any witt and will of their own . . . my word must be their law. . . . I would never come to give a child a blow; except in the case of obstinacy or some gross enormity. To be chased for a while out of my presence I would make to be looked upon, as the sorest punishment in the family. . . .[17]

Children raised in this type of home developed a hyperactive conscience. Charged with personal responsibility for their actions and deeply concerned to avoid offense, they were forced to discriminate for themselves between what their parents would approve or disapprove, between what was "right" and what was "wrong." With the development of full moral autonomy, this process of discrimination became divorced from the system of reinforcement that had engendered it: The individual's conscience (or superego) warned him against moral transgression and urged him on to a continual reform of himself.

This inner psychological dynamic pushed men and women onward in the pursuit of higher standards and demanded excellence and achievement, however those terms were defined. Mather was definite on this point as well. "'Tis not *Honest*, nor *Christian*," he wrote in 1701, "that a *Christian* should have no *Business* to do," sentiments which were echoed by John Adams three-quarters of a century later in a letter to his wife: "The education of our children is never out of my mind. Train them to virtue. Habituate them to industry, activity, and spirit. . . . For God's sake make your children *hardy*, *active*, and *industrious*; for strength, activity, and industry will be their only resource and dependence." Here then in the childtraining practices and the social values of certain dissenting Protestant sects (and perhaps also a certain class within those religious groups) was an important source of the entrepreneurial character structure. Here also was the threat of boundless discontent—a compulsiveness which could be harnessed only by a strict organization of activity. "The order which the Quakers are accustomed from childhood to apply to the distribution of their tasks, their thoughts, and every moment of their lives," a percipient French visitor to Philadelphia observed, "economizes time, activity and money." [18]

There were many differences between the Congregational creed of Thomas Hancock's father and the Quakerism of the Philadelphia Friends, but their members practiced a similar method of childtraining: a middle path which kept well clear of the extremes of authoritarian repression and parental neglect. Not all of their children became self-reliant adults imbued with a deep need for achievement. Sex roles, birth order, and the wider environment also affected the socialization process; and, in any event, inherited propensities could only be influenced within certain limits. Nonetheless, the results were impressive. Quakers constituted less than one-seventh of the population of Philadelphia in 1769, but they accounted for more than half of those who paid taxes in excess of £100. Of the seventeen wealthiest men in the city, twelve had been raised as Friends.

The intensity of the Quaker's motivation towards achievement had been complemented by a religious ethic which praised frugality and condemned self-indulgence and sensuality. Much in the manner of Thomas Hancock, who had reinvested rather than consumed the profits of the first decades of business, the

Friends placed severe constraints on consumption and in a disciplined, almost compulsive, manner saved for the future. Even in the absence of entrepreneurial character traits, the discipline imposed by Christian asceticism was conducive to economic development.

The new entrepreneurial personality was most prevalent in urban centers and among particular classes and religious groups, but the economic behavior patterns and materialistic values which accompanied (and/or reinforced) it knew no geographic or social limits. During the first two decades following the settlement of Kent, Connecticut, in 1738, its 772 male inhabitants engaged in more than 6,000 separate transactions in land. Plots were sold to newcomers and to the sons of established residents; or exchanged among members of the town. In the end the more astute inhabitants (and a few absentee speculators) emerged with a considerable profit; such dealings, in combination with the returns from farming or milling or storekeeping, created a group of rural-based traders, financiers, and moneylenders. At probate in 1724, the estate of Timothy Thrall of Windsor, Connecticut, contained store goods worth £411; land assessed at £1,145; and bonds, notes, and mortgages to the value of £2,923. This type of small-scale yet widespread capital accumulation played a crucial role in promoting the process of economic development in the north. It was the result not merely of the prime market for agricultural produce or the opportunities for gain offered by the active market in land but also, and perhaps most importantly, of the capitalistic ethos and behavior patterns which had become pervasive in the rural as well as the urban sector of the northern economy.

The differing capabilities of men in the pursuit of material possessions were registered eventually on the tax lists of the community. The distribution of wealth among the first generation of settlers in Chester County in Pennsylvania was relatively equitable, a reflection of the predominant position of the small landowners and the exigencies of life in a frontier society. Then, as some farmers prospered in the years after 1715—from a lucky choice of well-drained fertile fields, shrewd agricultural practice, or cunning manipulation of the market in land and commodities —and as other inhabitants diversified their economic activities, becoming the middlemen of the community, the extent of inequality gradually increased. As late as 1748 the poorest 30% of the taxpayers in Chester County could claim 13% of the county's wealth, but this proportion had dropped to 4% by 1802. During these five decades the top tenth of the taxable population (numbering 300 in 1748 and 720 in 1802) increased

Table 3.1

Distribution of Assessed Taxable Wealth in Chester County, Pennsylvania, 1693–1802

Taxpayers	Percentage of Total Wealth Held in						
	1693	1715	1730	1748	1760	1782	1800–18
Lowest 30%	17.4%	13.1%	9.8%	13.1%	6.3%	4.7%	3.9%
Next 30%	21.1	22.9	21.7	21.7	20.5	17.3	13.7
Next 30%	37.7	38.1	39.8	36.4	43.3	44.5	44.2
Top 10%	23.8	25.9	28.6	28.7	29.9	33.6	38.3
Total	257	670	1791	2998	4290	5291	7247

SOURCE: James Lemon and Gary Nash, "The Distribution of Wealth in Eighteenth C America . . . ," *J. Soc. H.* 2 (1968), Tables I and II.

its share of the assessed wealth from 28% to 38% of the total. A nearly identical secular trend appeared in Hingham, Massachusetts, where the wealthiest tenth of the taxpayers steadily accumulated a larger proportion of the town's resources during the first three quarters of the eighteenth century.

In neither of these agricultural areas did the proportion of wealth held by the most affluent section of the community reach the levels attained in the commercial cities, but the process by which it was accumulated was basically the same. The key elements, in rural and urban areas alike, were the growing scarcity of certain factors of production (which increased the economic leverage of those who controlled them) and the opportunities offered to merchants and creditors to provide processed goods and financial services to an expanding population. In Chester County, for example, the number of taxpayers tripled in the half century following 1730. By 1782 between 25% and 35% of all taxpayers were either tenant farmers or "inmates"—married artisans or laborers living in dwellings owned by others—who, each month, paid a part of their income in rent to the land- and house-owning members of the community, and yet another part to storekeepers and other creditors in return for services. The established property owners and middlemen thus amassed a disproportionate share of the growing wealth of the county. Because of their position they were able to secure—through rents, commission and interest charges, retail markups, and the like—a part of the income of many others.

This method of accumulating wealth was different from that practiced in the slave colonies, where the *entire* surplus product of the black slave was expropriated by his master. It

Chart 3.1

Percentage of Taxable Wealth Owned by the Top Tenth of the Taxpayers, 1675–1860

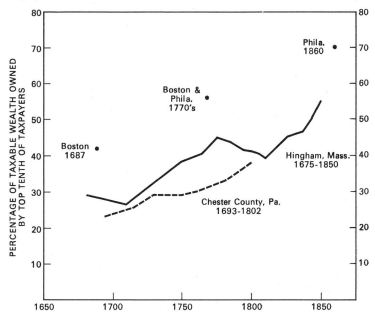

SOURCE: Tables 3.1 and 3.2; J. A. Henretta, "Economic Development and Social Structure in Colonial Boston," *WMQ* 22 (1965), Tables I and II; and, for Hingham, unpublished data compiled by Daniel Scott Smith. NOTE: Continuous data not available for Boston and Philadelphia.

was, rather, a system of agrarian and commercial capitalism in which a *part* of the output of many free men was funneled into the hands of a few. By 1774 the poorest 50% of all the adults who were potential wealth holders in the colonies of New Jersey, Delaware, and Pennsylvania owned only 13% of the total wealth of this region, as against the 40% held by the richest tenth of the population. But because of the general increase in prosperity (the result, in part, of the entrepreneurial activities of the affluent taxpayers), the standard of living of many members of the poorer half of the society was higher than that of their parents or grandparents. Concealed behind the increase in inequality (but part of the same process of economic development and social differentiation) was a significant rise in the absolute wealth of the community.

Indeed, it was this facet of the total evolutionary process that was the subject of most contemporary comment. "One half of the wealth of this city is owned by men who wear leather aprons;" a contributor to a Philadelphia newspaper claimed in the 1770's, "and the other half by those whose fathers or grand-fathers wore leather aprons." However valid as a statement of personal belief, the logic was deceptive and the remark misleading. Those who had benefited substantially from the labor of their parents numbered only 10% of the population, and this small group of wealthy taxpayers controlled 54% of the city's wealth in 1774. Moreover, even the present generation of artisans and shopkeepers constituted only half of the residents of the community. Below both of these relatively privileged groups were 40% of the free adult inhabitants; the members of this sizeable fraction of the society owned a pitiful 4% of the total wealth.

It was not this depressed section of the population, however, who controlled the development of Philadelphia or who conceived its myths and values. This was the prerogative of the successful, those long-time residents who saw about them only those craftsmen and storekeepers who had succeeded and

Table 3.2
Distribution by Net Worth: All Living Free Adult Potential Wealth Holders, American Middle Colonies and Philadelphia County, 1774

	Entire Middle Colonies		Philadelphia County Only	
	percentage of aggre-gate net worth	cumulative percentage of wealth	percentage of aggre-gate net worth	cumulative percentage of wealth
Poorest 10%	−0.4%	0 %	−0.1%	0 %
10–20	+1.5	+1.2	+0.6	+0.6
20–30	+2.5	+4	+1.6	+2
30–40	3.9	8	2.2	4
40–50	5.3	13	3.2	7
50–60	6.9	20	4.1	12
60–70	9.6	29	7.1	19
70–80	12.1	41	12.1	31
80–90	18.0	59	14.6	45
Richest 90–100	40.6	100	54.7	100
	100.0		100.0	

Source: Alice Hanson Jones, "Wealth Distribution in the American Middle Colonies . . . ," OAH Conference Paper, New Orleans, 1971, Tables 13 and 17.
Note: For definitions of net worth and potential wealth holders, see Jones "Wealth Estimates," EDCC 18, no. 4, pt. II (1970).

not the great numbers who had failed and floated away to other settlements. The descriptions of social reality composed by the members of this literate and articulate section of the community were optimistic not only because of the actual growth and prosperity of the city but also because they assumed that their own experience reflected that of the society as a whole. As always, the myths of the ruling class propagated a distorted, if attractive, version of social existence.

However skewed in their depiction of reality, these myths of social mobility and economic affluence were of crucial importance. They expressed, in an intangible, abstract form, the values and aspirations of the leading part of the community. Grudgingly acquiesced in by ordinary laborers; tacitly accepted by tenant farmers; and wholeheartedly embraced by small landowners, newly arrived indentured servants, hardworking artisans, and ambitious storekeepers, they constituted a set of shared beliefs which obscured (or perhaps justified) the acute differences in their respective material conditions.

Insofar as these elite and entrepreneurial values were internalized by the populace at large or assumed institutionalized form as role expectations of the adult members of the society, they bound this stratified community together and facilitated its continued economic expansion. Thus the White Oaks of Philadelphia—a society of relatively poor if respectable ship carpenters—instituted, as the high point of their year's social activity, an Annual Fishery which was modeled directly on the more elaborate and more prestigious festival celebrated by the gentry of the town. This conscious emulation of the social habits of their betters, this cultural mimesis, testified to the hold exercised on the minds and emotions of the lower status groups by the values and way of life of the wealthy merchants and gentry. Freer than the black slave, more prosperous than the poor white planter, blessed with a genuine opportunity for social mobility, the urban mechanic was, nevertheless, encompassed in a mental world not entirely of his own making.

The Social Basis of Provincial Politics

There were several levels of political activity in the colonies, each concerned with a different array of problems and each subject to a separate constituency. On the highest plane, the politics of empire were conducted primarily in London by aristocratic Englishmen and imperial bureaucrats with little personal knowledge of American affairs and by merchants and commercial groups with interests of their own to defend. Through their agents or allies in England the colonists in

America had a voice in the deliberations that took place in the Palace, in Parliament, and in the Plantation Office but it was weak and not often heard.

Local politics in America was equally impervious to imperial direction. In hundreds of towns, townships, and counties officials were elected and taxes levied by the resident inhabitants without direction or interference from London. These essentially autonomous systems of political power intersected on the provincial level: in the clash between the royal governor and the representative assemblies of the various colonies. The governor's task was to secure local support for imperial edicts and parliamentary legislation, if possible by persuasion but by patronage, threat, or bribery if necessary. All too often the weapons at his disposal (a few offices and military contracts, his own personal prestige and political abilities) were inadequate to the task.

These difficulties increased over time. No comprehensive and coherent colonial policy was conceived in London for implementation in America, and the patronage at the disposal of the governors was gradually appropriated by English ministers anxious to reward their own friends and supporters. An even more important factor in bringing about a slow decline in imperial authority was the appearance of an indigenous political elite. In the first generations of settlement most of the colonies lacked a distinct governing class or group of political leaders at the provincial level. Successful families might predominate in a given locality and royal governors might gather a small clique of supporters, but the ingredients of a functioning political system—a complex web of interest groups, family alliances, and regional factions—was completely lacking. Thus there was a period of "chaotic" factionalism in which there was "a ruthless competition for dominance, power, and economic advantage among rival groups of leading men, groups which were largely ad hoc and impermanent." [19]

This type of political activity—uncertain, constantly shifting, based on temporary alliances over specific issues—was the mark of a polity in which there was no sure center of social gravity. This chaotic state was characteristic of government throughout the colonies, except in the special circumstances created by the existence of the Puritan oligarchy in New England, during the first decades of settlement. It was true in Virginia until 1660 and in Maryland until 1689; it appeared as well upon the colonization of Pennsylvania, New Hampshire, and the Carolinas lasting, in each instance, for thirty or forty years. These conditions magnified the importance of the royal or proprietary governors, giving them effective authority out of proportion to the inherent powers of their office. This kaleidoscopic system of politics mirrored, on the governmental level, the unsettled social and economic structure of the community.

As social fluidity crystallized into coherent form, atomistic factionalism gave way to more stable and more predictable types of political activity. This evolution took two forms. In Virginia after 1720 and in South Carolina after 1740 the monopolization of wealth by a group of interrelated families with similar social interests and cultural values brought about the creation of a powerful political elite. The rise of a white colonial gentry in the West Indies had a similar result. In Antigua the provincial government was dominated between 1730 and 1775 by sixty-five leading families, those owning at least 300 acres of prime sugar-producing land. Fifty of these wealthy families were represented in the assembly during these years and thirty-nine in the council. Here, as in the southern colonies, the intense and bitter struggles characteristic of factional politics were submerged by the shared interests of the legislators. There were differences of opinion among individuals and struggles for power among families, but these contests were muted in tone and essentially superficial in character. They hinged on personal differences among men and not on deep economic, social, or religious cleavages in society.

The second, and more common, evolutionary political form was the emergence of a polity characterized by "stable" factionalism, with two or more relatively permanent interest groups contending for power. The classic case of this process of development was Rhode Island. Until the 1750's provincial politics in this small corporate colony had been virtually nonexistent, in part because of the absence of a strong executive branch of government. Each year the men selected by local communities of farmers predominated in the General Assembly and, in conjunction with the representatives from mercantile Newport, passed the few tax laws and general ordinances that were required. On nine occasions between 1710 and 1751 the agricultural interest enacted paper money bills designed to stimulate trade and relieve agrarian indebtedness; but apart from this particular schism between Newport and its hinterland, there were few permanent divisions within the assembly.

The emergence of Providence as a port city in competition with Newport effected a realignment of economic ties and created a system of factional politics based on sectional advantage. The spread of credit facilities and market contacts inward from the two urban centers prompted an intense civic rivalry which took political form in a bitter contest for control of the elective governorship. In 1755 the post was won by Stephen Hopkins, a merchant of Providence; this victory inaugurated a struggle for the governorship between the Hopkins family and the Ward family of Newport which lasted until the outbreak of the war for independence. The two family factions were agreed on questions of financial policy (succeeding finally in 1763 in winning assembly approval for a bill to control the value of currency) but differed sharply over the grant of monopolies, the apportionment of taxes, the bestowal of patronage, and other governmental actions which could be turned to sectional advantage. It was the prevailing strength of the Hopkins faction, guaranteed finally in the election of 1767, which resulted in the establishment of the College of Rhode Island (Brown University) in Providence rather than in Newport.

Thus the atomistic factionalism of provincial government in Rhode Island, based on the autonomy of small farming communities, had given way under the pressure of economic development to a more coherent political system dominated by merchants, lawyers, and their commercial allies resident in the urban centers. There were similar centralizing and stabilizing forces at work in other colonies as successful families translated their wealth and social prestige into political power on the provincial level. In New York a faction led by the Livingston family and based on support from the Hudson River aristocracy and dissenting religious sects battled for political hegemony with the Delanceys—Episcopalian in religion, mercantile in sympathy, and allied to the landowners of Westchester County. In the absence of political "parties," these family alliances based on social and religious interest groups had come to constitute the structural basis of provincial politics. Here also the diversity of the population made political activity open, competitive, and abusive—not at all conducive to the inculcation of habits of deference among the mass of the voters.

This emergence of an indigenous American polity, based solidly on the accumulated wealth and achieved status of a native-born elite, undermined the power of the royal governor. The deflation of imperial authority was greatest in those colonies, such as Virginia, where there were few differences among the representatives which could be exploited to the advantage of the Crown, but the process was everywhere the same. Only the socially and politically undeveloped colonies could be easily managed in the interest of the mother country. One such case was Georgia where the predominance of Scottish mercantile credit, the small settler population, and the astute political machinations of Governor Wright almost kept the colony out of the independence movement. Another was remote, sparsely settled New Hampshire where Governor Wentworth —himself a member of the leading family in the province—

used mast and timber contracts from the royal navy to control the assembly in the three decades preceding the outbreak of war. These exceptions explained the rule: only where there was no strong provincial elite or where its interests were identical with those of the governor could the imperial representative have more than a modicum of power.

As old families and established groups tightened their grip on the institutions of government during the first three-quarters of the eighteenth century, American politics became more elitist and oligarchic. Fewer and fewer settlers could justly observe, with Cadwallader Colden, that "the most opulent families, in our own memory, have risen from the lowest ranks of the people." [20] Even in relatively democratic Connecticut the 600 offices above town level were filled by only 400 different men (because of plural officeholding) in the 1750's; and in any one year over half of these officials were members of the one hundred most prominent families. A few decades later, John Adams remarked:

Go into every village in New England and you will find that the office of justice of the peace, and even the place of representative, which has ever depended only on the freest election of the people, have generally descended from generation to generation, in three or four families at most.[21]

Politics had become predictable. The great mass of ordinary men voted for the members of those families who had proved their astuteness in economic affairs and whose large houses and social prestige clearly marked them out for the management of the affairs of state.

The difference between the politics of the northern colonies and those in the South did not lie primarily in the extent of the franchise, but rather in the proportion of men who were genuinely eligible for office. In Virginia, Maryland, and much of South Carolina all of the black population and 75% of the white inhabitants were automatically excluded, by color or condition, from an active role in the decision making process. Political life was the prerogative of the privileged members of this quasi-aristocratic society: capable, well-read men who were, in a very real sense, born to rule. In these regions of colonial America a place in the county court or the legislature was effectively limited to nominees chosen from among the top 10% of the total adult male population.

The social spectrum of political representation and active participation in the North was about twice as large. The absence of a large slave population and a cultural heritage of independence had resulted in a less highly stratified society; and the greater diversity of economic activities had brought moderate affluence to a greater proportion of the total population, especially in the predominant rural sector. There were the glimmerings of an established oligarchy in New York, with its mass of tenant farmers presided over by members of the Livingston, Van Courtland, or Van Rensselaer families—and even in Massachusetts, where 40% of the top officials in thirteen towns were drawn from their four leading families. But there was also more competition for office among men of considerable property and less deference paid to them by those of ordinary means, especially in the heterogeneous middle colonies. If its abusive tone, open character, and social, religious, and sectional diversity occasionally gave the royal or proprietary governor greater leverage and more room to maneuver, the emphasis on local autonomy and the democratic thrust of the provincial politics of the North rendered it as impervious to imperial direction and control as that of the less internally divided colonies to the south.

Conflict and Consensus

Common allegiance to the British Crown produced similarities in language, culture, and political institutions in the various American colonies but it could not prevent (or conceal) their fundamental divergences in social development. The economic base and the composition of the population varied from one region to another; and so also did the value systems, behavior patterns, and character structures of their inhabitants. Within each area, however, the fragments, or facets, of social life formed a coherent and interdependent whole. Each of these social systems had a number of functionally critical qualities; and these can be isolated, as a set of abstractions, for comparison and contrast.

The society of the West Indies was "plural" in nature. It was composed of two distinct sociocultural sections divided along racial lines; and each of these subcultures preserved, to a considerable extent, its own institutions and way of life. There were different patterns of marriage, family life, and property ownership between blacks and whites; different principles governed religious worship and social intercourse. For all their differences in language and tribal background, the African slaves had more in common among themselves than most of them did with their white masters.

The disparity in racial origins and in material condition determined the nature of authority and of political life. The two subsystems were held together by physical force, not moral consent. There was no common allegiance to a set of political principles; no unconscious affirmation of a central set of values which sanctioned the legitimacy of the social order. Indeed, it was the policy of the dominant white minority to demarcate clearly its superiority over the black majority and to discourage acculturation and assimilation (however much miscegenation might be tolerated).

The hegemony of the whites was maintained by their control of the government and, most important of all, the military. Independent companies of British troops were permanently stationed in most of the islands of the West Indies; and periodic attempts to transfer them to other parts of the empire elicited strong protests from those merchants and planters who had the most to lose if white law and order were not maintained. The social order was so fragile and the danger of slave insurrection (perhaps abetted by the neighboring French or Spanish) so great that there was no alternative to the dependence on brute military force as the first guarantee of political authority. Even this was not always successful. In Jamaica, black Maroons waged a successful guerrilla war against white planters and British troops during the 1730's and secured de facto independence for their communities on a remote corner of the island.

The same fears of rebellion were present in South Carolina and accounted for the willingness of the provincial assembly to subsidize the British regulars stationed in that predominantly black colony. South Carolina was the scene, nevertheless, of the only black uprising of major significance on the continent during the colonial period. In 1739 fifty to one hundred blacks rose in bloody revolt and marched off to join the Spanish in Florida before being dispersed by the white militia. The constant fear of black rebellion left a deep mark on this society, for it demanded the institutionalization of violence as the basis of social stability.

Despite reliance on force and a strict caste division between the races, the society of the southern American colonies was not plural in character. The widely dispersed black population was unable to maintain a viable religion and culture of its own. Moreover, the gradual acculturization of native-born slaves through the total-institution of slavery gradually lessened the crude dependence on force. As time passed, elements of "consensus" and of moral persuasion began to infuse the system of social control. This was especially the case among the poor white planters who quickly learned to accept their subordinate place in the social hierarchy. Thus, although sharply divided along the lines of race and class, this society (except in the backcountry) was relatively stable; conflict was latent, not manifest.

By contrast, New England society was a model of the consensus made possible by homogeneity. British troops were never stationed in these settlements until 1768 and their presence then was an important factor in bringing about armed revolt by the xenophobic resident population. There had been previous outbreaks of violence against customs officials and other royal bureaucrats, likewise the agents of an alien and external power. There had also been a good many uprisings which were extra-institutional in character: "mobs" composed of a fair cross-section of the population took action, for example, against deviant elements (such as prostitutes, carriers of contagious diseases, and those who sought to hoard food or manipulate its price) who seemed to constitute a danger to the moral or physical health of the community. As a rule these mass police actions received the tacit support of the local officials. Lacking a powerful constabulary and overwhelmingly white, Anglo-Saxon, and dissenting Protestant in composition, these communities mobilized the entire body politic for the task of preserving order.

This system of social self-control was possible because of the relative uniformity of thought and condition among the members of these towns. Access to many communities in New England was strictly regulated by the resident population, and undesirable aliens were constantly "warned out." These rigid standards of social (and often religious) selection were designed to insure that these settlements remained restricted to like-minded inhabitants. This quest for unanimity was bolstered by a religious ideology which stressed self-restraint and selfless-ness in dealings with others; by a system of childtraining which fostered a strong moral conscience and an acute sense of right and wrong; and by cultural habits and social expectations which placed a high value on conformity to accepted standards. Once the members of a town meeting had achieved consensus on a given issue, their decision assumed an ethical significance all were bound to respect.

Those who would not heed the voice of the community were encouraged to leave or, upon occasion, actually expelled. There was no toleration of diversity in this homogeneous region; no philosophical commitment to the rule of the majority. "The major part of those who were present were [farmers]," the merchants of Salem, Massachusetts, argued when protesting against a tax schedule which imposed high rates on their financial assets, "and the vote then passed was properly their vote and not the vote of the whole body of the town." [22] The metaphor—with its implication of a mutually dependent and interconnected polity in which the well-being of one member affected the condition of all—was completely appropriate. It reflected the social and cultural homogeneity of most of rural New England and the intuitive rejection by most of its inhabitants of a world in which there was a diversity of value systems; they had no historical experience of such complexity.

The cultural difference between the original Dutch settlers and their English conquerors had helped to provoke Leisler's rebellion in New York in 1689; and the result had been permanent stationing of a detachment of British troops in the colony. Subsequent migration of thousands of Germans and Scotch-Irish Presbyterians into Dutch New York (and the neighboring provinces of New Jersey and Pennsylvania, which were already the home of a sizable Quaker population) introduced even more diversity into the social complexity of this region. And yet these colonies never degenerated into plural societies ruled only by naked force.

New England democracy, a "democracy devoid of legitimate difference, dissent, and conflict," [23] had a very different character from that developed by the more heterogeneous society of the middle colonies. A political system based on compromise and accommodation gradually (and grudgingly) emerged in this area during the course of the eighteenth century, giving institutional legitimacy and an encompassing constitutional form to its cultural diversity. Political factionalism was rife in these provinces—was perhaps more intense here than anywhere in the British empire—but these legislative struggles served to prevent a resort to physical force and political coercion. All religious and cultural factions, even eventually the rough Scotch-Irish Presbyterians of the frontier regions, were accepted into the polity on the basis of equality. Consensus was limited to representation and participation; not, as in New England, to the substance of politics. But this was sufficient to preserve social stability while generating a competitive type of politics which eventually produced (in the persons of Aaron Burr, DeWitt Clinton, and Martin Van Buren) the first really professional politicians in American history.

If the middle colonies lacked the homogeneous solidarity of New England or the enforced stability of southern slave society during the eighteenth century, these provinces were also spared their rigorous psychological or martial systems of social control. The internal coherence of the middle colonies did not derive from the existence of dependent personalities created by huge disparities in wealth and status or from the institutionalized violence of slavery; nor did it rely on invocation of a conformity in thought and action which stultified individual self-expression by channeling it into accepted forms. It was not completely accidental that the freedom of the press to criticize government officials was first clearly enunciated in New York—in the Zenger case of 1735. And the grounds of defense, which admitted the libel but justified it as being true, adumbrated a new principle of law. Forced by the contingencies of history to deal with diversity, the inhabitants of the middle colonies were slowly accommodating their laws, political systems, and personal mental outlooks to their unpredictable new world of social and cultural complexity.

At midcentury these problems had assumed a new sense of urgency, not only in the middle colonies, but also in areas less well-equipped by experience or inclination to deal with them. Beginning in 1740 there were a series of interrelated crises in American society as the inherent tendencies of two generations of rapid population growth, extensive economic development, and increased social diversity rushed forward to fulfillment. In more than one colony these new tensions were to pull the inherited web of social authority and political power to the breaking point.

Notes to Chapter Three

1. The formulation is Eric Fromm's, as quoted in David M. Potter, *People of Plenty: Economic Abundance and the American Character* (Chicago: University of Chicago Press, 1954), p. 11.
2. Frank J. Klingberg, *An Appraisal of the Negro in Colonial South Carolina* (Washington: Associated Publishers), p. 29.
3. Bernard Bailyn, "Politics and Social Structure in Virginia," in Stanley N. Katz, ed., *Colonial America: Essays in Politics and Social Development* (Boston: Little, Brown, 1971), p. 154.
4. See Lawrence Stone, "Social Mobility in England, 1500–1700," *P&P* 33 (1966): 23–24; and Peter Laslett, *The World We Have Lost* (New York: Scribner, 1968), pp. 61–64, whose simile I have borrowed.
5. Winthrop D. Jordan, *White Over Black; American Attitudes Toward the Negro, 1550–1812* (Chapel Hill: University of North Carolina Press, 1968), pp. 108–109.
6. "The Autobiography of the Reverend Devereux Jaratt, 1732–1793," introduction and notes by Douglass Adair, *WMQ* 9 (1952) : 361.
7. Leonard W. Labaree, ed., *The Papers of Benjamin Franklin*, 12 vols. (New Haven, Conn.: Yale University Press, 1956–1970), vol. 8, pp. 341–342; and New York Historical Society, Colden Papers, *Collections*, vol. 51, pp. 30–31.
8. F. R. Dulles, *Labor in America: A History*, 3rd rev. ed. (New York: Crowell, 1966), p. 11.
9. Reprinted from the Boston *Gazette*, *WMQ* 23 (1966) : 146–147.
10. Stuart Bruchey, *The Roots of American Economic Growth, 1607–1861* (New York: Harper & Row, 1965), pp. 194–195.

11. Patricia Holbert Menk, ed., "D. M. Erskine: Letters from America, 1798–1799," *WMQ* 6 (1949): 276.
12. Richard Bushman, *From Puritan to Yankee: Character and the Social Order in Connecticut, 1690–1765* (Cambridge: Harvard University Press, 1967), p. 18.
13. John Demos, "Underlying Themes in the Witchcraft of Seventeenth-Century New England," in Katz, *Colonial America*, p. 130 n.
14. Bushman, op. cit., p. 6.
15. Charles Wilson, *England's Apprenticeship, 1607–1763* (New York: St. Martin, 1965), p. xi.
16. Elizabeth B. Schlesinger, "Cotton Mather and His Children," *WMQ* 10 (1953): 183–186.
17. Arthur W. Calhoun, *A Social History of the American Family*, 3 vols. (New York: Barnes & Noble, 1960), vol. 1, p. 113.
18. F. B. Tolles, "Benjamin Franklin's Business Mentors: The Philadelphia Quaker Merchants," *WMQ* 4 (1947): 69.
19. Jack P. Greene, "Changing Interpretations of Early American Politics," in R. A. Billington, ed., *The Reinterpretation of Early American History* (San Marino, Calif.: Huntington Library, 1966), p. 176.
20. Bernard Bailyn, *The Origins of American Politics* (New York: Knopf, 1968), pp. 131–132.
21. J. R. Pole, "Historians and the Problem of Early American Democracy," *Amer. Hist. Rev.* 67 (1962): 646.
22. Michael Zuckerman, "The Social Context of Democracy in Massachusetts," *WMQ* 25 (1968): 542.
23. Ibid., pp. 539–540.

Before 1765 the inhabitants of the North American colonies were loyal, if somewhat fractious and uncooperative, subjects of the British Crown. There had been no significant challenge to imperial authority since 1689 when the overthrow of the Stuarts in the Glorious Revolution in England had encouraged rebellions against a number of their appointees in America. For three generations the colonists had accepted the relatively mild restrictions imposed by the Laws of Trade and Navigation and had prospered. For its part the home government had acquiesced in the development of the local representative assemblies and watched without animadversion the evolution of a rather complex and autonomous economic system.

Then, rather suddenly, the imperial authorities began to tighten the bonds of empire. Beginning in the 1760's, the British parliament began a sustained campaign to reimpose its sovereignty over the American settlements and to regulate more closely the course of their internal development. This resolve took concrete form in a series of measures designed to increase imperial revenues in America and to subject colonial trade to more rigorous administrative controls. Within a dozen years these measures—hardly oppressive by any standards and only tentatively and partially implemented—had produced an armed revolt in most of the American colonies.

The response seemed completely out of proportion to the stimulus. And so, in a narrow sense, it was. The momentous effect produced by the new imperial legislation was less the result of its intrinsic character than of the context into which it was introduced. For three-quarters of a century the Americans had ruled themselves, without interference from London; any alteration in this established pattern—which had come to appear as the given, the natural, state of affairs—was certain to meet resistance.

THE CRISIS OF AMERICAN COLONIAL SOCIETY

Moreover, the settlers had been arguing and fighting among themselves since 1740, as they sought to alleviate the strains placed upon their traditional institutions and values by a sustained period of rapid growth. For nearly a generation a succession of religious struggles, economic disturbances, and armed conflicts had shaken the foundations of social stability, creating a tense social environment conducive to an aggressive, even violent, reaction to new and unexpected pressures. Injected into the highly charged atmosphere of a volatile society with a penchant for independence, the new British regulations produced an explosion which all but shattered the once-impregnable edifice of imperial authority.

Westward Expansion and Armed Conflict

Since the late 1740's various members of the Board of Trade, the advisory agency on American matters within the British government, had perceived both the growing autonomy of the American settlements and the increasing tensions within many of them, and had proposed new types of measures designed to deal with these developments. In 1749 the Board seriously considered the dispatch of royal troops to suppress the land riots which had broken out in New Jersey, the first occasion during the entire eighteenth century when events in any of the continental colonies had seemed to require such a drastic measure.

In fact, this uprising of small tenant farmers against landlords and speculators was symptomatic of widespread discontent in many of the longer-settled agricultural regions. In New Jersey, the basic problem was the engrossment of land by wealthy proprietors, a situation which invited a political solution; but elsewhere, the troubles stemmed from the more fundamental pressure of population upon depleted landed resources. One index of this menacing development was the large number of unmarried single men living at home because they could no longer be easily absorbed into the local economy. Twenty-three percent of the white population of Bristol, Rhode Island, in 1774 was composed of single men and women over the age of 16, and 16% of all taxpayers in Chester County, Pennsylvania, in 1760 were single freemen over the age of 21.

Each year some members of this mobile and potentially volatile section of the population moved off to the frontier in search of better opportunities. This migration alleviated some of the problems faced by the overcrowded communities of the East; it also generated a series of bitter battles over disputed land claims in the western regions. During the 1750's a group of farmers in Connecticut created the Susquehannah Company in order to undertake colonization of the Wyoming Valley in Pennsylvania. By 1774 the Company (which by this time had become a speculative enterprise) had settled 2,000 colonists in Pennsylvania and had won the support of the Connecticut Assembly for the extension of that colony's legal jurisdiction into the area.

This direct challenge to the land rights of the Penn family and to the authority of the Pennsylvania legislature brought the two colonies to the verge of war. Indeed, sporadic fighting had broken out between those holding land grants from Pennsylvania authorities and the intruders from Connecticut. Within New England itself, the situation was equally acute. Armed conflict had taken place between residents of New York and the Green Mountain Boys of New Hampshire over land claims in the future state of Vermont; and there were other outbreaks of violence along the borders separating New York from Massachusetts and Connecticut.

The pattern was clear. The result of a century of sustained population growth was a massive migration into the interior along the entire American frontier and the reopening of crucial questions about long-disputed western boundaries. In 1745 the New England colonies raised a large expeditionary force for an attack on the French fortress of Louisburg in Nova Scotia in order to safeguard their fishing industry (which had served as an alternative source of employment for those forced off the land) and to inhibit French settlement in the interior. Similar expansionist sentiments appeared in the middle and the southern colonies during these same years. Hundreds of settlers began to push across the mountains toward the fertile lands of the Ohio River valley, producing requests for military assistance from colonial governments and prompting the creation of land companies seeking title to this rich agricultural area. By 1754 this pressure from poor settlers, wealthy speculators, and colonial politicians had led to a confrontation between French and American military forces in the backwoods of Pennsylvania and to the outbreak of a general war which was neither sought nor welcomed by the leading statesmen of Europe.

The Seven Years' War led to permanent expulsion of the French government from Canada. It also ensured British control of the interior of North America, which, in turn, created a new series of conflicts between the American settlers and the mother country. To guarantee its sovereignty and to lessen the danger of a new war with the Indians, the British government issued a Proclamation in 1763 restricting settlement to the east of a line drawn down the crest of the Appalachian mountains; and to maintain the inviolability of this boundary, it proceeded to station troops from the regular army at strategic points within the interior. The anger of land-hungry farmers and eager speculators was soon directed against the imperial authorities. For the next decade influential colonists with an interest in London sought to have this restrictionist settlement policy reversed, while thousands of ordinary Americans repudiated British authority directly by moving into the prohibited western lands.

The fear of this unregulated mass migration of white settlers into lands belonging to the Indian tribes had been one of the major factors underlying the British decision to maintain an army of 10,000 men in America following the end of the war. Another consideration which figured prominently in this crucial commitment to a military presence was the obvious need for a garrison force in the newly captured provinces of Nova Scotia, Canada, and Florida. Finally, there was the feeling among some members of the British ministry—such as Charles Townshend and the Earl of Halifax, both of whom had urged the dispatch of troops to New Jersey a decade before—that the steady trend toward colonial autonomy should be broken by resolute action. As one memorandum prepared in the Plantation Office put it: "Troops and Fortifications will be very necessary for Great Britain to keep up in her Colonys, if she intends to secure their Dependence on Her. . . ."[1]

Troops were first used, however, to resolve one of the many land disputes which had suddenly arisen all across the continent. At the request of local authorities a battalion of British regulars routed squatters from the estates of the rich landlords of the Hudson River valley and thus guaranteed, by force of arms, the land claims of these New Yorkers against those of the settlers who had migrated from neighboring Connecticut and Massachusetts. The reports in the New England press of this seemingly arbitrary use of military force, with their emphasis on looting and indiscriminate destruction, reinforced the fears of many colonists of the dangers to their liberty posed by a standing army over which they had little, if any, control. Indeed, the adverse political reaction produced by this hasty intervention was sufficient to secure a ministerial rebuke for General Gage, the Commander-in-Chief of the British forces, and to ensure that regular troops would not be used again in the settlement of domestic colonial conflicts.

Yet this was precisely the moment when a respected and neutral imperial police force was most needed in the colonies. For in addition to the conflicts generated by the pressure of population upon resources in New England, there were other armed confrontations in the colonies to the south. During the late 1760's government authority and social order disintegrated

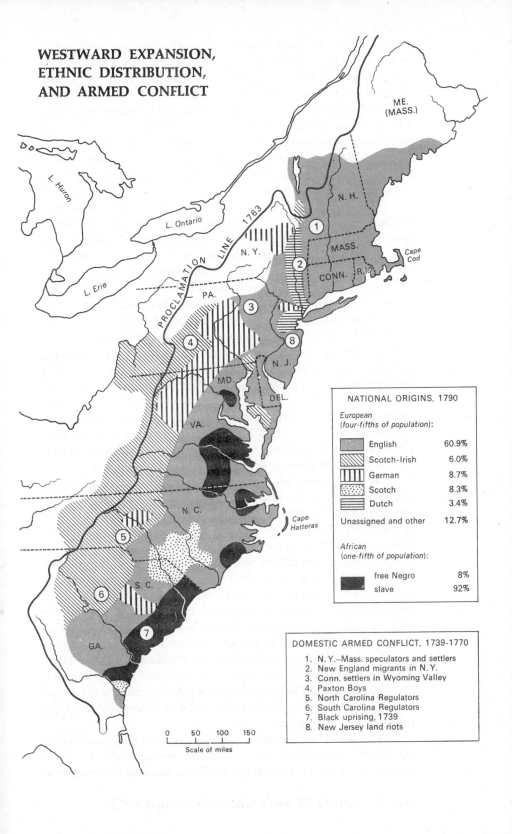

WESTWARD EXPANSION, ETHNIC DISTRIBUTION, AND ARMED CONFLICT

ME.
(MASS.)

L. Huron

L. Ontario

PROCLAMATION LINE 1763

L. Erie

N. H.

N. Y.

MASS.

CONN.   R.I.

Cape
Cod

PA.

N. J.

MD.

DEL.

VA.

N. C.

Cape
Hatteras

S. C.

GA.

1
2
3
4
8
5
6
7

NATIONAL ORIGINS, 1790

European
(four-fifths of population):

	English	60.9%
	Scotch-Irish	6.0%
	German	8.7%
	Scotch	8.3%
	Dutch	3.4%
Unassigned and other		12.7%

African
(one-fifth of population):

| | free Negro | 8% |
| | slave | 92% |

DOMESTIC ARMED CONFLICT, 1739-1770

1. N. Y.–Mass. speculators and settlers
2. New England migrants in N. Y.
3. Conn. settlers in Wyoming Valley
4. Paxton Boys
5. North Carolina Regulators
6. South Carolina Regulators
7. Black uprising, 1739
8. New Jersey land riots

0   50   100   150

Scale of miles

completely in the backcountry of South Carolina, and actual fighting broke out in the interior regions of North Carolina and Pennsylvania. These struggles were not the relatively simple disputes over land rights which had brought violence to the unsettled frontier of the North, but disputes which encompassed a much wider range of issues: political representation of newly established communities in the provincial assemblies; sectional discrimination in taxation; administrative corruption; Indian policy; and, suffusing them all, a basic confrontation among antagonistic ethnic groups.

The origins of these encounters lay in two related events: the large-scale migration of non-English settlers into the American colonies during the first half of the eighteenth century and their settlement in the less-crowded and less-accessible areas of the interior. In 1700 most of the white population (with the significant exception of the Dutch settlers in New York and New Jersey) had been of English ancestry, but this predominance had steadily decreased in the face of sustained immigration from other parts of the British Isles and from continental Europe. William Penn deliberately encouraged the settlement of Germans in his colony, establishing them in townships of their own and thus facilitating the preservation of their language, customs, and religion. This influx of German colonists extended to New York, where shiploads of refugees from the Palatine were welcomed as tenant farmers as early as 1707; and to Virginia and the Carolinas, where the backcountry was gradually filled by the migration of Germans moving down the Shenandoah Valley.

By 1790, when the first census revealed the full extent of ethnic diversity in the United States, those of German ancestry constituted nearly 9% of the total white population. In Pennsylvania the proportion was nearly four times as great, while in New York and New Jersey the large concentration of settlers of Dutch descent constituted another political and cultural force of considerable magnitude. This basic alteration in the composition of the population was one of the prime causes of the open and competitive factional character of politics in the middle colonies. Indeed, the balance of power was sufficiently fine in this region that the political hegemony exercised by those of English ancestry was threatened by coalitions composed of various other ethnic groups. In Pennsylvania, one observer noted, Baptists, Presbyterians, and German Lutherans had combined to "attempt a general confederacy of the three societies in opposition to the ruling party [of Quakers]."

The arrival of thousands of Scotch-Irish migrants during the middle decades of the eighteenth century added a new element of diversity and instability. These Scottish Presbyterians

Table 4.1
Ethnic Distribution of the White Population in 1790:
Selected States

State	English	Scotch	Scotch-Irish	Irish	German	Dutch	Unassigned or Other
Massachusetts	82.0%	4.4%	2.6%	1.3%	0.3%	0.2%	9.2%
New York	52.0	7.0	5.1	3.0	8.2	17.5	7.2
Pennsylvania	35.3	8.6	11.0	3.5	33.3	1.8	6.5
Virginia	68.5	10.2	6.2	5.5	6.3	0.3	3.0
South Carolina	60.2	15.1	9.4	4.4	5.0	0.4	5.5
All states and territories	60.9	8.3	6.0	3.7	8.7	3.4	9.0

SOURCE: *Historical Statistics*, Ser. Z 20.

had settled in Ireland during the previous century in order to secure the dependence of that Catholic country to the British Crown, but now found themselves the victims of an ethnic and religious system of discrimination almost as extensive and onerous as that applied to the Catholic population. The Test Act of 1704 reserved public office to members of the Church of England, while mercantile legislation subordinated the Irish woolen industries to those of the mother country. A succession of bad harvests in the late 1720's was a final and irreparable blow to the hopes of thousands. In July of 1728 seventeen ships were jammed into Ulster ports boarding emigrants and over 3,000 people left for America during the course of the summer alone.

Once in the colonies many of these settlers moved on to the frontier; and their letters to those still in Ireland inaugurated a process of chain-migration as whole kinship groups and villages joined relatives and neighbors in America. Eight percent of the population of Maine was of Scotch-Irish extraction in 1790, while the proportion reached 9% in South Carolina, and 11% in Georgia and in Pennsylvania. Bitter at the treatment they had received in Ireland, these Ulstermen were not prepared to accept without question the British Proclamation of 1763 restricting the bounds of their American settlements. Nor were they willing to permit the eastern and English sectors of the colonies to dominate their lives or deny them a voice in the affairs of state.

The first overt conflict came in Pennsylvania in 1763. A group of Scotch-Irish settlers massacred a tribe of peaceful

Indians who were under the nominal protection of the Quaker-dominated provincial government. This barbarism, although provoked by Indian raids on farms established on tribal lands, also reflected resentment at the unwillingness of the Assembly to sanction an armed expansion into the interior of the colony. Because representation was apportioned so that the three eastern counties elected twice as many members as the five counties to the west, the settlers on the frontier were unable to exert much political leverage. They resorted, therefore, to direct action. Following the massacre, the Paxton Boys led 250 armed frontiersmen in a determined march on Philadelphia. Only the mediation of Benjamin Franklin, who met the dissident group at Lancaster, stemmed this advance and averted a confrontation between the Scotch-Irish Presbyterians and a militia of mechanics and tradesmen hastily armed for the defense of the city.

When a similar type of conflict between the interests of the west and those of the east developed in North Carolina, there was no tradition of political compromise to aid in the resolution of the dispute. Here, as in Pennsylvania, the backcountry was composed of a heterogeneous population of Germans and Scotch-Irish. There were, in addition, thousands of recent migrants from Scotland (10 to 15% of the entire white population in 1790) who had been forced from their homeland by the pressure of population upon depleted agricultural holdings, rising rents, and the repression visited upon the countryside by the English government following the failure of the Jacobite uprising of 1745. The distribution of political power in North Carolina was similar as well, with control of the provincial Assembly lodged firmly in the hands of slaveholders of English descent resident in the seaboard regions.

These sectional divisions generated a series of local uprisings in the backcountry in the late 1760's. The residents of Orange County began by complaining of extortionate fees exacted by officials appointed by the governor; the corrupt management of elections by the provincially nominated sheriffs; and the imposition of tax schedules which discriminated against the less-developed economy of the interior. When these grievances were ignored, a Regulator Movement organized opposition to the provincial authorities. By 1768 crowds of men and women were releasing their arrested leaders from jail, forcing the closing of courts hearing cases for debt and for nonpayment of taxes, and setting fire to the properties of unpopular judges. The response of the royal governor, strongly backed by the provincial Assembly, was to raise the eastern militia in order to put down this agitation by the force of arms. In May of 1771, the

Regulators of North Carolina were put to flight at the battle of the Alamance River; and their leaders subsequently prosecuted, convicted, and put to death.

Regional tensions were nearly as acute in South Carolina, but in this predominately black colony they never reached the stage of armed conflict because the militia of the lowland counties was immobilized by the pervasive fear of a slave revolt. The provincial government took no action in 1766 when groups of bandits began a campaign of arson and robbery against those who had settled in upland regions. In this political vacuum, the task of maintaining order was assumed by another group of Regulators. This vigilante organization first suppressed the outlaw bands and then sought to control the lives of the "lower people," those hunters and squatters who lived at the fringe of respectable society and who seemed to constitute a threat to the stability of the region.

This arbitrary (if understandable) assumption of political authority by the Regulators resulted in the appearance of another extra-legal movement. The members of the Moderation, some of whom had previously served as provincial justices of the peace, questioned the legitimacy of Regulator rule and demanded a return to more established methods of maintaining law and order. In March of 1769 a pitched battle between 600 supporters of each of these rival backcountry groups was narrowly averted. Finally impressed by the seriousness of the situation, the provincial Assembly created four new judicial circuits, each with the highest jurisdiction in civil and criminal cases and each with provisions for trials by a jury composed of residents of the immediate area. With this grant of judicial autonomy, the inhabitants of the interior of South Carolina had achieved one of the goals demanded by the Regulators of North Carolina; but they, like most of the residents of the American interior, lacked equal political representation in the provincial Assembly and an equitable tax schedule.

Local factors—the composition of the population, a tradition of political compromise, the presence of racial as well as ethnic divisions—dictated the specific outcome in each colony, but the divergent results could not conceal the wider pattern: The expansion of settlement into the interior had exacerbated political conflict and created severe social cleavages within each of the American settlements. The traditional system of representation had not been sufficiently flexible to accommodate itself to the new distribution of population and thus give form and order to emergent social forces. By 1770 most disputes had achieved a temporary resolution; but everywhere in the backcountry there were grievances that would find renewed expression upon the outbreak of the war with England and that would take an explicitly political form in the constitutional conventions called to establish the new institutions of state government.

Of even greater importance was the fact that for the first time in the history of English settlement in America, white men were turning to physical force as the ultimate arbiter of their differences. In the past those in the English colonies had used armed force to dispossess the aboriginal peoples from their lands, to suppress black slave revolts, and to resist the expansion of the French. But, except on rare occasions, such as Bacon's Rebellion in Virginia in 1675 and the uprisings in Maryland, New York, and Massachusetts in 1689, the colonists had not sought a military solution to their own political and social problems.

Now, in the third quarter of the eighteenth century, the situation had changed. In New England the tensions induced by soil depletion, higher mortality rates, and a surplus agricultural population had produced a determined expansion to the west and north and widespread (but small-scale) violence among land claimants. In the colonies to the south the heterogeneity of the population gave sectional disputes a more coherent and an even more dangerous character. To those of English ancestry the Scotch, Scotch-Irish, and Germans were nearly as alien as the French against whom they had fought for centuries. Political and economic conflicts that might have been settled by constitutional means were escalated, by the intensity of ethnic prejudice, into armed confrontations. Ultimately, this cultural polarization of society would be revived and increased by the war for independence; in New York and Pennsylvania and in the Carolinas, ethnic identity would be a prime determinant of allegiance to the Loyalist or Patriot side.

There was a third factor, in addition to land hunger and cultural diversity, that accounted for the increasing incidence of political violence. This was the militarization of colonial society produced by the wars against the French. There were more arms and ammunition now available in America than ever before and more men who were experienced in their use. The years of fighting had also broken down the prohibitions placed by civilized society on the use of force. Men who had taken up arms against Louisburg in 1745 or against the French and Indians between 1754 and 1763 had become accustomed to using physical violence to defend their property or to attain their personal interests. Emotionally and intellectually they were prepared to use force, whether the object was to win a disputed land claim in New England; to defy the discriminatory policies of provincial governments dominated by eastern interests; or, eventually, to resist the new British measures of taxation and control.

The immediate effect of the militarization of society by the Seven Years' War was to raise the intensity of intracolonial disputes; a second result was to increase the probability of an armed confrontation between the colonies and the mother country. For the first time in their history the American settlers had among their numbers a large contingent of officers and soldiers with actual battlefield experience; a group of merchants with considerable expertise in military logistics; and governmental leaders acquainted with the problems of wartime mobilization and finance. Beyond this, the population as a whole was familiar with the successful use of military force for the achievement of national goals. In 1775 political violence was not an unknown quantity for thousands of Americans, but a central part of their individual lives.

The Great Awakening

The increasing ethnic diversity of the colonies was accompanied by a growth of religious controversy. The appearance of new cultural groups in the middle and southern colonies brought a corresponding expansion in the number of religious sects and constituted a direct challenge to the extant principles of doctrinal orthodoxy. Only Pennsylvania, with its guarantee of complete religious liberty, largely escaped the problems posed by the existence of many different denominations within a polity in which state support (and tax monies) went to an established church. Elsewhere, the most prevalent type of relationship between church and state resembled the multiple establishment created in New York in 1664—each settlement was permitted to choose its own pastor and church. When Governor Gooch invited the Scotch-Irish Presbyterians to settle along the Virginia frontier in the 1720's and 1730's (to serve as a buffer against Indian attack), he granted them freedom of worship and exempted them from the support of the established Church of England.

The evolution toward a society of sectarian diversity and religious liberty was slowest in New England, where the homogeneity of the population and the paucity of non-English immigrants permitted more traditional attitudes to remain unquestioned. During the seventeenth century the Puritans of Massachusetts Bay had resorted to deportation (and, in a few cases, to judicial murder) to rid their settlements of Quakers, and these exclusionist and repressive attitudes lingered on for decades. It was only in 1708 that Connecticut granted Baptists,

Anglicans, and Quakers the legal right to worship (while continuing to exclude Roman Catholics), and only in 1727 that the members of these religious groups were exempted from the compulsory support of the established Congregational churches. This latter concession was contingent upon the presentation of a certificate testifying to the individual's monetary support of his own church—a reservation that revealed the continuing strength of the belief that men were too depraved to support religion on a voluntary basis and that it was the duty of the state to guarantee the financial viability of religious institutions.

This alliance between two of the major institutions of American society was subjected to tremendous strain by the outbreak of intense and far-reaching controversies within nearly all of the churches. These internal cleavages were the result of disagreements over questions of religious doctrine and church practice. Many ministers and congregations had gradually turned away from the harsh seventeenth-century Calvinistic beliefs which had stressed the innate evil of man and the overwhelming omnipotence of a wrathful God. They substituted instead an Arminian creed which depicted a more loving Savior and allowed that men might be able to ascertain the fundamentals of religion through the use of their natural reason.

This shift in doctrinal emphasis was accompanied by changes in church organization. By 1700 most churches in New England had accepted the Half-Way Covenant of 1662, which stipulated that the children of the "elect" automatically became part-members of the church even though they themselves had not had a conversion experience. With this broadening of the qualifications for religious participation came the assumption that salvation might not be dependent completely on the free gift of grace from God, but might be facilitated by membership in a religious organization.

This process of change was apparent in all of the colonies, but it was most obvious in New England where Puritan Congregationalism had lost the cutting edge of its Calvinist theology, its exclusiveness of membership, and the power of the laity of the individual churches to determine religious dogma and practice. These changes were at once a declension—a deterioration of original purity—and a maturation of a new type of religious organization under the pressure of new social conditions. Puritan Congregationalism, initially the institutional manifestation of a number of small, self-defined groups of "saints," had evolved into a denomination with a formal structure uniting the clergy of the various churches and with a membership drawn from the entire community. It was, in fact, well on its way to becoming an established church in the traditional Catholic sense: a hierarchically organized religion into which all members of the society were accepted at birth.

This trend toward centralization, universality, and formalism was abruptly halted by the Great Awakening, the great revival of faith and piety which affected all classes and all sections of American society during the first half of the 1740's. Religious revivals had been led by Theodore Frelinghuysen in the Dutch Reformed Church during the 1720's and later by William and Gilbert Tennant among the Presbyterians and by Jonathan Edwards among the Congregationalists. But these local stirrings of enthusiastic religion were insignificant when compared to the stir created by the arrival in the colonies in 1740 of George Whitefield, the great English evangelist.

In its harsh theological content and fervent forensic style, the preaching of Whitefield and the other revivalists recalled a more primitive mode of religious experience, one which appealed to the emotions and fears of men and women and not to their hopes and intellects. In this respect the message of the Awakening represented both the working out of an internal dialectic within the Protestant churches in America (as the dry formalism of recent religious practice generated its own antithesis) and the conditions of the external colonial environment (for the great emphasis on the after-life hinted at disillusionment, if not despair, about the condition of the world). Wherever the great preachers—Whitefield, Edwards, Tennant, and Davenport—went, they were met by huge, enthusiastic, almost hysterical crowds who listened in awe and trembling to descriptions of an omnipotent God who "held each sinner by a thin thread over the abyss of *hell*." And everywhere this gospel of a wrathful, yet ultimately forgiving, God was taken up by ordinary men who had been deeply moved and who now felt themselves compelled to testify publicly to the power of the New Light which had suddenly illuminated their hearts. Within a year of Whitefield's arrival there were dozens of itinerant preachers propounding the Word of God to all those who would hear.

The intense piety which now suffused the lives of hundreds of thousands of colonists, and the overriding concern with the after-life, was undoubtedly the result, in part, of the impression made by the great diphtheria epidemic that had just swept through the colonies with a force equal to that of the Awakening itself. Perhaps as many as 20,000 settlers, most of them children, fell victim to the disease, while those who survived were suddenly and overwhelmingly reminded of the tenuousness of life and of the inevitability of death. The feeling of utter helplessness in the face of an epidemic that could not be stayed by the frail hand of man was readily translated into religious terms as the punishment enacted by an avenging God on those who had departed from the paths of devotion and righteousness.

The consciousness of dependence and despair fostered by bacteriological disaster was accentuated by economic recession. The outbreak of the War of Jenkins' Ear in the West Indies in 1739 disrupted the lucrative trade between North America and the islands; and eruption of a general European war a few years later cut deeply into the profits of the tobacco trade. The level of wholesale commodity prices in America dropped by nearly 20% between 1740 and 1745,* and the per capita value of British imports dropped precipitously at the same time. Coming at the end of a two-decade slump in business activity, this wartime recession was particularly damaging. By 1745 the American standard of living had dropped to its lowest point during the first three-quarters of the eighteenth century. (See Chart 4.2.)

Neither this general economic decline nor the recent epidemiological crisis accounted completely for the extraordinary character of the response to the message carried by the revivalists. Indeed, much of the importance of these events stemmed from the fact that they were superimposed upon an already critical social and economic situation in hundreds of local communities throughout the colonies—the result of a century of sustained population growth. One index of this demographic crisis was the rapid increase in the extent of premarital sexual

Chart 4.1
Premarital Conceptions in Hingham, Massachusetts, 1650–1875

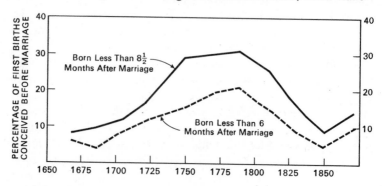

Source: Unpublished data compiled by Daniel Scott Smith.

*From an index number of 67 to 58, five-year moving averages computed with the price level of 1850–1859 as the base period of 100.

intercourse during these years. In Bristol, Rhode Island, fully one-half of the women married between 1740 and 1760 bore a child within eight months, while in Hingham, Massachusetts, the proportion of premarital conceptions grew from 10% in 1700 to 30% in 1750.

This alteration in sexual behavior did not endanger the traditional nuclear family structure (since conception was followed by marriage and not by illegitimate birth), but it did reflect profound changes in economic conditions and in the relations between many parents and their children. The laws of most of the colonies required parental consent for the first marriage of their children and, in the past, this permission had usually depended on the conclusion of a satisfactory property settlement between the parents of the engaged pair. In this agricultural society of freeholders, marriage had always been as much concerned with the transmission of property between generations as with the emotional desires of those involved. The "love" of the couple for each other would be the product of the union, not its cause.

This concept of marriage as primarily a property settlement intimately connected with the landed wealth of the entire family was now breaking down in the face of new social conditions. Dangerously subdivided farms at home and the lure of greater opportunities elsewhere had diminished the control of many parents over the lives of their children. At the same time the increasing predominance of personal wealth (in the form of cash, mortgages, loans, and movable goods) over landed property had broken the automatic connection between the marriage of male offspring and the transfer or division of the farm. Economic conditions were such that the traditional arranged marriages could readily be replaced by sexual relationships based largely on the free choice of those involved; and it was this type of more personal and more romantic union which was steadily becoming more important.

This shift in mores, like all crucial social transformations, was neither completely understood by parents—who attempted to force the lives of their children into the constricting mold of their own experience—nor accepted by their religious institutions, which stood forth as the guardians of the older cultural practices. Eventually the feelings of tension and guilt induced by this widespread repudiation of parental, religious, and social authority were assuaged by the total psychological submission which took place during the Great Awakening. In the town of Braintree, Massachusetts, in 1728, "Joseph P———— and Lydia his wife made a confession before the church . . . for the sin of fornication committed with each other before marriage," and between that date and 1744 the records of the church were filled with such confessions of incontinence.[2]

Both the increase in premarital sexual intercourse and the psychological tensions which it produced were, to a large extent, the reflection of economic circumstances which struck particularly hard at the prospects of the young. Those children who came to maturity during the 1730's in settlements that had been founded between 1691 and 1715 found that the landed resources of family and community were no longer sufficient to enable them to obtain an estate and marry during their 20's. Frustrated in matters of the world, they found solace in apocalyptical religion. During the period of the revival in Norton, Massachusetts, the average age of male admissions to communion was 29.9 years (as compared to 39.7 years before 1740), and 57% of the new members were between the critical ages of 20 and 30. One-quarter of these new communicants were laborers, forced to compete in the wage economy by the lack of land; and only 36% owned more than thirty acres (as compared to 79% of those admitted in previous decades). Religion and the quest for an after-life served as an opiate for the poor, the defeated, and the hopeless.

In the past many New England communities had faced the problem of a surplus agricultural population and had resolved it unobtrusively through migration or economic differentiation. Now, however, these outlets were partially closed by economic recession and by a pessimism induced by the epidemiological crisis. Here was a fertile ground for the revivalists' message of eternal salvation; and it was in those communities, such as Norton, in which the decline in the disease environment and in financial prosperity was compounded by land hunger that the Awakening commanded the most support and had the longest effect. All of the American settlements were affected by Whitefield and his followers, but it was the pattern of local social and economic conditions that determined the intensity of the response.

Whatever the precise causal sequence, the result was much the same. Those who had defied religious and social sanctions in lusting after wealth, power, or sexual pleasure found solace in submission to an omnipotent yet loving God and justification in the revivalists' exhortation to look within themselves, to the promptings of their own consciences, as the ultimate arbiter of right and wrong. In the end, the thousands who embraced the Awakening denied the power of social institutions to judge the character of their lives and placed their trust instead in the Inner

Light, the voice of God which had spoken to them directly in the conversion experience.

This inversion of the locus of authority constituted a profound and immediate threat to the traditional rulers of religion and of society. In an influential pamphlet of 1740 Gilbert Tennant warned church members of the *Dangers of an Unconverted Ministry* and asserted that only those who had actually experienced conversion had God's authority to preach. The danger posed by this doctrine and by the scores of itinerant preachers were suddenly apparent to hundreds of established ministers, who now drew back in horror at the monster they had helped to unleash. Branding the revivalists as "innovators, disturbers of the peace, of the church, sowers of heresies and sedition," the Old Lights sought political support to buttress their privileged position. Many Connecticut ministers who had welcomed Whitefield to their pulpits in 1740 praised the banning of itineracy by the Assembly two years later and closed their churches to the great evangelist when he returned to the colony in 1744. In Virginia, the Anglican-controlled House of Burgesses passed a series of strict laws in an attempt to control the "missionary Presbyterians" who had moved in from the frontier to spread their message in the eastern parts of the colony.

This legal repression served only to undermine still further the faltering religious and political authority it sought to preserve. A series of bitter battles shook the Connecticut Assembly during the 1740's as the New Lights attempted to repeal the law against itineracy and to secure the tax exemptions granted to the non-Congregational churches in 1727. Eventually these struggles assumed a regional alignment as the small farmers and socially mobile merchants of the more recently settled eastern region called for the issuance of more paper money and the expansion of settlement into Pennsylvania, two proposals designed to alleviate the conditions that had made this area so very receptive to the revival. Opposition to these measures came, for the most part, from the longer settled regions of the colony, inhabited by the defenders of economic as well as religious conservatism.

Equally intense struggles took place on the local level as each faction demanded the installation of a minister of its own choosing. Many congregations split in two when their members were unable to agree on appointments and on church practice and dogma. Ultimately, these bifurcations undermined the strength of the New Light movement. The first major schism came when the more radical Separatists, who demanded a return to complete congregational autonomy and a membership strictly limited to the visible Saints, broke off from those who were attempting to reform Congregationalism from within. Then, during the 1750's, the Separatists themselves divided over the question of infant baptism. Maintaining that adult baptism was a logical extension of the principle of a visible sainthood founded on a conversion experience, many Separatists joined established Baptist groups or founded new churches of their own. By the 1770's there were at least 120 Baptist congregations in New England and the influence of the sect was growing even more rapidly among the lower strata of the population in the western sections of Virginia.

As the conservative ministry had warned from the beginning, the repudiation of established institutional authority could lead only to a process of continual fragmentation within the Protestant churches. The New Lights had fixed the locus of divine authority within the heart of every believer; once unleashed, the sovereignty of the individual conscience knew no bounds and respected no dogma. "Does not the core of all this difficulty lie in this," Isaac Backus—a Separatist minister turned Baptist—asked rhetorically in replying to a detractor in 1768, "that the common people [justly] claim as good a right to judge and act for themselves in matters of religion as civil rulers or the learned clergy?" [3]

Indeed, the implications of the decline in religious oligarchy and orthodoxy were even more extensive and profound than Backus realized, for the Awakening served to legitimize the right of groups and of individuals to oppose or criticize a wide range of governmental measures. "Coercive uniformity," proclaimed Ezra Stiles in 1760," is neither necessary in politics nor religion." [4] These sentiments were echoed, a generation later, by James Madison in Number 51 of the Federalist Papers: "In a free government," Madison declared, "the security for civil rights must be the same as that for religious rights. It consists in the one case in the multiplicity of interests, and in the other in the multiplicity of sects." [5] These abstract statements of principle merely reflected the fact that the religious sovereignty of the individual conscience had been transformed, in the minds of thousands of ordinary Americans, into the political sovereignty of the individual voter. A Pennsylvania mechanic wrote to the *Independent Gazetteer* in 1784:

All of the miseries of mankind have arisen from freemen not maintaining and exercising their own sentiments. No reason can be given why a free people should not be equally independent in . . . their political as well as their religious persuasions. [6]

Both Old and New Lights joined in the protest against the Stamp Act in Connecticut in 1765, but the difference in their approach was more significant than the similarity of their stance. The Old Lights, those whose lives had always been oriented to the demands of external authority, sought redress through the traditional institutions of imperial government; while the heirs of the revival, those whose attitudes had been shaped by a generation of resistance to constituted authority, participated in disproportionate numbers in the extra-legal activities of the Sons of Liberty. The personal testimony of John Adams, himself a conservative Patriot, revealed in the most decisive and eloquent terms the ultimate political ramifications of the Awakening. In his attack on the Writs of Assistance, Adams reported, James Otis

> ... asserted, that every man, merely natural, was an independent sovereign, subject to no law, but the law written on his heart, and revealed to him by his Maker, in the constitution of his nature, and in the inspiration of his understanding and conscience. His right to his life, his liberty, no created being could rightfully contest. . . .[7]

"Young as I was, and ignorant as I was," Adams continued, "I shuttered at the doctrine he taught; and I have all my life shuttered, and still shutter, at the consequences that may be drawn from such premises."[8]

When the Americans revolted against British authority in 1776, they did so in the name of an ideology of popular sovereignty and of political equality which had already become deeply interwoven into the fabric of colonial society. The American family structure, with its traditions of partible inheritance and autonomous nuclear households, had accustomed entire generations to a system of equal social relationships among brothers and sisters and aunts and uncles. This crucial, if intangible, private emphasis on equality eventually took an explicitly political and public form in the 1780's—in the massive repudiation of the Society of Cincinnati because of its provision that membership was to pass to the eldest male descendents of the military officers who founded it. During the Awakening this predisposition toward a diffusion of authority had been strengthened, in hundreds of communities, by the appearance of religious sects founded on the principle of the priesthood of all believers and by the widespread repudiation of existing religious and political structures of power.

The republican institutions of government created by the new state constitutions only confirmed in political fact and legal form a preexisting transformation in social behavior and psychological outlook. The process of making (in John Jay's words) "sovereigns [out] of subjects" had begun much earlier in the

American past: in the appearance of a distinctive type of family structure; in the maturation of forms of representative government based on the English model; and, finally, in the metamorphosis in the locus and the nature of authority which accompanied (and, in a sense, constituted) the Great Awakening. The inability of the traditional holders of power during the 1740's to control the lives of their children or to regulate the religious activities of the New Lights testified to the inroads made by the process of social and economic evolution on the patriarchal and authoritarian system inherited from the seventeenth century, a system which represented the antithesis of the republican values of legal equality and individual liberty now incorporated in the public values of the new American nation.

The Crisis of Economy and Society

Some of the strongest ties binding the colonies to the mother country were commercial in nature. Most of the goods exported from the American colonies to Europe were handled by British merchants and, by the third quarter of the eighteenth century, the settlements in America had emerged as one of the principal markets for British manufactured goods. Before 1755 the colonists had realized sufficient returns from their shipping earnings and from their exports of tobacco, rice, wheat, and fish to pay for these processed goods. Then, rather suddenly, the Americans went deeply into debt to their British suppliers. By 1760 the total indebtedness of the colonies amounted to £2 million and by 1772, when it sparked a credit crisis in Britain, the American debt had risen to more than £4 million.

This deterioration in the American balance of payments position took place at a time when the export sector of the economy was experiencing an unprecedented period of prosperity. The quantity of tobacco and of rice exported from the southern colonies reached an all-time high in the 1760's and early 1770's, and the international market price of both commodities was at a high (and slightly rising) level during the entire period. Wheat prices were increasing even more dramatically, as the result of a series of poor crops in Europe in the late 1760's. The permanent transition of England from a grain-exporting to a grain-importing nation took place at this time (as a result of the diversion of men and resources into the nonagricultural sector of the economy); and this development opened up new markets for American producers, as European buyers turned to the colonies as a new source of supply. Between 1765 and 1769 the tonnage of the ships clearing from Philadelphia to southern European ports increased three-fold because of this demand for wheat. The relative scarcity of grain also turned the terms of trade with the West Indies in favor of the northern colonies. In 1775 a Boston merchant could obtain five gallons of molasses in exchange for a single bushel of wheat, whereas three decades before the ratio had been only three to one.

Neither the high prices paid for colonial exports nor their increased quantity was sufficient to accumulate enough foreign exchange to offset an even more dramatic rise in the value of imported commodities. In the five-year period centering on 1750, British goods worth £1.11 million had been imported by America each year; a decade later the average annual value of imports had risen to £2.12 million. In per capita terms, the consumption of British goods had risen from 19 shillings in 1750 to 26 shillings in 1760, a clear indication of a significant increase in the standard of living.

This new prosperity was based on very tenuous foundations: it was not being paid for out of current earnings but by a lien on future production. In the five years between 1768 and 1772, the value of goods imported into the American colonies exceeded the income derived from all sources by more than £2 million. Only the money pumped into the colonies by the British Treasury reduced this huge deficit to a tolerable level. At least £1.5 million of the colonial debit during this five-year period was offset by British expenditures related to the maintenance of the fifteen battalions of regular troops now stationed in America.

Indeed, military spending constituted the crucial factor in determining the performance of the American economy during

Table 4.2
The Pattern of Trade, 1768–1772
(in thousands of £ sterling in current prices)

	Great Britain	Southern Europe	West Indies	Africa	Total
New England	−2,501	543	1,379	113	−466
Middle colonies	−3,704	1,071	722	1	−1,910
Southern colonies	−359	873	348	−682	180
	−6,564	2,487	2,449	−568	−2,196
	Estimated British military expenditures				1,500
	Continental Balance of Payments Deficit				−696

Source: From J. F. Shepard and G. M. Walton, "Estimates of Invisible Earnings in the Balance of Payments of the British North American Colonies, 1768–1772," *JEH* 29 (1969), Table 8.

the entire third quarter of the eighteenth century. The dramatic increase in imports which initiated the deterioration in the international economic position of the colonies began, in per capita terms, only in 1756—following the outbreak of the Seven Years' War in America. There had been a surge in imports a decade earlier, but this had not been a key turning point in the financial development of the colonies. Part of this earlier rise was merely a temporary resurgence following the dislocations in shipping brought about by the wars of the early 1740's (the depression which had played an important role in the Great Awakening); the rest was the result of a very gradual increase in the foreign demand for American commodities. Taken together, these two developments were only sufficient to raise the value of per capita imports in the early 1750's to the level maintained during the first decades of the century, a level which represented the pro-

Chart 4.2
Population, British Imports, and American Wholesale Prices: American Colonies, 1700–1775

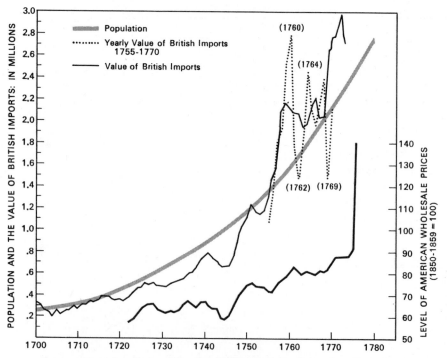

SOURCE: Data has been taken from *Historical Statistics*, Ser. Z 1, Z 336; and John J. McCusker, "The Current Value of English Exports, 1697 to 1800," *WMQ* 28 (1971), Table III.

NOTE: Values are expressed as 5-yr. moving averages in £ sterling at current prices.

ductive capacity and purchasing power of the American economy under the most favorable peacetime conditions.

This economic equilibrium was shattered by the Seven Years' War. Men, arms, and money poured out of Great Britain and into the colonies. The increased demand for goods and services in America brought a sudden prosperity to farmers, artisans, and merchants. The rise in wholesale prices from an index figure of 69.5 in 1756 to 83.5 in 1763 was in part the result of a greatly increased supply of paper money, issued by the various colonial legislatures to pay for military purchases and backed by British specie or the income from future taxes. But a significant portion of this increase in prices was the result of a massive jump in demand, and was therefore translated into greater profits for producers and middlemen alike. The greater amount of money in circulation and the increased purchasing power of the colonists resulted in a strong demand for imported goods. British manufactures poured into America between 1756 and 1760; and then the rapid decline in military spending brought this artificial boom to an abrupt end.

Barring a dramatic increase in exports or the renewal of the British military subsidy, the Americans could only maintain the wartime level of imports by going into debt to their British suppliers. By 1764, the value of British exports to the mainland colonies had again climbed to a high level, but this increase in consumption had been purchased at a heavy price. The postwar recession brought bankruptcy and disgrace to those who had seriously overexpanded their financial commitments during the years of lavish subsidies and easy credit. "I think we have a gloomy prospect before us," Chief Justice Allen reported from Philadelphia in 1765, "as there are of late some Persons failed, who were in no way suspected, and a probability of some others, as the whisper goes." [9]

Introduced into the depressing economic climate created by financial retrenchment and business failures, the new British measures of taxation and control assumed a more menacing character than their content warranted. The tightening up of the colonial Customs Service had begun to drain funds into the coffers of the imperial government even before the end of the war. "Since you Sailed from here our Officers have recd Orders not to Enter foreign Molasses as heretofore," a merchant of Salem, Massachusetts, warned one of his captains in 1758,

The Vessells that have arrived since those orders have been admitted to Enter about One Eighth or Tenth part of their Cargo paying 6d Sterling p. gall. Duty for what is entered—which is more than twice as much as was given before.[10]

By 1765 the American Customs Service was collecting more than £30,000 a year in duties, a tremendous change both in financial and psychological terms from the annual revenue of less than £2,000 during the long years of salutary neglect. And just at the time that specie was being drained from the colonies, the Currency Act of 1764 enjoined the colonial legislatures from printing paper money in order to stimulate business activity by creating a currency inflation.

The Stamp Act of 1765 was the most threatening measure of all, not only because of the huge sums that it was expected to raise but also because this revenue was to be used to maintain the British troops now stationed in America. The military subsidy that had been the initial driving force behind the recent rise in the colonial standard of living would come to an end. In addition, Americans would be required to assume a burden they had never before carried. The stakes of the contest had now risen to the £400,000 per year required to supply and to pay the British garrison; and with this shift in the dimensions of the financial debate, traditional constitutional arguments took on a more vivid significance. In 1764 Thomas Cushing, the Speaker of the Massachusetts Assembly, had argued that the new Sugar Act was "contrary to a fundamental Principall of our Constitution vizt. That all Taxes ought to originate with the people;" [11] but only upon the arrival of the stamped papers in America did this ideological argument receive the active popular support required to transform it into a powerful political force.

Violent resistance to the Stamp Act served to focus attention on the mother country as the ultimate cause of the financial difficulties faced by many of the colonists. In 1766 one Virginian recalled that a debt of £1,000 had once seemed excessive, but that

ten times that sum is now spoke of with indifference and thought no great burthen on Some Estates. . . . Indeed . . . , in 1740 I don't remember to have seen such a thing as a turkey carpet in the Country except a small thing in the bedchamber. Now nothing are so common as Turkey or Wilton Carpetts, the whole furniture, Roomes, Elegant and every appearance of opulence. [12]

This extravagance generated widespread calls for a return to a more simple and more frugal mode of existence but, as George Washington explained in a letter to a friend, the planters of his acquaintance had grown accustomed to their new style of life and were "ashamed" to admit that their estates could not bear the cost.

It was not among the Great Planters, however, that the

resentment against British merchants and manufacturers was most pronounced. For the Chesapeake gentry, foreign indebtedness was a perennial problem, and one with which they had learned to live—however much they might complain of the rapacity of the British middlemen. This was not the case with the poor white farmers of Virginia, who had been subsidized in the years after 1740 by Scottish merchant houses rather than by local entrepreneurs. Nor was this the normal state of affairs among the northern agricultural producers, who had traditionally paid for British imports from the returns of current production and had restricted their wants accordingly. For the publicists and preachers of these sections of the American population, debt was not a justifiable method of stimulating business activity but a moral failing which led inexorably to a weakening of character. John Adams spoke for hundreds of concerned ministers and worried pamphleteers when he condemned the "vicious, luxurious and effeminate Appetites, Passions, and Habits" created by rising consumption of British manufactures.

Divided within and among themselves between desire for a higher standard of living and commitment to the traditional virtues of discipline, self-restraint, and frugality, the American settlers continued to increase their purchases of imports even while they confessed their inability to pay. In the end, they projected their diffuse fears and anxieties outward, against the British, discerning in the combined activities of the merchants and ministers of the mother country a cunning plot to undermine the moral and economic independence of the colonies by encouraging frivolous imports and then to enslave the inhabitants by the imposition of a heavy burden of taxation. This rationalization was at once absurd and convincing, bizarre yet understandable, vague but operative: In the Stamp Act Congress held in New York late in 1765, the delegates responded to this myth of their own making by resolving to cease the importation of British goods until the new measures of taxation were repealed.

This nonimportation agreement was a political tactic designed to coerce Parliament to respect colonial interests; a moral remedy for the consumptive disease that was eating away at the spiritual health of American society; and a temporary solution to the deteriorating international financial position of the American settlements. As such it had a powerful appeal to various groups within the population. Members of the colonial assemblies, men familiar with the cynical world of power, praised its realistic approach, while the xenophobic members of the Sons of Liberty welcomed its firm declaration of economic independence. Finally, the merchants, many of whom had huge stocks of British goods on hand (after the surge in imports in 1763 and 1764), accepted the new policy because it offered them the opportunity both to reduce swollen inventories and to protest against taxes and controls which had already affected their business activities. Similar considerations prompted the merchants of New York to issue a new call for a nonimportation agreement following the passage of the Townshend Duties in 1768.

This economic coercion was eminently successful. Petitions from British merchants trading to America were instrumental in securing the repeal of the Stamp Act in 1766; and the great drop in the value of colonial imports from Great Britain in 1769 was an important factor in winning a partial repeal of the Townshend duties. Only the tax on tea was retained as a symbol of parliamentary supremacy.

In their effects on American public opinion, the two non-importation agreements were even more significant. They underlined the present state of economic dependence on Great Britain while offering a definite nationalistically oriented alternative. "Manufacture as much as possible and say nothing," Benjamin Franklin advised his countrymen at one stage in the controversy,[13] and many northern towns (especially those in over-populated New England) responded by establishing textile works to provide domestic sources of clothing and sailcloth. These municipal efforts were supplemented by an increase in the private production of woolens. The wearing of homespun clothes became a sign of patriotism while the display of imported finery was condemned as an attack on economic self-sufficiency. The commercial activity which had once bound the colonies and the mother country firmly together had become, in the eyes of many Americans, a system of economic imperialism in which the relatively undeveloped colonies were being placed at the mercy of British merchants and manufacturers. As one radical polemicist in New York City charged in an attack on those Patriots who had simply protested against internal taxation,

... they have on the whole rather betrayed than defended the cause ... tho' they condemn the Stamp-Act, [they] would have us at the mercy of the British Parliament in every article but taxation.[14]

If the non-importation agreements pointed the way toward a national economic policy of self-sufficiency and self-determination (thus winning the support of artisans and craftsmen in the port cities), they did nothing to diminish the dependence on or the demand for British goods. In the period from 1771 to 1774, the value of imported commodities was 47% higher than it had

Table 4.3
Balance of Payments on Current Account, 1768–1772
(*in thousands of £ sterling*)

	1768	1769	1770	1771	1772	Total
New England	121	317	155	−769	−290	−466
Middle colonies	−568	164	−188	−976	−342	−1,910
Southern colonies	218	335	120	−200	−194	180
	−229	816	87	−2,044	−826	−2,196

SOURCE: See Table 4.2.
NOTE: The figures for the southern colonies are somewhat misleading, since many of their imports were transshipped from the northern ports.

been between 1765 and 1768. And the colonial balance of payments, which had shown a positive result during the period of nonimportation, deteriorated rapidly once the boycott was lifted. By 1772, the Americans were once again deeply in debt to their British suppliers, a fact that would heighten the emotional impact of the new tax on tea and lead to new measures of resistance.

The Chesapeake planters did not rebel in 1776 simply to avoid the repayment of British debts of more than £2 million; nor did the northern merchants and their legal allies fabricate elaborate constitutional arguments merely to protect their threatened financial position—for men rarely act in such direct and uncomplicated ways. This is not to say that economic factors did not play a crucial role in the coming of the American war for independence. The tensions introduced into colonial society by the great increase in the per capita consumption of British goods in the years after 1755 added a psychological dimension to the friction over constitutional principles. The nagging, enervating sensation of economic dependence experienced by thousands of colonists because of the large commercial debt owed to British merchants gave both financial and emotional impetus to the demand for "no taxation without representation." They had personally experienced the corroding effects of private debts and reacted instinctively when it appeared that their present burdens would be compounded by public taxes. Moreover, British manufactures now threatened the livelihood of the urban craftsmen; British commercial regulations had suddenly altered the frame of reference of the northern merchants; British taxes loomed as a new danger to the political autonomy of the economically dependent Chesapeake gentry—all of which struck directly at that sense of independence, economic, political, psychological, which had come to be a defining feature of the American social order.

The Disintegration of Imperial Authority

Whether it assumes the form of revolutionary upheaval or evolutionary development, historical change always takes place in a multidimensional social space in which the lines of causation are so numerous and so tangled that it is only with the greatest difficulty that their relative significance can be fully understood. The analysis of the origins of the American war for independence offers no exception to this rule. In retrospect, it is clear that the gradual emergence of an indigenous leadership class able to exert control over society through its wealth and prestige and through its predominance in strong and relatively representative institutions of government had fulfilled one of the crucial preconditions for a successful movement for self-determination. Equally apparent is the fact that three generations of rapid economic and demographic growth had created the structural base required for colonial autonomy, and had induced changes in family life, religious practice, ethnic composition, and social authority which challenged the ideological principles and political institutions upon which American society had been based. But if these developments supplied the prerequisites for political upheaval leading to independence (requirements which were not completely fulfilled in the smaller, more dependent, and plural society of the West Indies), they did not make it inevitable.

A second series of causes, superimposed upon the conflicts and tendencies inherent in the process of social evolution on the American mainland, increased the likelihood of a political breakdown within the British empire. The Seven Years' War—the first of the long series of confrontations between England and France which had impinged directly and immediately on the colonists—prompted a growing militarization of society, an economic cycle of prosperity and recession, and a cultural xenophobia produced by large-scale contacts between American "provincials" and the arrogant and status-conscious officers and men of the British regular army. Yet even these disruptive and dangerous forces did not, in themselves, lead inescapably toward political violence.

It was only when these preconditions and these forces were overlayed by yet another layer of conflict that their inherent tendencies were made manifest and channeled into a movement for American independence. This was the campaign begun by the home government to bring the colonies more firmly under imperial control. This effort, planned and directed in the first instance by men at the middle level of the English bureaucracy, did not simply appear out of an historical vacuum. It was, rather, the logical, if belated, response of British officials and ministers to the same series of developments which had made colonial independence a definite possibility. Beginning in the late 1740's imperial bureaucrats had perceived the growing maturity of the American settlements and had begun to devise measures to curtail this trend toward autonomy. This task was then made more urgent by the Seven Years' War, which diminished still further the powers of the royal governors in America (who were forced to meet Assembly demands in order to secure financial support for the military effort) and which lessened the dependence of the colonists on the mother country by removing the French from Canada. The process was dialectical and self-reinforcing; the very strength and confidence of the American settlements had generated a British movement for the reform of the imperial administrative system.

This campaign began even before the end of the Seven Years' War. In 1762 a Revenue Act ended the absentee system which had undermined the efficiency of the American Customs Service and also directed the royal navy to assist in the apprehension of smugglers. Then came the Proclamation of 1763 and the Currency Act of 1764 which subjected other areas of American life to direct imperial supervision. And these innovations were quickly followed by yet another revenue measure, the Sugar Act of 1764, which imposed tighter controls on coastal shipping and extended the jurisdiction of the vice-admiralty courts, in which customs offenses were tried without a jury. And just as these new and largely unprecedented laws were being implemented in America, well-publicized discussions were taking place in London with regard to the best method by which the colonists could defray the cost of the greatly enlarged British garrison.

The simple announcement of these new regulations in such rapid succession would have been sufficient to raise considerable alarm among settlers whose affairs had escaped close imperial scrutiny for three generations. When they were followed, almost immediately, by a series of legal prosecutions, the impact was even greater. The Writs of Assistance case in Boston in the early 1760's attracted the most attention at the time, but there were other customs cases in Charleston, South Carolina, and two important legal battles in New York involving the tenure of judges and the right of trial by jury. These disputes between local residents and the royal authorities received extensive coverage in the colonial newspapers, which precisely at this time began to devote significantly more space to American news. By the time the ministry headed by George Grenville decided to impose a direct tax, many colonists were deeply disturbed by the British reform program and were extremely suspicious of the ultimate intentions of the imperial government.

The extent of the fear, hostility, and tension created by the sudden imposition of tight administrative controls and new taxes in the midst of a period of economic uncertainty and recession was revealed in 1765. The passage of the Stamp Act triggered a massive wave of American resistance. In New York City on October 31, the day before the Act was to go into effect, two hundred merchants vowed to cease the importation of British goods. Large numbers of storekeepers and tradesmen immediately promised their support; and the members of both groups then joined mechanics, sailors, and laborers in a mass protest meeting on the Common. On the following night more than 2,000 residents of the city surrounded the fort where the stamps were being guarded and then plundered the house of a British officer. The continuance of these nightly demonstrations and the inability of the local collector to implement the Act prompted the Lieutenant Governor to call upon General Gage to use the military garrison to rout the protestors by force. "Fire from the Fort," Gage replied, "might disperse the Mob, [but] it would not quell them; and the consequence would in all appearance be an Insurrection . . . the Commencement of a Civil War." [15]

The Americans had embarked upon a campaign of overt intimidation and physical violence to secure their ends, and the imperial officials and forces lacked sufficient power to deter them. In Albany, New York, and in Charleston, South Carolina, local merchants joined in nonimportation agreements; and groups of townspeople, calling themselves the Sons of Liberty and consisting of men from all ranks of society (but composed mostly of the artisans and workers who constituted the bulk of the urban population), forcibly prevented the distribution of the stamps and secured the resignations of the designated collectors. In Boston the mob did not stop until it had destroyed the house of Lieutenant Governor Hutchinson. In Philadelphia it was only the counter-demonstration organized by the White Oaks (who were supporters of Benjamin Franklin) which prevented the destruction of the residence of John Hughes, Franklin's associate and the new tax collector. In nearly every continental colony British authority had been tried and found wanting. Nowhere were the forces of imperial law and order strong enough, or determined enough, to prevail; and only in a few places was local support forthcoming to shore up the crumbling facade of imperial authority.

Political violence in the 1770's: American patriots attempt to nullify parliamentary legislation by mob action directed against customs officials and
other supporters of British authority.

The events of 1765 exposed the tenuous character of
British power in America and finally dispelled the aura of imperial legitimacy which decades of abrasive factional politics had
not been able to erode. Previously the disputes between the royal
governors and the assemblies had consisted primarily of routin-
ized conflicts within a political system whose basic principles and
legal procedures were not questioned. Now the various colonial

elites had not only repudiated the representatives of the imperial government but called upon the population for support through extra-institutional action.

This cleavage within the ranks of the traditional leaders of American society was of crucial significance. It unleashed anti-imperial sentiments long present among certain groups of the settlers but theretofore suppressed or discouraged by the local colonial authorities. "The spark of liberty is not yet extinct among our people," wrote one Virginia planter, "and if properly fanned by the Gentlemen of Influence will, I make no doubt, burst out again into a flame." [16] Because of its firm political and psychological control over the rest of society, the Chesapeake gentry could view the expression of popular Anglophobic sentiments with equanimity; they could control the anger and actions of the poor white planters and direct it much as they pleased.

The situation was far different in most of the urban centers of the North. There the anti-imperial animus of lower status groups was both more acute and more independent of external control. In 1747 the Boston town meeting had expressed its "Abhorrence" of a riot by local sailors and other lower class residents of the town following a nighttime impressment sweep by the royal navy. The merchants and public officials had protested by citing an Act passed in the sixth year of the reign of Queen Anne which, they alleged, exempted the American colonies from impressment. In 1765, the social and economic elite of Boston had forsaken this moderating role, and the legal and the violent modes of opposition to unpopular imperial measures had become one. In New York City, a similar type of political alteration resulted in appeals for universal resistance to the Stamp Act. "To overthrow it," one publicist proclaimed, "nothing is wanted but your own Resolution, for great is the Authority and Power of the People." [17]

If the lines of class were temporarily obscured by the nearly universal opposition to the Stamp Act, the effect of the imperial crisis was to accentuate the divergent interests within colonial society and to endanger the paramount position of many of its traditional leaders. By 1770 Philadelphia ship carpenters—in the White Oak Society—who had traditionally embraced the values of the merchant elite, had broken their alliance with the Quaker merchants over the issue of nonimportation, and had joined with the Presbyterian party and the Sons of Liberty in their forthright attack against British rule and against the hegemony of the wealthy, eastern, and English leaders of Pennsylvania politics.

The invisible mental bonds that had tied the various strata of colonial society together were thus weakened, even as those that had bound the empire together as a single political entity were being completely broken. By 1773 well-educated Americans were asserting that British actions had "openly dissolved the pact of society," leaving "every one to provide for his own security in the best manner he can." [18] And John Allen, whose influential *Oration on Liberty* was read, according to John Adams, to "large Circles of the common People", was to argue that,

For my part, I cannot see how any Man in America, can properly break the Laws of England. The whole lies here, the laws of America only are broke, let the offender then be tryed by the law he has broke.[19]

The laborious rehearsal of legal precedents, which had formed the basis of the defense of colonial rights and privileges in the past, was thus replaced by a simple statement of self-evident fact.

Allen's sentiments were gradually elaborated into a more coherent, more intellectual, form by the leaders of the Patriot forces, many of whom had been trained in the law. "The Lawyers are the Source from whence the Clamors have flowed in every Province," General Gage informed his superiors at the time of the Stamp Act crisis. Most members of the American bar remained loyal to the Crown because of their inability to reconcile opposition to constituted authority with a lifetime practice of English law. But those lawyers who did become Patriots supplied the protest movement with a consistent intellectual focus and meaning, and in 1776 twenty-five lawyers appeared among the fifty-six signatories of the Declaration of Independence.

In their construction of an ideology of resistance to British authority, the Patriot leaders built upon a series of assumptions and principles formulated by Whig ideologists and politicians in England and already incorporated into the vocabulary of American politics. Concerned with the arbitrary power exercised by the Stuart Kings in the years before 1689, the early English Whigs had sought to limit the authority of the Crown and to increase the power of the legislative branch of the government. These ideas had been especially appealing to many members of the colonial assemblies, where the prerogative powers of the royal governors were often greater than those of the King himself, and where representative government was still in its infancy. Then, during the middle decades of the eighteenth century, Americans fell heir to a corpus of political thought formulated by a relatively small group of anti-Walpolian dissenting Whigs, who stressed the dangers to liberty posed by the ability of the King and his ministers to manipulate Parliament through patronage, bribes, and other forms of covert influence. These ideas were perceived by colonial publicists and legislators to apply with particular force in America, where royal governors were attempting, with every means at their disposal, to create a subservient majority within each of the representative assemblies.

To those Americans who viewed the world through the prism of Whig political thought, the events of the immediate past took on a most disturbing and most sinister meaning. The new measures of imperial taxation and control had followed immediately upon the accession of King George III in 1760. And to those colonists who pondered the patterns of history, it seemed as if the despotism of the Stuarts, defeated by force of arms in England and in the colonies in 1689, had been resurrected in a new form in the young and the strong-willed Hanoverian monarch—a despotism which was all the more serious because it was aided and abetted by a corrupted Parliament. In these dire circumstances many American settlers felt they had no one to look to but themselves if they wished to defend their traditional liberties.

With this realization by a large section of the American political elite—a comprehension shaped by the peculiar concept of reality embodied in the Whig intellectual tradition—the anti-imperial tendencies inherent in American politics suddenly became manifest. This change in political climate was firmly exploited by lower status groups, whose motivations were determined by their own less-ideologically influenced perceptions of the British threat. "What can a Governor do, without the assistance of the Governed?" an imperial customs official wrote plaintively from Philadelphia in 1770, "What can the Magistrates do, unless they are supported by their fellow Citizens? What can the King's Officers do, if they make themselves obnoxious to the people amongst whom they reside?" [20]

Sensing this loss of authority, the British ministry redeployed its American garrisons in an attempt to restore its monopoly of force. Troops stationed in the conquered provinces of Canada were transferred to the northern port cities, as were some of the men stationed along the frontier. With this reversal of military priorities, few efforts were made to stem the flow of settlers to the west, despite the growing danger of an Indian war. Unable any longer to rule the settled regions of the American colonies by consent, the imperial government had been forced to resort to the primitive logic of deterrence.

This policy might have succeeded if it had been combined with a political strategy designed to regain the confidence of the leading members and most influential social groups within the colonial population. Peace and unity were still possible, Benjamin Franklin argued in 1769, if Great Britain would *"repeal* the laws, *renounce* the right, *recall* the troops, *refund* the money, and *return* to the old method of requisition."[21] But the British ministry was unable to deal in a pragmatic and flexible way with the practical and constitutional questions raised by the recent confrontations. Even an intelligent and well-placed individual like Thomas Hutchinson—the American-born Governor of Massachusetts who had questioned the wisdom of the Stamp Act— was unable to shake himself loose from the outworn dogma of the past. "I know of no line," he wrote in the early 1770's, "that can be drawn between the supreme authority of Parliament and the total independence of the colonies."[22]

The ability of the British government to deal constructively with the imperial crisis was also hampered by political instability at home. There were six different ministries in the fifteen years preceding the outbreak of war, and the frequent changes of policies and personnel served to disrupt the lines of personal influence and destroy mutual trust. These practical difficulties were compounded by the growing self-confidence and intransigence of Parliament itself, a development which assumed a tangible form in the hardening of the official attitude toward popular demonstrations. The threat of mob violence had been one factor which had deterred Sir Robert Walpole from proceeding with his plan to raise revenue by means of a domestic excise tax in 1733. And twenty years later the danger of disturbances in London forced Henry Pelham and his brother, the Duke of Newcastle, to repeal an act for the naturalization of Jews that they had guided through Parliament less than six months before.

By 1760 a new generation of ministers had assumed the key offices of government. These men were less prepared than their cautious predecessors to tolerate or to heed extra-institutional protests: the food riots of 1766 were harshly suppressed by military force; and two years later the ministry excluded John Wilkes from his seat in Parliament, despite widespread popular demonstrations—an action which confirmed the fears of many colonists about the threat to their own political rights and liberties. When the Gordon riots broke out in 1780, the British government again acted decisively and with armed force: troops killed 285 protesters, while the mob itself was not responsible for the loss of a single life.

The constitutional intransigence of the home government and its readiness to use force to secure its ends resulted in a series of potentially dangerous confrontations between British troops and dissident colonists. Before 1765 the usual opponents of the various American mobs had been lonely customs officials who were forced, by their lack of power, to effect a compromise between their royal instructions and the demands of the local inhabitants. With the arrival of British troops, the two sides were more evenly matched; and a new element of instability was added to an already tense situation. Beginning in 1768, when a detachment of the regular army was sent to Boston to protect the customs officials, a series of minor disputes broke out between the townspeople and the army. Discontent over the attention paid to local women by the troops was exacerbated when the poorly paid soldiers began competing with townsmen for jobs. Suffusing all of these conflicts was a pervasive hostility to the forces of occupation which led to the harboring of deserters and to continual acts of provocation. The breaking point came in March of 1770 when the troops fired on an unruly crowd, killing five persons.

The mere presence of British regulars had not restored law and order. Indeed, it had unlocked a new dimension of conflict, one that threatened to lead to violence on a large scale. For three years the home government wavered in its resolution, removing the army from Boston to an island in the harbor and avoiding the introduction of any legislation that might revive American resistance. Then, in 1773, the Tea Act renewed the constitutional struggle, and revived American support for those radical Patriots who had warned of British perfidy. Like Grenville and Townshend before him, Lord North, the new chief minister, was not content to declare the sovereignty of Parliament and to wait for time (and gradual political pressure) to win the acquiescence of the colonists. He felt compelled to exercise Parliamentary authority and thus to obtain overt acknowledgement of British suzerainty.

From this point on, events moved logically and inescapably toward violence and war. Following a vote by the town meeting of Portsmouth, New Hampshire, an angry crowd forced the merchants to whom the newly taxed tea was consigned to reship it to Halifax, Nova Scotia. In Philadelphia, Charleston, and other port cities the Sons of Liberty compelled local officials to store the newly arrived tea in locked warehouses. While in Boston, the traditional center of anti-imperial agitation, 342 chests of tea were destroyed by a small group of radicals who had the support of the town meeting.

As in 1765 there was open, massive, and violent resistance to British authority. But now the stakes were higher, for the lines of constitutional conflict were clearly drawn; there was a capable group of radical Patriots in America determined to push for complete independence; and the British government was no longer willing to tolerate further acts of insubordination. In the spring of 1775 the ministry sent orders to General Gage to close the Massachusetts Assembly (which had been proscribed by the Coercive Acts but which was meeting illegally outside Boston) and to seize its leaders and the arms and ammunition stockpiled by the colonial militia. For the first time in the decade-long confrontation, the imperial authorities were themselves prepared to use armed force in an aggressive pursuit of their goals.

For their part, the radical American patriots were ready to use violence to establish a federation of independent states with governments based firmly on the principles of popular sovereignty and representative government. In the ten years since the Stamp Act crisis the colonists had moved from resistance to revolution. Forced by the debate over taxation to formulate a coherent statement of their aims and beliefs, the Patriot leadership had begun with the ideology of constitutional rights bequeathed to them by the English Whigs and then, influenced by more radical demands (from urban artisans and freeholding farmers) for self-determination and political equality, moved beyond this negative formulation to conceive a more positive vision of the American future: an ideology of independence and of republicanism that reflected both the traditional autonomy of American political institutions and the new locus of religious and civil authority within the conscience of each and every citizen.

Notes to Chapter Four

1. John Shy, *Toward Lexington: The Role of the British Army in the Coming of the American Revolution* (Princeton: Princeton University Press, 1965), p. 65.
2. Arthur W. Calhoun, *A Social History of the American Family* (New York: Barnes & Noble, 1960), vol. 1, p. 132.
3. William G. McLoughlin, *Isaac Backus and the American Pietistic Tradition* (Boston: Little, Brown, 1967), p. 23.
4. Richard Hofstadter, *The Idea of a Party System: The Rise of Legitimate Opposition in the United States* (Berkeley: University of California Press, 1969), p. 59.
5. Ibid., p. 63.
6. Leonard Bernstein, "The Working People of Philadelphia," *Penna. Mag. Hist. Biog.* 74 (1950): 327.
7. Lawrence Gipson, *The Coming of the Revolution, 1763–1775* (New York: Harper & Row, 1954), p. 38.
8. Ibid.
9. Edmund S. and Helen M. Morgan, *The Stamp Act Crisis: Prologue to Revolution* (Chapel Hill: University of North Carolina Press, 1953), p. 48.

10. Thomas C. Barrow, *Trade and Empire: The British Customs Service in Colonial America, 1660–1775* (Cambridge: Harvard University Press, 1967), p. 142.
11. Massachusetts Historical Society, *Collections* 74 (1918): 145–146.
12. Emory G. Evans, "Planter Indebtedness and the Coming of the Revolution in Virginia," *WMQ* 19 (1962) : 519.
13. Charles M. Andrews, *The Colonial Background of the American Revolution*, rev. ed. (New Haven: Yale University Press, 1931), pp. 149–150.
14. Bernard Friedman, "The Shaping of the Radical Consciousness in Provincial New York," *Jour. Amer. Hist.* 56 (1970) : 790.
15. F. L. Engelman, "Cadwallader Colden and the New York Stamp Act Riots," *WMQ* 10 (1953): 575–576.
16. J. R. Pole, "Representation and Authority in Virginia from the Revolution to Reform," *JSH* 24 (1958) : 28.
17. Friedman, op. cit., p. 797.
18. Benjamin W. Labaree, *The Boston Tea Party* (New York: Oxford University Press, 1964), p. 111.
19. John Bumsted and Charles Clark, "New England's Tom Paine: John Allen and the Spirit of Liberty," *WMQ* 21 (1964) : 568.
20. Barrow, op. cit., p. 246.
21. Richard Koebner, *Empire* (New York: Cambridge University Press, 1961), p. 115.
22. William Nelson, *The American Tory* (New York: Oxford University Press, 1962), pp. 32–33.

During the years that followed the Declaration of Independence nearly all of the institutions and values which had been inherited from the mother country and haphazardly adapted to the exigencies of the American environment were discussed and debated wherever men and women gathered: in private houses and public taverns, in town meetings and legislative assemblies. Those rules and customs which had ceased to govern social conduct were stricken from the statute books; and behavior and habits (such as the use of aristocratic titles) deemed to be incompatible with republican values were discouraged by new laws or by more informal means of coercion.

The result, in the end, was a new social conception of reality, a half-legal, half-unconscious system of values and way of looking at the world. It embodied the ways in which citizens of the new American republics were expected to deal with each other in their economic and social lives and specified the proper relationship between individuals and their political superiors. Not all men and women would abide by the new rules and informal understandings, both because no society ever achieves complete internal coherence and because, like all such codes of conduct, they discriminated against some social groups to the advantage of others.

Nevertheless, this new value system conformed more closely to the ways in which Americans wanted to act (and were acting) than did the older imperial-patriarchal system of social order and authority. This relationship between ideas and reality, between institutions and behavior, was dialectical and dynamic: the values and expectations adumbrated during the imperial crisis and given institutional expression during the first generation following independence formed the context within which the next century of American social development would take place. And, then, they too would pass away, superceded by ideas and organizations

WAR AND SOCIAL CHANGE

5

more appropriate to life in a complex urban and industrial society.

In retrospect, these adjustments assume a deceptively easy, almost automatic and inevitable character. They were not so in practice. Those who had been born into the old society and taught from infancy to accept its precepts as given, unalterable, and self-evident fought a determined battle to insure its preservation, as the example of the Old Lights and the Loyalists clearly demonstrated. Moreover, certain crucial aspects of the new ideological conception of reality—the mythic structure that comprised the public values of the new republican states—were contradicted by the material conditions of American social and economic life, by the gross inequalities in wealth, status, and power among the formally equal citizenry.

There were still other conflicts: Various interest groups had grown powerful during the colonial period and now struggled with one another to exert their influence within the emerging institutions of government and to achieve universal acceptance of their beliefs. Even before the end of the war, Americans found themselves divided on fundamental questions of economic priorities and the distribution of political power. By destroying the established system of government and authority, the quest for home rule had made it possible for previously powerless groups to raise the question of who should rule at home.

The Disruptions of War

The armed struggle for independence was a long and economically costly conflict. The New England fishing industry, which had accounted for 10% of the commodity exports from the continent in 1770, was temporarily destroyed. The lucrative production of indigo in the Carolinas, dependent on British subsidies, was likewise extinguished by the war, never to recover. The trade in imports was also severely affected, since the war was fought against the country that had previously monopolized the colonies' supply of manufactured goods and consumed or handled at least 40% of all American exports. The tobacco colonies were particularly hard hit by the disruption of the traditional channels of commerce. Some Chesapeake planters sought to trade directly with European customers, defying the naval blockade, while others stored their nonnutritive crop for postwar sale and converted their plantations to the cultivation of foodstuffs.

The agricultural regions of the North were better equipped to deal with the exigencies of the wartime economy. Wheat, bread, and livestock were still in great demand in the West Indies and in southern Europe, and trade with these regions continued despite the dangers posed by the royal navy and privateers. There was also a great domestic demand for foodstuffs, since agricultural output had been cut by the inability to replace old farm equipment; by the loss of a significant fraction of the male laboring force; and by the periodic depredations of livestock, fodder, and grain by the soldiers of both armies.

The most serious consequences were felt in the cities, whose very existence was dependent on commercial activity. Boston, New York, Philadelphia, Charleston, and Newport were all occupied for a time by British troops; and even when the army had departed, the naval squadrons and privateers which lurked outside their harbors continued to disrupt trade. The income from shipbuilding and from commercial transactions declined abruptly, undermining the entire economy of the urban areas. Unemployed shipwrights, dock laborers, masons, coopers, and bakers drifted off into the countryside to find work on farms or in small villages; joined the Continental army; or, if they had Loyalist sympathies, departed with the forces of occupation. The population of New York City declined from 21,000 in 1774 to less than half that number in 1783. Even in 1790, after nearly a decade of peace, the proportion of Americans living in towns of 2,500 or more people was only 5.7% of the total population, the lowest peacetime proportion in more than half a century.

The decline in the relative size of the urban population provided an accurate indication of the great short-run cost of the war for independence. The disruptions produced by the fighting itself, by the loss of established markets and sources of credit, and by the depreciation of capital resources and lack of new investment created a period of economic stagnation which lasted for two decades. The value of continental exports to Great Britain and the British West Indies had averaged $7.5 million per year between 1771 and 1773, but this total dropped to an average of only $5.8 million between 1785 and 1787. The proportion of American exports taken directly by other nations increased from 30 to 50% of the total between these two periods, but this penetration of new markets was not sufficient to maintain the per capita level of exports. By 1790 the value of exports in per capita terms was only two-thirds as large as in 1774, and there was a corresponding decrease in the volume of foreign imports. Given the failure of domestic manufacturers and artisans to increase their production during these years, the decline in overseas trade brought a fall in the American standard of living and with it an increase in the probability of conflict between competing economic groups.

These commercial difficulties were exacerbated by the dramatic rise in governmental expenditures on military activities.

Table 5.1
American Exports, 1770–1793
(in millions)

Period	To Great Britain	To British West Indies	To Others	Total	American Population
1771–1773	$5.3	$2.2	$3.2	$10.7	2.4
1785–1787	4.4	1.4	5.8	11.6	3.6
1792–1793	4.3	1.2	5.5	11.0	4.2

Source: Compiled from Gordon C. Bjork, "The Weaning of the American Economy: Independence, Market Changes, and Economic Development," *JEH* 24 (1964), Tables 2 and 3.

Gifts and loans from the French monarchy provided invaluable assistance to the struggling Americans at various stages of the war, but the total French contribution did not begin to compare with the money, men, and supplies poured into the colonies by Britain during the Seven Years' War. In order to raise sufficient funds to pay and maintain the Continental army, the Congress was forced to borrow large sums of money, first at home and then, when domestic sources proved insufficient, from foreign bankers. By 1783 the Dutch had invested $10 million in the success of the American cause.

Neither these loans nor the sums extracted from state governments (which were reluctant to levy heavy taxes) were sufficient to defray the growing expenses of the national army. The Continental Congress began, therefore, to buy needed supplies from farmers and artisans with paper currency, seeking to maintain the value of these bills by pledging their redemption with future tax receipts. By 1779 Congress had issued $191 million worth of Continental currency, but the states had collected taxes adequate to retire only $120 million of the old bills. A growing fear that the currency would not be redeemed for its face value led to a steady depreciation in its purchasing power. By 1777 it took $3 in Continental bills to buy goods that could be purchased for $1 in gold or silver, and this ratio continued to increase: to 7 to 1 in 1778; 42 to 1 in 1779; 100 to 1 in 1780; and, finally, to 146 to 1 in 1781, when the currency ceased to have any value as money.

This inflationary trend was accentuated by the fiscal policies of the state governments, many of whom also issued large amounts of paper money. In Maryland a bag of salt which cost

$1 in 1777 was valued at $3,900 three years later, while the price in paper currency of a bushel of wheat increased by a factor of 5,000. Most of this increase was "artificial," in that it stemmed from the enormous increase in the supply of money; but there was also a real shortage of goods. Even after an embargo had been placed upon the export of foodstuffs from Philadelphia in 1779, the price of flour in terms of gold or silver was 113% above its prewar level.

The abrupt and dramatic rise in prices engendered both by the general currency inflation and by the rapid growth in the demand for scarce goods produced widespread appeals for governmental control of prices and wages. At the end of 1776 delegates from the New England states met at Providence to set prices for domestic commodities and imported goods, and a similar meeting at New Haven in the following year established wage guidelines as well. Farmers, mechanics, and manufacturers were enjoined to restrict the increase in the cost of goods and services to a level 75% greater than that of 1774, while tradesmen were allowed a rise of 25%.

These political controls were generally ineffective. Farmers refused to sell their goods at the established prices, either hoarding them or engaging in blackmarket sales to merchants with military contracts. To correct these abuses the Massachusetts legislature passed an "Act to prevent Monopoly and Oppression" in 1777; but was forced to confess, three years later, that the law had led to "such a stagnation of Business and such a withholding of articles as has obliged the People to give up its measure or submit to starving." [1]

The increasing price of foodstuffs struck hardest at the poorer inhabitants of the cities, those whose businesses or job opportunities had suffered because of the war and who were unable to grow food of their own. These new hardships accelerated the political mobilization of this section of the urban community, a process that was already well advanced. In 1770 a Philadelphia mechanic had attacked "a certain Company of leading men" who had traditionally taken it upon themselves "to nominate persons and to settle the ticket, for Assembly-men, Commissioners, Assessors, etc, without ever permitting the affirmative or negative voice of a Mechanic to interfere." And this growing consciousness among the artisan class of their "Right to *speak* and *think* for themselves" resulted in the creation of a Mechanics Association in 1774.[2] By 1779, when British withdrawal from the city produced a period of severe inflation and food shortage, this middle strata of the city's population was well organized and prepared to act. In May a crowd seized a merchant, accused him of exporting flour desperately needed within the city, and then forced the town meeting to set whole-sale and retail prices for thirty-two commodities.

Previously only the members of the wealthier or better-educated classes of American society had established formal groups for political purposes. As early as the 1720's electoral activities in Philadelphia were managed by the Gentlemen's Club and by the Leather Apron Club, which had been organized by the governor in order to mobilize support among the artisans for his political program. There were scores of associations composed solely of members of lower-status groups—such as the Cordwainers Fire Company—but it was only under the pressure of wartime conditions that these organizations were transformed from social fraternities into political-interest groups. In 1779 the tanners, curriers, cordwainers, and other leather workers refused to abide by the price schedule established by the Philadelphia town meeting and formed an association to defend the interests of their trades.

By the end of the war formal organizations of artisans and mechanics were playing an active role in the political process in all of the major American cities. More members of this class could now exercise the franchise because of the lowering of the property qualifications for voting (in Newburyport, Massachusetts, 86% of the adult males were eligible to vote in 1785 as against 60% in 1773), and trade organizations had now been accepted as an integral and a legitimate part of the urban social order. In a parade honoring George Washington in Boston, forty-six trades marched in alphabetical order behind the government officials, merchants, and professional men who led the procession. The order of march reflected the continuing assumption of a graded social and economic hierarchy, but the flags carried by these occupational associations (in a similar procession in Philadelphia celebrating the ratification of the federal Constitution in 1789) challenged the traditional hegemony of the wealthy and the well-born. The flag of the weavers, "a rampant lion in a green field, holding a shuttle in his dexter paw," was inscribed with the motto "may the government protect us," while the banner of the bricklayers proclaimed that "both buildings and rulers are the works of our hands." [3]

The effect of the war and of the ensuing years of economic stagnation had been to make abundantly manifest the distinct interests of the lower-status groups within the northern urban population and to establish these middle-class groups of artisans as an important force in the political process. A second result of these years was no less important. The active manipulation of prices and wages in the war economy underlined the power of governmental bodies (now free of external British control) to alter the context within which business activity took place. This, in turn, encouraged the political mobilization of rural producers. During the war commercial farmers had joined in political coalitions with middlemen, government contractors, and merchants in opposing the regulation of prices—for it was in the financial interest of all of these groups to secure the free and untrammeled movement of the market mechanism. They had been opposed both in the streets and in the councils of government by urban craftsmen, who demanded the control of prices, and by representatives of subsistence farmers who had few commodities to sell on the market and whose economic position was being eroded by rising taxes and the high price of manufactured goods.

The war had widened the economic cleavages in society and had demonstrated, as never before, that affluence and poverty were as much political or social as natural phenomena, the results of a system of production and distribution which discriminated unfairly against some while permitting others to achieve windfall profits. "Fellows who would have cleaned my shoes five years ago, have amassed fortunes, and are riding in chariots," James Warren protested to John Adams from Boston in 1779, and such envious sentiments were echoed by many others during the economically depressed decade of the 1780's.[4] Some of the most acute complaints were voiced by hard-pressed agricultural debtors who needed ready supplies of credit to repay old obligations and to reestablish their farms on a solid basis. By 1785, seven of the new American states had issued substantial amounts of paper currency in an attempt to meet the financial demands of the farming population.

When merchants and other creditors opposed this remedial legislation and pressed for a "hard" currency backed by tax revenues, they initiated a series of fierce political battles. In Massachusetts in 1786 the representatives from the depressed western section of the state secured approval in the lower house of the legislature for measures which regulated legal fees and provided for a new issue of currency. When these bills were defeated in the Senate—in which eastern creditor interests were disproportionately represented—the towns of the west met in extralegal conventions to condemn the legislation, to demand repeal of excise taxes, and to insist upon the regulation of legal fees. Then, under the leadership of Captain Daniel Shays, a former officer in the Continental army, the inhabitants began to close the courts in order to protect their property from sale for default on mortgage and taxation payments. The people had banded together, as they had a dozen years before, "in order," as one of them put it, "for the Suppressing of tyrannical government." The allusion was not lost on contemporaries. "The people," the arch-conservative Fisher Ames commented, "have turned against their teachers the doctrines, which were inculcated to effect the late revolution." [5]

In Massachusetts (as in North Carolina a generation earlier) the struggle had been fought along sectional lines, but the points at issue were essentially economic in character. In every colony there were large numbers of men, mostly farmers, who needed tax exemptions, a moratorium on debt repayments, or an inflationary monetary policy in order to safeguard their standard of living and their property during this period of financial stagnation and rising taxes. In the northern states, where freeholders constituted a large percentage of the total rural population and where the political system was relatively representative, the needs of the agriculturalists were eventually, if grudgingly, met. The Massachusetts militia put down the Shaysites by force, but in the following year the legislature moved to meet some of the demands of the western farmers.

A similar trend was apparent in the South as well. In Maryland, where the new state constitution excluded thousands of small debt-ridden planters from an active part in the political process by high property qualifications for voting and officeholding, the demand for an expansionist fiscal policy came from a group of wealthy speculators who had become deeply involved in a number of precarious ventures during the war and who stood to be ruined by continued financial deflation. Here, as in neighboring Virginia, such splits within the ranks of the wealthy planters offered the poor white farmers their first opportunity in generations to secure an economic program that was suited to their own interests. In 1783 and again in 1785 delegates from the counties in the Southside of Virginia—a newly settled region in which half of the white adult males owned land—secured the postponement of tax collection measures supported in the state legislature by delegates from the Northern Neck, a region dominated by wealthy planters with large numbers of slaves and tenants.

As James Madison pointed out at the time, most of these political battles were not fought between "the Class with, and the class without property," but among different groups of property holders: rich planter and poor; merchant creditor and agricultural debtor; banker and artisan borrower. There was a large (and a growing) landless rural population—30% of the adult males in Chester County, Pennsylvania, in 1782, and at least 11% in Kent, Connecticut, in 1796—but this submerged and scattered agricultural proletariat was without political power or political awareness. The battles in the legislatures were fought between different groups of capitalistically oriented property owners and producers, who were competing against each other in the marketplace and in the political institutions that determined tax and monetary policy.

These were old conflicts in American history, now made increasingly acute by the economic depression, the increased potential for remedial government action following the removal of imperial controls, and—perhaps most importantly—the increasing sectional differences both within and among the states. Previously agricultural creditors and debtors had lived next to each other in the same district; however divided on financial matters, they were united by a shared social experience and by their allegiance to a common system of values. With westward expansion of settlement and the appearance of specialized financial institutions in the East, the scale of economic differentiation had increased and had assumed a geographic character. By 1820, 14% of the entire American population lived in regions added since 1790 (and as many more in the newly settled western sections of states like New York and Pennsylvania). Those who lent and those who borrowed were no longer neighbors engaged in the same type of productive activity. And the agricultural unrest and regional conflict which found violent expression in Shays' Rebellion in Massachusetts would appear again during the course of the nineteenth century among Jacksonian farmers in Ohio and Kentucky, Grangers in Indiana and Illinois, and Populists in Kansas and the Dakotas. By 1790, the struggle between the small western agricultural capitalists and the eastern entrepreneurs of commerce, transportation, industry, and finance was on the verge of becoming a structural feature of American life.

In the vastness of the American West this conflict between rich and poor, between aspiring farmer and established entrepreneur, would be given an articulate and violent expression completely foreign to the shape and character of the eighteenth century. The diversity and the expanse of life was growing too large to be encompassed within the tight social, psychological, and ideological bounds of the traditional systems of elite control. Therein lay the possibility of a genuinely democratic society.

The Parameters of Change

During the war for independence itself, the political battles among artisans, farmers, and merchants were dwarfed by the more fundamental cleavage between Patriots and Loyalists. Loyalism first appeared as a definable political force in 1774, when the passage of the Coercive Acts elicited a call from Boston for the imposition of new economic sanctions against Great Britain. To blunt this appeal, a group of political conservatives in

New York proposed a general Congress in order to seek an over-all political settlement with the mother country. When the First Continental Congress met in Philadelphia in the autumn of 1774, John Dickinson and Joseph Galloway, two influential delegates from Pennsylvania, sought to rally "men of loyal principles" behind a final attempt at reconciliation. But the bloc of delegates from the middle colonies (where the competitive nature of politics had accustomed the leadership to seek compromise rather than confrontation) was not large enough to counteract the emotional pleas and organizational skill of the Anglophobic New Englanders and the voting strength of the Virginians (whose fears of the "low, levelling principles" of the men from Massachusetts were outweighed by their suspicions of British intentions). Galloway's plan for an American Parliament failed by a single vote, and he and his allies were unable to prevent the passage of new resolutions of nonimportation and nonexportation.

Conservative by inclination, concerned to avoid conflict rather than to foment it, and doubtful themselves about the wisdom or even the legality of the new imperial legislation, the Loyalists had waited too long before mustering their supporters. By the time they had emerged as a third force to mediate between the Patriots and Parliament, the situation was already desperate. In December 1774, when Governor Wentworth of New Hampshire attempted to raise an armed force to prevent the Patriots from seizing weapons from the fort at Portsmouth, he could only assemble one sheriff, two justices of the peace, four provincial councillors, and two of his personal secretaries. Even a month later, after extensive canvassing, Wentworth's new Tory Association boasted but fifty-nine members, fourteen of whom were his own relatives. The rest of the populace was either unwilling to become involved or deterred by its fear of the Sons of Liberty.

The arrival of large contingents of British troops prompted more of the settlers to declare their allegiance to the political institutions under which they had been born and raised. At least 25,000 Americans fought for the Crown in regular army units and thousands more served in the militia seeking to maintain imperial authority in pacified areas. In many localities, such as upstate New York and the Carolina backcountry, the split between Patriots and Loyalists followed the lines of long-existing class and ethnic differences. Angered by the prewar suppression of their land claims by the Whig landlords, New York tenant farmers flocked to the Tory cause, as did many disgruntled settlers in the uplands of the South. Here, as elsewhere, the withdrawal of British forces triggered a massive migration; more than 100,000 Americans left their homeland during these years, migrating to Canada, the West Indies, or even back to Great Britain itself.

The character of the exodus was as important as its size. Although most of the emigrants were farmers by occupation, families of urban, commercial, and governmental backgrounds were represented in disproportionate numbers. This regional and class bias in Loyalism was apparent in Virginia, where few members of the planter aristocracy embraced the Tory cause—in part at least because the oligarchic character of colonial politics in the Chesapeake had prevented the appearance of abusive factionalism; and also in New England, where membership in the Church of England (in the otherwise homogeneous society of Dissenters) was a crucial determinant of continuing allegiance to the Crown. Of the forty-seven barristers practicing law in Massachusetts in 1774, seventeen fled the province during the war while another fourteen remained behind as Tory sympathizers or reluctant Patriots. Most imperial officials had departed by the end of the war, and so also had many of the influential northern merchants who had held lucrative military contracts in the years following the Seven Years' War. Death and downward social mobility had always taken a toll of those at the apex of society, but the vacuum suddenly created by the emigration of Anglicans, barristers, merchants, and imperial officials from the American port cities was much larger than that produced by the normal process of social evolution.

This void was quickly filled by those who had previously been excluded from the top positions of wealth and status by the intermarried group of families who had enjoyed the confidence and the favors of the royal governor. The Lowells, Higginsons, Jacksons, and Cabots transferred their interests and residences from Essex county to the Boston area between 1777 and 1794, forming the nucleus of a new social and economic elite. And many established residents of the city used the opportunities offered by the war to improve their position. Eighteen merchants and three shipowners were among the twenty-six purchasers of land confiscated from eight Loyalists in Suffolk County and sold by the state of Massachusetts at public auction. There was a modicum of social mobility in these areas of high Loyalist emigration, as well-to-do Patriots replaced wealthy Tories at the top of the social order, but there was no democratization of wealth. The profile of social stratification was just as skewed by inequality in 1790 as it had been in 1774.

If the war for independence did not alter, either directly or indirectly, the distribution of wealth in America, it did undermine—if only temporarily—the oligarchical control of the legislatures by wealthy planters and merchants. In this, the growing self-consciousness of the artisan class was one factor and another was the new ideology of republicanism which explicitly legitimized the sovereign power of the entire white male population; but most important was the increased representation of the interior regions in the new state governments. This geographic shift in the locus of political power had begun in 1775, as anxious eastern Patriots had sought the support of western residents for the prosecution of the war. Representation in the extralegal congresses and conventions assembled in the various states was determined primarily on the basis of population (rather than by traditional geographic boundaries), and this served to increase the proportion of delegates from the agricultural hinterland. The larger size of these bodies created still more openings for men of moderate means and small accomplishments. The new House of Burgesses, one Virginian commented in 1776, was

composed of men not quite so well dressed, nor so politely educated, nor so highly born as some Assemblies I have formerly seen. . . . [But, he concluded,] They are the People's men (and the People in general are right).[6]

The voters had not repudiated those wealthy leaders who had led the movement for independence, but because of the change in the basis of apportionment these men now constituted a much smaller and much less powerful group within the representative bodies. Before the war, 85% of the assemblymen from the six colonies of New York, New Hampshire, New Jersey, Maryland, Virginia, and South Carolina owned wealth in excess of £2,000; and even in supposedly democratic Massachusetts men from the wealthy class had furnished over half of the total number of representatives in 1765. By 1784 this percentage had dropped to 22% in Massachusetts, and there were corresponding decreases in the other states. Less than one in five of the delegates to the colonial assemblies in the third quarter of the eighteenth century had been artisans or yeoman farmers, but in the aftermath of war and reapportionment these social groups now constituted a majority in some of the northern legislatures and a powerful minority in the southern assemblies.

Yet the strength of these democratic forces was not sufficient to overcome the vested interests of wealth and prestige in the more oligarchic regions. The lowland planters of South Carolina controlled the legislature of that state until after 1800, when reapportionment finally shifted power to the upland districts (where a new elite was now forming, based on the production of cotton by slave labor). And it was only in 1829–1830 that a Constitutional Convention in Virginia abolished high property qualifications for voting and instituted an equitable system of sectional representation. In northern states, where many of these reforms were achieved by 1780, the deference paid to the traditional leadership enabled it to retain effective control of the new state governments. Nevertheless, these assemblies were somewhat more representative of the total white adult male population than the institutions of the late colonial period had been; and the presence of ordinary men in the halls of government had broken the once automatic identification between established wealth and political power.

This alteration in the complexion and composition of governmental institutions was significant and, in a certain sense, "revolutionary." But it occurred only in certain states and then only because the foundations had been laid in the preceding decades, by the implacable westward march of thousands of settlers. It was, in reality, the "completion" of a long process of social evolution, simply speeded up and given a positive articulation by the war for independence and the new republican ideology.

And so it was in other areas of American life as well. Except for the disruptions produced by the war itself and by the Loyalist emigration—which *were* historically new developments—most of the changes that took place during these years represented the culmination of previous trends. President Dwight of Yale might proclaim that the years between 1774 and 1783 had unhinged "the principles, the morality, and the religion of the country more than could have been done by a peace of forty years" but what he could not see, because he stood too close to events, was that this acceleration of the historical process had followed along *linear* lines of development. Connecticut and Rhode Island did not even bother to call constitutional conventions in 1776, but simply continued the (basically republican) institutions of government established by their seventeenth-century colonial charters. And most of the other states retained the traditional property qualifications for voting and officeholding, lowering them somewhat, but now bestowing constitutional sanction on the traditional assumption that only those with a stake in society could be safely trusted with its management.

In the immediate aftermath of independence merchants, planters, lawyers, and entrepreneurs had been well placed by their past achievements and power to stamp their imprint on the newly molded forms of political authority. Some previously disadvantaged groups, like the militant farmers of the interior and the urban artisans, had also been sufficiently prepared by past events that they were able to seize the historical moment and realize some of their goals through purposeful political and social action. But other deprived groups were unable to make use of the opportunity created by the demise of established authority to improve their place in American life. Blacks, propertyless whites, and women were not permitted much of a role in the unfolding historical drama; although the ideology of republicanism and liberty under whose banner the war was fought spoke directly to their condition.

I wish most sincerely [Abigail Adams declared in 1774] there was not a Slave in the province. It always appeared a most iniquitous Scheme to me—[to] fight ourselves for what we are daily robbing and plundering from those who have as good a right to freedom as we have.[1]

The glaring inconsistency of the existence of slavery in a supposedly free society prompted the whites of five northern states to abolish the institution. But such action did not touch the overwhelming majority of the black population, which was being steadily condemned to an ever more subordinate position in the social order of the South. And because the northern legislation was enacted by the dominant racial caste for reasons of its own (rather than as the result of purposeful action by the oppressed blacks themselves), its effect was minimal. In Massachusetts the law declaring the end of legal slavery was accompanied by another which prohibited the marriage of whites to Indians, blacks, and mulattoes. Given the pervasive racism among the members of the dominant white caste, the new legal freedom was meaningless; the consciences of many northern whites were clear, but northern blacks remained in a condition of social, economic, and political subordination.

The continuing dependence of the black even in the northern states proved that racial oppression was not the result of a single factor that could be removed by the legislative enactment of legal freedom, but that it was, in effect, "overdetermined"— the product of an interlocking series of causes which were extremely resistant to change. The mere award of basic civil rights meant little in the face of racial discrimination and systematic denial of economic and social opportunity. Indeed, the experience of the blacks (both in the North in the aftermath of independence and in the South in the years after 1865) revealed the tragic limitations of the ideology of liberty and equality enunciated during the struggle with Great Britain. The right to the "enjoyment of life, liberty, and property according to standing laws" guaranteed by the Massachusetts Constitution of 1780 (and by similar provisions in the basic charters of the other states) merely established legal equality for the adult male inhabitants; neither society nor government accepted an obligation to insure that this abstract civil right would be translated into economic autonomy and social dignity for all men.

Nor did the new ideology and institutions of republicanism automatically generate an improvement in the status and the condition of the women of the society. In 1777 the extraordinarily astute Abigail Adams chided her husband that she and other American women would "not hold ourselves bound by any laws in which we have no voice or representation," [8] but the depressed position of women during the colonial period robbed this stand of any political force. Women were subject to the legal control of their fathers until the age of 21 and upon marriage, as Blackstone's *Commentaries* of 1768 stated, "the very being or legal existence of the woman is suspended . . . or at least is incorporated and consolidated into that of the husband." [9]

This system of "domestic servitude" (as John Stuart Mill was to call it) was only one aspect of the oppression under which women suffered. Like blacks, their inferior social position was "overdetermined," by a complex and constricting web of laws, habits, and traditions. "Women in New England," Timothy Dwight noted with approval, "are employed only in and about the house, and in the proper business of the sex." Because such sexist attitudes were anchored in the social and economic reality of American life, they commanded wide support. As one anti-feminist male pointed out during the debate over universal adult suffrage in New Jersey in 1799,

Women generally, are neither by nature, nor habit, nor education, nor by their necessary condition in society fitted to perform this duty with credit to themselves or advantage to the public. . . .[10]

Trained from childhood to assume the role of housekeepers; taught that they were naturally inferior to men; denied the right to hold property while married; systematically excluded from responsible professional positions (even that of midwife, by status-seeking male physicians during the 1780's); and encouraged to bear children at frequent intervals—American women faced too many social, cultural, psychological, and biological obstacles to be able to assume a full and an independent role in the society. The appearance of a feminist movement that would demand for women the republican civil rights guaranteed to free white and black men was contingent upon the disappearance of at least some of the customs and practices that had systematically condemned women to a position of inferiority in society.

The first signs of this process were apparent well before 1815. The decline in the frequency of arranged marriages during the eighteenth century had already decreased the power of the father over his female offspring, and had given to the woman herself a somewhat greater role in the determination of her own future. This emancipation from the paternal will was, at best, an ambiguous legacy from the colonial period; for, if marriage based on romantic love gave women a wider choice of partners it also introduced the blinding and often irrational impulse of sexual passion into the selection process. And, even more importantly, it diminished the protective role of the father over the future well-being of his daughter; in a society of pronounced sexual inequality, this attenuation of paternal solicitude could only work to the advantage of the husband and the subordination of the wife.

Indeed, this very sharpening of sexual politics within the conjugal unit may have constituted an important element in bringing about the appearance of a feminist movement. The process of social and economic evolution had made women more independent, and literally forced them to respond in a creative fashion to the unsettling realities of their new position. The dynamics of these fundamental social changes were apparent in many eastern communities in which the migration of male inhabitants to the frontier had created a surplus of women. Fifteen percent of the female children born to one group of parents in Hingham, Massachusetts, between 1721 and 1760 remained spinsters at least until the age of 45, and there was a similar increase in the number of never-married women in Bristol, Rhode Island, during these same years. Whatever the psychological and sexual hardships of spinsterhood, these women had the ownership and control of their own property. And because they were freed from the onerous task of bearing and raising huge numbers of children, they could devote their time and energy to other socially productive activities. During the nineteenth century these women entered into the work force on an independent basis—as the clerk in a store, as a teacher in a public or church school, or even as a poorly paid worker in a textile mill—and thus broke another of the invisible social chains that had traditionally bound the members of the female caste.

The final precondition for the creation of a feminist movement was the appearance of organizations limited to women and run by them. These historically new associations, which began to appear in the United States around 1800, were initially religious in character, formed by the women of a congregation to raise money for missionary activities and to plan social functions. For the first time American women were not divided among separate households, but united in organizations of their own. Equally important, they were addressing themselves to the types of social questions traditionally reserved to men. By the 1830's there were more than one hundred female antislavery societies in the United States, and it was out of these groups that the Women's Rights Movement gradually developed. "In striving to strike *his* [the black man's] irons off," Abby Kelley, an early feminist, later recalled, "we found most surely, that *we* were manacled *ourselves.*" [11]

The liberation of blacks and of women was intimately connected because both occupied the same type of structural position within the American social order. Both were members of a caste, one racial and the other sexual, into which one was received at birth and could never escape. Moreover, the majority of the members of both groups in 1775 (and still in 1815) were the legal chattels of the white male section of the population. Finally, both were encased within societal institutions which either by accident or design insured that they would be confined to menial occupations and denied the opportunity to develop the full potential of their minds and personalities. Those few women and blacks who lived outside the systems of social control embodied in the male-dominated family and the white-dominated institution of slavery found that sexism and racism still denied them an equal place in American life. They joined those who were white and male, but also poor and propertyless, as members of the hidden and oppressed *majority.*

The freedoms won in war and sanctified in the new constitutions were limited, in the main, to those who were white and male and propertied. As such, they reiterated and reinforced the character of the society as it appeared at the end of the colonial period. The Patriot leaders did not envision a new social order and the governments they created did not attempt to alter existing religious beliefs; the distribution of wealth; or the barriers of sexual, racial, and class status. The limited nature of the goals of the insurrectionists underlined the fact that this was not a "total" revolution (such as that in France between 1789 and 1799, in Russia in 1917, or in China in 1949) in which previously disadvantaged or powerless groups sought to use political power to effect a dramatic change in the basic nature of society. It was, rather, a movement for home rule led, managed, and ultimately controlled by groups who occupied privileged positions in the society. For these men, those who were already the dominant members of the indigenous social system, independence itself was justification enough for the costs and the sufferings of war.

For the others, those men and women who constituted the majority of the population, the most important result of these years was the "simple" revolution in ideology. Generated initially by the transformation in the structure of society and authority; precipitated by the imperial crisis; and embodied in the republican institutions of the new nation, the ideology of liberty, equality, and popular sovereignty represented a dynamic force for reform with an inner logic of its own. As Benjamin Rush observed in 1787,

The American war is over, but this is far from being the case with the American revolution. On the contrary, nothing but the first act of the great drama is closed. It remains yet to establish and perfect our new forms of government.

The potential power of the new republican ideology to effect the transformation of an unjust, unequal, and oppressive social order represented the redeeming feature of the American independence movement, elevating it above a self-interested evasion of imperial responsibilities by a privileged colonial elite, and constituted its most impressive legacy to future generations of Americans. Whatever the harsh reality (and menacing tendencies) of the social and economic system from which they sprang, the public myths and values of the new republics would be used as intellectual, psychological, and emotional levers by those who sought a different type of society. "Man and Woman were created equals," Lucretia Mott proclaimed during her struggle for the abolition of slavery and the emancipation of women, "[and were] provided by the Creator with inalienable rights. . . ."

Law and Social Process

Other wars for national independence have produced political systems controlled by charismatic leaders, who rule by virtue of their own personal authority; by military regimes based on force and the active suppression of dissent; or by authoritarian groups, who rule through a facade of representative institutions. None of these theoretically possible outcomes transpired in America (although there were, especially in the more oligarchic regions in the South, great similarities to the last of these models).

Upon the breakdown of royal authority, the provincial assemblies and the local town meetings and county courts expanded the range of their traditional functions and assumed the tasks of the imperial government. The legitimacy of this de facto transfer of power was quickly confirmed by the new state constitutions, all of which were written and ratified in the five years between 1776 and 1780. Political stability was not endangered, since the people at large readily accepted the new institutions of government and the status accorded to those men engaged in governing. There was no breakdown in the state's monopoly of power, no dramatic repudiation of the old habit of obedience, and no questioning of the necessity to reestablish a political system based on rational rules of legal authority.

This peaceful, dignified, and permanent transfer of legitimate authority indicated that "the observance of law and belief in law" had themselves become enduring parts of the American system of values.[12] This development had been facilitated, during the colonial period, by the existence of relatively well-developed institutions of government and of a complex and coherent political culture. The continuous creation of new statutes and the orderly amendment of existing legislation had encouraged the inhabitants to look to legal processes and procedures to deal with the problems posed by rapid social change. The character of the economic system, with its heavy dependence on written contracts, property titles, and negotiable bills of credit—all of which were enforceable at law—also accustomed men to place their faith in legal institutions. The growing importance and prestige of the court system and the legal profession after 1725 also contributed to the formation of a legally oriented culture. Behind the overt manifestations of respect for the legal process was an inner psychological commitment, buttressed in New England by the Puritan system of childhood training that prompted the internalization of moral codes and elsewhere by the widespread social approval given to law-abiding behavior and responsible conduct. The results of this multifaceted and multilayered process of social evolution became apparent at the time of independence. There were bitter conflicts among various interest groups over the structure of the new governments and the content of new legislation, but no one doubted that the republics they were creating would be, as John Adams put it, "governments of laws and not of men."

This deep adherence to legal procedures played an important role in shaping the character of the social process itself. The guarantees of property and of legal privacy written into the state and federal constitutions established not only the substantive values of the society—which the law was expected to sustain—but also a firm commitment to the procedural safeguards offered by the legal system. Thus, the Fifth Amendment to the federal Constitution prohibited the new national government from depriving any person of his liberty or property "without due process of law." This institutionalization of inherited English legal procedures in the new American constitutions represented an attempt by the Patriot leaders (many of whom were lawyers) to legitimate a system of arbitration and reconciliation that would be immune from political interference and private passion. Conflict would be subsumed within the bounds of the law; and the courts would resolve disputes among individuals and between the state and its citizens without a resort to force or to legislative enactment.

The legal system itself had some claim to being a politically neutral institution. But the law, as enacted by the legislatures and evolved by judicial decision, contained a definite system of social values. Until 1831 the laws of New York permitted imprisonment for debt even when there was no evidence of fraud. Here was the use of criminal penalties for offences amenable to treatment by simple resort to the procedures of civil law. Even commercial fraud might have been handled without reference to the penal code (with the guilty party made responsible for reimbursement), but most of the state legislatures made fraud a criminal offense.

Whether the specified penalties were criminal or civil was, in a certain sense, irrelevant. For the fact of overwhelming importance was the intervention of the political state, through the mechanism of the legal process, in the economic life of the society. The legislative sanction given to the laws of contract added the weight of social legitimacy and state power to private transactions of the marketplace and committed the government to the active defense of the rights of property through criminal prosecutions or through the provision of a civil court system.

The character of the evolving relationship between the state and the individual with regard to property rights was revealed by the debates over confiscation of Loyalist estates. In New York the public interest was given a certain precedence by the declaration of "the sovereignty of the people of this State in respect to all property within the same," but elsewhere there was a greater hesitancy to deny the natural right to property for which the war was, at least in part, being fought. In Massachusetts, most of the Loyalist confiscations were carried out under the terms of a long-standing "Act to Provide for the Payment of Debts." In these cases the state did not expropriate Loyalist property, but undertook its sale on the application of a creditor, a procedure which was completely consistent with a conservative Whig interpretation of property rights.[13]

This emphasis on the sanctity of individual property (quite remarkable in the heat of a civil war) extended as well to the laws of contract. There were some lawyers and judges in Massachusetts, such as Francis Dana and Theophilus Parsons, who argued that "the existing rights of the public" should not be infringed by the action of private parties to a contract; and they declared such contracts invalid on the grounds that they were injurious to the public welfare.[14] This older, almost Tory (and almost socialist), interpretation of contract law did not ultimately prevail. The general tendency of American law during the nineteenth century was to support the bargains made in the market by private individuals, whatever the social cost. This principle was given final sanction when the authors of the federal Constitution in 1787 included a clause prohibiting the several states from passing "any law impairing the obligations of contract."

The dichotomy between the public interest and the property rights of the individual was revealed, in a slightly different form, in the gradual transformation of the laws relating to the ownership of real estate. In New England during the eighteenth century the royal governors and the corporate assemblies had granted land in fee simple, a form of conveyance which gave the grantee or the purchaser complete and unrestricted control of the property. In most of the other colonies, however, land grants carried a stipulation for the annual payment of a small quit-rent to the Crown or the proprietor. This was not a normal rent, with a value proportional to the worth of the property, but a fixed sum in money or produce which symbolized the fact that the ultimate ownership of the land remained with the Crown (although the resident owner could freely dispose of his real estate in accord with the laws of the colony).

The weakness of royal rule in America meant that these annual duties were rarely paid and, with independence, quit-rents were abolished in every state except New York—where they were retained as a nominal charge due to the state itself. The culmination of this trend in property law came in the Ordinance of 1785, which outlined land regulations for the states that were to be carved out of the Northwest Territory, the great national domain which stretched from the Ohio to the Mississippi Rivers. Adopting the attitude that it held the land in trust for the sovereign people, the federal government did not seek a quit-rent or attempt to retain ultimate ownership. The Ordinance specified, rather, that the land was to pass in fee simple from the government to the first purchaser.

There was one respect, however, in which the Ordinance reiterated the traditional limitations on property rights of the individual. The charters of most of the colonies had reserved one-fifth of the returns from all mines and minerals for the use of the Crown, and this concept of the intrinsic right of the state to extract a portion of the mineral wealth continued to command respect. The Ordinance of 1785 reserved one-third of the output of all gold, silver, lead, and copper mines for the use of the federal government.

This attempt to reserve some of the natural resources of the country for public use proved abortive. When the federal Congress attempted, between 1807 and 1847, to implement the policy incorporated into the Ordinance by leasing (rather than selling) public lands containing rich deposits of lead in Missouri and Wisconsin, local residents refused to comply, mining the land as if they owned it. The practice of the eighteenth century had created the assumption that land was to be treated just as any other tradable commodity. And in the end this commitment to the primacy of individual property rights forced the abandonment of this effort to retain part of the nation's mineral wealth for the public. The principles of American republicanism, founded as they were on capitalist rights of property, stood in opposition to the traditional public control embodied in the sovereignty of the Crown.

Republican and capitalist assumptions thus combined with powers inherent in the state to provide much of the impetus behind the gradual expansion of the market mechanism. When the colonial assemblies had levied taxes payable in specie or paper currency (rather than in kind or in labor), they had induced—indeed, virtually compelled—men and women to participate in the market economy. The provision of an extensive court system and a coherent body of legal rules governing property transactions were also crucial political contributions to the functioning of the American economy. Less than fifty pages of Blackstone's four-volume *Commentaries on the Laws of England* (1769 edition) dealt with business contracts, but Judge Kent's *Commentaries on American Law* of 1830 devoted an entire volume (out of four) to contracts and commercial matters. The growing importance of commercial law, both in America and in England, reflected the fact that the working of the "invisible hand" of the market (as postulated by Adam Smith) was contingent on the existence of an elaborate system of legal rules and social expectations. Each member of society had to feel confident that if he acted in a rational economic fashion, others would react in reciprocal, equally predictable, and legally enforceable ways.

By the time of independence the market had become one of the most conspicuous institutions of American society. This was especially the case in the northern regions where other forms of social mobilization, such as the impressment of labor for public works and a master's control over his servants, had gradually atrophied during the course of the eighteenth century. In these urban or commercially oriented areas, the market mechanism had become the main device by which men, money, and resources were directed into productive activities. With this transition from external coercion to the free participation of individuals in the marketplace, the economic system of the states to the north and west of Pennsylvania took on a much different character from that in the racially divided settlements to the south. The southern colonies, inextricably entangled in the slave system—with its

conscription and direction of labor by the threat of violent force
—continued to depend on that older and more primitive means
of work discipline.

And yet the market, despite its elegance and modernity,
was also a coercive system. If this was not immediately obvious,
it was only because of the indirect type of compulsion exerted by
the market mechanism. If men and women were to eat and to
live in a market economy, they *had* to strike a wage bargain with
an employer or produce goods that could be sold. But because
they were left *physically* free to choose the way in which they
would deal with the demands of the market, they had a somewhat greater range of choice than those who were servants,
slaves, or conscripted laborers. These options were not unlimited;
the freedom of the marketplace was not absolute. The individual
was under great pressure to migrate to an area where land or
jobs were available; to live in districts or houses with rents he
could afford; to accept the type of work that was offered by an
employer—for the alternative, in each case, was financial disaster
and personal hardship.

The power of the market to mobilize men and money was
well appreciated by the entrepreneurs of American society, for
they were the men who had created the market. And just as these
businessmen had once attempted to secure from the state a
strong legal foundation for the market economy, so now they
sought specific governmental support for its expansion. The
ideological justification for this political intervention derived
from the republican premise that government was the servant of
the people, working to expand the common-wealth of the society.
And, beginning in 1780, it became widely accepted that one of
the prime tasks of the various American governments—federal,
state, and local—was the promotion of economic development.
"It is a grave error to suppose that the duty of a state stops with
the establishment of those institutions which are necessary to the
existence of government. . . ," Chief Justice Black of Pennsylvania declared in a court decision in 1853, "To aid, encourage,
and stimulate commerce, domestic and foreign, is a duty of the
sovereign, as plain and universally recognized as any other."

This aid to business enterprise took various forms. Some
were direct extensions of the mercantilist practices contained in
the British Acts of Trade and Navigation. The Tonnage Act,
passed by the federal Congress in 1789, restricted all shipping
between American ports to vessels owned by citizens of the
United States and levied a special duty of fifty cents a ton on
goods imported into the country in ships that were foreign built
or foreign owned. A Tariff Act, passed in the same year, was
intended to raise revenue, but within a generation it had been

amended to impose high protective duties on a variety of foreign manufactures. This legislation was more successful in balancing the federal budget (providing two-thirds of all national government income between 1790 and 1860) and in creating bitter sectional feeling between North and South than in stimulating expansion and technological innovation in crucial import-substituting industries; but it did subsidize a number of domestic manufacturers (at the public expense) by raising the price of imported goods.

This federal program of economic nationalism was complemented, on the state level, by a variety of governmental measures. In the thirty years between 1789 and 1819, the various state governments issued more than 2,500 charters to business corporations, giving them a privileged legal status and making it easier for them to attract investment capital. By this means the legislatures attempted to direct private resources into those enterprises that would provide the social overhead capital needed for rapid economic growth. Of the 326 charters issued before 1800, 207 (or 63%) were for the construction of turnpikes, bridges, and canals—the transportation system which was a fundamental prerequisite for the expansion of the market economy. By 1812, the Commonwealth of Pennsylvania had chartered 55 turnpike companies, while New York had granted articles of incorporation to 57 and Massachusetts to 105.

Governmental participation in the construction of canals went far beyond the bestowal of legal privileges. The capital cost of canals was so great that it was only in New England, with its dense concentration of population, that the prospect of private profits was great enough to attract a sufficient number of investors. Elsewhere, the state governments took the initiative, seeking to enlarge the productive capacity of the community by opening up the interior for development. Of the total investment of $132 million in the canals of the Trans-Alleghany region between 1815 and 1860, $117 million (or 89%) was contributed by state governments and only $15 million by private individuals and companies. The use of public money enabled these regions to be opened up long before private financing could have done so. By a massive intervention in the market economy, the states hoped to realize, for their citizens, the great social profits to be obtained by the expansion of settlement and production.

Direct involvement of the state governments in the operations of the market mechanism proceeded furthest in Pennsylvania. Beginning in 1809, with the grant of a loan to private individuals for the construction of a steel mill, the Commonwealth began to play an active role in business enterprises outside of the field of transportation. Arguing simply that "works of

(Buffalo and Erie County Historical Society)

This scene, on the state-subsidized Erie Canal near Buffalo, New York, suggests the effect of improved water transportation on the development of commerce and industry and on the growth of inland urban areas.

public importance deserve public encouragement," the state government expanded its investments in these mixed public and private enterprises until in 1844 it was financially involved in more than 150 separate companies.[15]

This purposeful intervention of the government into economic affairs gave a measure of public direction to a market mechanism whose primary function was to resolve bargains among private individuals without express regard for the good of society. These developmental projects also served to increase the rate of investment and capital accumulation, for the states used their preeminent financial position (guaranteed by the sovereign power of taxation) to underwrite huge bond issues that otherwise would have seemed too speculative and too dangerous to foreign or domestic investors.

As the financial resources of the new nation expanded during the nineteenth century, the various state governments gradually exchanged the role of proprietor for that of regulator. This switch in emphasis and activity, which had been implicit in the ideology of American public development from the very beginning, left the financing of new projects in the hands of banks and other specialized monetary institutions. That these new agencies were able to assume this crucial role was also the result, in large measure, of the encouragement given to the creation of a private banking system by the state governments.

One of the major factors in inhibiting the flow of surplus capital into productive investments during the colonial period had been the absence of a banking system. Financing for mercantile and manufacturing ventures was arranged through business partnerships, short-term joint-stock ventures, or private loans made between merchants. From this informal system of credit a more specialized structure began to emerge during the war for independence. The first president of the Bank of North America wrote from Philadelphia, in 1784, that

When the bank was first opened here, we adopted the only safe method to avoid confusion. Educated as merchants, we resolved to pursue the road we were best acquainted with. We established our books on a simple mercantile plan, and this mode . . . pointed out by experience alone, has carried us through so far without a material loss or even mistake of any consequence.[16]

By the time the First Bank of the United States was established by a federal charter in 1791, there were local banks in New York, Massachusetts, and Maryland, as well as in Pennsylvania. The important services rendered by these institutions, especially in extending short-term credit to merchants who needed money immediately in order to pay for shipments of imported goods, brought a rapid increase in their numbers. There were twenty-one banks in the United States by 1795 and ninety by 1812. The combined specie holdings of these institutions by the end of this period amounted to more than $15 million and they had more than $52 million either out at loan or circulating as negotiable bills of credit. The monetary stability of this private financial system owed something to the activities of the First Bank of the United States, which accepted bank notes in payment of federal taxes and then presented them for redemption, a procedure that forced the banks to maintain sufficient reserves of specie.

With the creation of a complex and comprehensive system of banking, the United States entered a new stage in its financial development. Markets, rational economic behavior, and money have appeared together, as part of a single integrated system of commercial exchange, in many parts of the world at different times in history; but seldom has this relatively simple mechanism been superceded by a more elaborate system of financial relations based on business firms, complex institutions of credit, and a deliberate search for technological innovations and new forms of economic enterprise. Yet, as the nineteenth century began, precisely this transition was beginning to take place in the economically more advanced urban regions of America.

The number of patents (another state-created and state-supported property right) issued by the United States government for new inventions increased from an average of 20 per year between 1790 and 1795 to 200 per year between 1808 and 1824. Concurrently, new types of financial institutions began to evolve. Shortly after 1800 the merchant house of Alexander Brown and Sons of Baltimore deemphasized its trade in commodities and began to specialize in "paper" transactions—charging merchants a fee of 2% for buying bills of exchange drawn on foreign banks and then redeeming them in Europe or using them to speculate in the international money market. In Philadelphia the firm of S. and M. Allen and Sons began to provide a specialized financial service of another type: it promoted a system of lotteries to raise capital for investment purposes. This method of raising funds was so successful (because it provided a means of tapping the small savings of thousands) that the number of offices run by the Allens grew from 3 in 1809 to 60 in 1827.

By 1815, the system of merchant capitalism that had been the driving force behind the American economic development of the eighteenth century was in the process of becoming a specialized structure within which the once-indivisible functions of trading, insuring, financing, and banking would be performed by separate institutions. Although the merchant entrepreneurs still occupied the center of the stage, these men, whose fathers or grandfathers or former employers had begun in trade and then diversified their activities as the empirical situation had demanded, were now being replaced by a wide variety of different men, each of whom concerned himself only with a particular type of financial activity. If these new actors had less range, versatility, and audacity than their predecessors, they were more accomplished practitioners of their separate vocations. With this division of labor, the commercial advances of the previous century were consolidated in a new series of organizational relationships. The next economic advance would begin at a higher and more efficient technical level.

Taken alone, or even together, the creation of a new financial structure, the massive intervention of the states in the market economy, and the articulation of a legal framework based on capitalistic values were not sufficient to unleash the sustained process of economic growth needed to initiate transition to an industrial society. This would require a fundamental shift in population and production to the western regions and the urban areas of the United States—not to be accomplished by a few legislators, entrepreneurs, and bankers within a few decades. The process could, however, be encouraged and accelerated by the presence of a value system and an institutional infrastructure designed to promote rapid economic growth. By 1815 the necessary configuration of ideas and agencies had begun to appear in America: The banking network was providing short-term credits to merchants and amassing domestic capital for long-term investments; the device of the public corporation, by providing governmental backing for private enterprises, was attracting much-needed foreign capital; and the federal tariff and the developmental projects of the states were working through the market mechanism to induce or attract or coerce the diversion of men, money, and resources into manufacturing enterprises or into exploitation of the interior.

All of these economic developments were based, in the last analysis, on political decisions. And the extent of this governmental involvement in business activity was a new element in American history. Certainly, in the past, the British state had given some support to colonial interest groups, and some of its mercantilist policies (such as the subsidies for indigo and naval stores) had worked to the advantage of the colonists. But in the aftermath of independence the full weight of the American state was thrown behind the innovating entrepreneur and the achievement-oriented capitalist—giving them special charters; funnelling public money through their hands; perfecting a legal framework suited to their needs; and embodying their values in new legislation.

These policies were defended by those who made them as contributing to the material welfare of the community. And that they did, there can be no doubt. But some men at the time took a slightly different reading of the situation. "In this country," wrote one Pennsylvanian, "sovereignty is vested in the people themselves, and whatever power is granted to corporations, is so much abstracted from the people themselves." This also was true. In the name of economic development, the American system of governmental assistance to business enterprise had, through the private corporation and the market mechanism, helped to create a financial and commercial oligarchy in the northern cities of the United States.

The economic growth stimulated by this state intervention did increase the common-wealth of the society, but primarily by increasing the private fortunes of the wealthier citizens of the new nation. The farmer or the worker who waited for the benefits to "trickle down" through the market mechanism found the rewards much less substantial than did the entrepreneurs, who were the direct beneficiaries of this aid and assistance. This was so not only because these men handled much larger volumes of goods and money but also because the public managers of these early governmental enterprises were often large private investors in the same companies. The policies they pursued were calculated as much with reference to their private interests as to the public good.

Like the law itself, the American system of governmental aid was not socially neutral. It purchased gains in the gross national product at the cost of a growing inequality of wealth— and the disparities in social status and political power that would inevitably follow. But this, perhaps, was only to be expected. The definition given to republicanism by the Patriot leaders was founded on the sanctity of private property; and the new legislatures were still controlled, for the most part, by those planters, merchants, lawyers, and entrepreneurs who had led the revolt against Great Britain and who were now in a position to use their wealth, family connections, and personal abilities to increase their position of dominance in an increasingly competitive and capitalist economic and social system.

Notes to Chapter Five

1. Richard B. Morris, ed., *The Era of the American Revolution* (Magnolia, Mass.: Peter Smith, n.d.), pp. 118–119.
2. Leonard Bernstein, "The Working People of Philadelphia," *Penna. Mag. Hist. Biog.* 74 (1950): 327.
3. David Montgomery, "The Working Classes of the Pre-industrial American City, 1780–1830," *Labor History* 9 (1968): 13–14.
4. Richard D. Brown, "The Confiscation and Disposition of Loyalists' Estates in Suffolk County, Massachusetts," *WMQ* 21 (1964): 548.
5. David H. Fisher, "The Myth of the Essex Junto," *WMQ* 21 (1964): 205.
6. Jackson T. Main, "Government by the People: The American Revolution and the Democratization of the Legislatures," *WMQ* 23 (1966): 407.
7. Edmund Morgan, "The Puritan Ethic and the American Revolution," *WMQ* 24 (1967): 22–23.
8. Andrew Sinclair, *The Emancipation of the American Woman*, original title (1965) *The Better Half*, 2nd ed. (New York: Harper & Row, 1970), p. 30.
9. Kate Millet, *Sexual Politics* (New York: Doubleday, 1970), p. 68.
10. Arthur W. Calhoun, *A Social History of the American Family*, 3 vols. (New York: Barnes & Noble, 1960), vol. 1, p. 188.
11. Sinclair, op. cit., p. 37.
12. James Willard Hurst, *Law and Social Process in United States History*, 1960 (New York: DaCapo, 1971 reprint), p. 15.
13. See Brown, op. cit.
14. Fisher, op. cit., pp. 202–203.
15. Louis Hartz, *Economic Policy and Democratic Thought: Pennsylvania, 1776–1860* (Magnolia, Mass.: Peter Smith, n.d.), passim.
16. Bray Hammond, *Banks and Politics in America from the Revolution to the Civil War* (Princeton: Princeton University Press, 1957), p. 66.

The two types of preindustrial society that had existed, in rudimentary form, in America in 1700 were still present a century later. The size and the complexity of these social systems had increased during the interim, but there had been no fundamental or permanent alteration in their structure. The potential for internal development was not yet exhausted, and there still remained the possibility of external expansion. Indeed, the final maturation of the slave society of the southern part of the United States would only take place between 1820 and 1860, in lands far to the south and west of its original Chesapeake home. There, finally, the full economic, cultural, and ecological implications of the institution of racial slavery in a preindustrial society would become fully manifest.

The more dynamic freeholding society of the North had an evolutionary "time-scale" of shorter duration. By 1815 it had already arrived at a point from which it would either stagnate (as the rural-based economy of the South was to do after 1860) or undergo metamorphosis into a new type of social order. By 1860 the issue had been settled: Transition to an urban and industrial society was well advanced in the northeastern part of the United States and its system of freehold agriculture had spread into the rich lands of the Middle West. The civil war which followed was, in the final analysis, a struggle between two fundamentally different forms of social organization—the one inherited from the eighteenth century and the other pointing toward the twentieth century.

The foundations for this struggle between the slave and the free states had been laid in the decades before 1775, but it was only after 1815 that the expansion of cotton production in the South, the growing industrialization of the Northeast, and the settlement of the West magnified the differences between the two systems of social and economic life. During the intervening years the inhabitants

PREINDUSTRIAL AMERICA: THE MATURATION

of the two regions could cooperate, without undue conflict, in the achievement of national goals: winning independence in two wars against Great Britain; fabricating and testing the new republican institutions of government; and beginning the settlement of the vast interior of the continent. It was the very successes of the Americans during these years that, ironically enough, led ultimately to the tragic failure of civil war. Independence, the federal Constitution of 1787, and westward expansion all sharpened sectional antagonisms while making it possible for one region to threaten the economic interests and way of life of the other through control of the central government.

As yet these bitter conflicts lay in the future. The disruptions caused by wars in America and in Europe at the end of the eighteenth century had served momentarily to retard the century-long trend toward sectional differentiation and animosity. The years between 1775 and 1815 constituted a period of arrested social and economic development; for a generation and a half the momentum of change slowed, permitting a coherent consolidation of the developments of the eighteenth century. Here, at last, was the maturation of the preindustrial social order.

The Limiting Parameters of the Preindustrial Economy

By the traditional standards of the preindustrial world, the performance of the American economy had been remarkable, even outstanding. This point was made by Thomas Jefferson in a report from Paris in 1787.

Of twenty millions of people [in France] . . . , there are nineteen million more wretched, more accursed in every circumstance of human existence than the most conspicuously wretched individual of the whole United States.[1]

Like most members of his caste, Jefferson simply ignored the 750,000 Americans (nearly 20% of the entire population) who were blacks or slaves; but he was on somewhat surer ground with regard to the white population. The annual per capita income of the white residents of the American middle colonies in 1774 was $71, an amount which compared favorably with the figure of $100 achieved by the more highly developed English economy by the end of the eighteenth century.

This difference underlined, nevertheless, the severe limitations on output in a preindustrial agricultural economy. England had ceased to be a grain-exporting nation in the 1760's, as a result of the increasing diversion of labor and resources into the more-productive nonagricultural sector of the economy; and by 1811 only 34.7% of all English families were directly engaged in agriculture. This was less than half of the American proportion (83.7% in 1810) and this in itself accounted for much of the variation in the levels of per capita income between the two economies. For the yearly output of a worker in a nonagricultural occupation in the United States during the first half of the nineteenth century was nearly double that of a farm laborer.

There was another factor, in addition to the predominance of the agricultural sector, that had retarded the expansion of the American per capita gross national product. This was the extremely high proportion of dependent children in the population, the result of the high birth and low childhood mortality rates. In 1774, in Connecticut, 32.1% of the total population was 9 years of age or younger; and the proportion for the entire United States in 1800 was even higher—34.6% of all inhabitants fell within the bounds of this relatively unproductive age group. Eventually these children would provide welcome additions to the work force, but in the short run they constituted a heavy drain on the meager capital resources of the society.

During the eighteenth century the American settlers had compensated for these economic and demographic liabilities by developing a strong export trade in agricultural commodities. Indeed, this foreign trade had become the crucial factor in determining variations in the standard of living. American prosperity had deteriorated after 1775 because of the decline in commerce, and it began to return only upon the revival of international trade in the late 1780's. By 1793 the value of per capita imports into the United States had regained the level reached in the American colonies in the early 1770's. And, then, with the continuance of the wars of the French Revolution in Europe, the value of imports shot upwards, raising the American standard of living to a new high.

Unlike the import boom that took place in the late 1750's, this expansion in American per capita consumption of foreign goods was financed almost completely out of current earnings. The foreign liabilities of the United States amounted to $61.1 million in 1790 and to $62.0 million fifteen years later, despite the fact that goods worth $700 million had been imported during the intervening period for domestic consumption. As in the past, the cost of these goods was offset in part by the sale of American commodities in foreign markets. Roughly 80% of these exports still came from the agricultural sector of the economy (in the form of flour, tobacco, rice, meat, and—increasingly—cotton),

Chart 6.1

Population, Imports, Exports, and Shipping Earnings, 1760–1830

(in U.S. dollars)

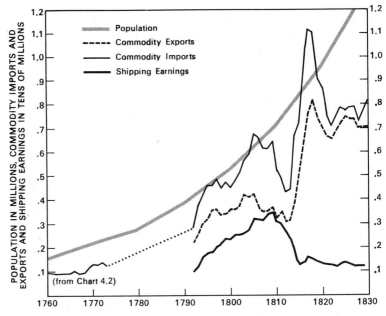

SOURCE: Computed from data in Douglass C. North, *The Economic Growth of the United States, 1790–1860* (Norton, 1966), Tables B–III, E–III, B–VIII, C–VIII, A–III.

NOTE: The value of pre-1775 commodity imports has been translated into dollars by the formula: £1 sterling of 1774 is equal to $4.50 U.S. dollars of 1792. See A. H. Jones, "Wealth Estimates," *EDCC* 18, no. 4, pt. II, 125.

Imports, exports, and earnings are 5-yr. moving averages in U.S. dollars.

while the bulk of the rest were derived from the extractive industries of lumbering (11%) and fishing (5%). These traditional exports were now earning more foreign exchange than in the 1780's because of the growing European demand for American farm products during wartime, and also because of the high (and rising) prices paid for these commodities between 1788 and 1814. These factors combined to lift the total value of American exports from $20 million per year in the 1790's to nearly $70 million per year by the 1820's (although even this dramatic increase was not sufficient to match the growth in population).

The import costs not defrayed by this expansion of exports were financed by the freight earnings accumulated by American merchant vessels. This was also a traditional item in the balance of payments account, only now the level of these merchant receipts was much higher than ever before. Unable to ship products to and from their colonies in their own vessels

Table 6.1
United States Balance of Payments: Selected Years and Aggregate, 1790–1819
(in millions of dollars)

Fiscal Year	Exports (Excluding Reexports)	Imports for Domestic Consumption	Specie Movements	Freight Earnings	Ship Sales	Insurance	Interest Charges	Yearly Balance	Cumulative Balance at End of Year
1789									−60.0
1790	19.9	−23.5	1.0	5.9	0.2	−1.0	−3.6	−1.1	−61.1
1800	21.8	−44.1	2.0	26.2	0.8	−3.7	−4.8	−1.8	−82.3
1810	42.3	−64.9	−2.0	39.5	1.0	−3.6	−5.5	6.8	−72.9
1819	70.1	−93.5	1.0	15.2	0.6	−1.9	−6.2	−14.7	−176.0
Total: 1790–1819	1170.4	−1725.7	12.9	628.8	21.7	−81.0	−143.1	−116.0	

SOURCE: Derived from D. C. North, "The United States Balance of Payments, 1790–1860," in *Trends*, Table A–4.

NOTE: These figures include the debt of $88.5 million (most of it accumulated between 1816 and 1818) repudiated by American citizens —the source table did not.

because of privateers and of blockading fleets, the European nations turned to the United States merchant marine. As "neutral carriers," American ships were legally protected from armed attack as long as certain customs requirements were fulfilled. Commodities from the British and French West Indies were transported in American ships to ports in the United States and then reexported to their European destination, and a reverse procedure was followed on the return trip. This circuitous pattern of trade was more expensive in terms of freight rates; but since most customs duties were refunded upon reexportation and since the risk of capture was greatly reduced, the gains accruing to the warring nations of Europe far outweighed the liabilities.

For the merchants and the inhabitants of the urban seaports, the results were equally beneficial. Freight earnings averaged more than $20 million a year in the ten years between 1793 and 1802 (as against $6.5 million between 1790 and 1792) and more than $31 million per annum for the ten years beginning in 1803. For more than two decades these earnings constituted the largest source of American foreign exchange, with a value greater than any single commodity export. Even when the charges of $3 to $5 million per year paid to British firms for marine insurance were deducted from these totals, the credits earned through the provision of commercial services provided more than enough revenue to pay for the large import bill. And because more American trade was now being conducted in domestically owned vessels (the proportion rising from 60% in 1790 to 85% in 1815), the balance of payments position of the United States was improved still further.

Finally, these commercial earnings raised the level of business activity in the seaport cities, and generated—through the multiplier effect—enough new jobs to raise the number of urban residents in New England and the middle Atlantic states to more than 10% of their total populations by 1810. Many of these new urban laborers and craftsmen were absorbed by the shipbuilding industry, for domestic shipyards provided most of the vessels that raised the tonnage of shipping owned by American merchants from 355,000 tons in 1790 to 1,089,000 tons in 1808.

This surge of productive activity and prosperity demonstrated the considerable economic advances which could be made within the framework of the export-oriented and mercantile-financed economy of the eighteenth century. It also revealed, if less dramatically than in the 1750's and 1760's, the tenuous character of an economic expansion based upon favorable external conditions and wartime shipping or military subsidies. In 1807 the embargo disrupted the lucrative reexport trade. And when commercial patterns returned to normal in Europe in 1815,

Table 6.2
Percentage of Total Population Resident in Towns of 2,500 or More

Region	1770	1780	1790	1800	1810	1820	1830	1840
New England	—	—	7.5%	8.2%	10.1%	10.5%	14.0%	19.4%
Middle Atlantic	—	—	8.7	10.2	11.5	11.3	14.2	18.1
South Atlantic	—	—	2.3	3.4	4.5	5.5	6.2	7.7
Entire United States	7.0%	—	5.7%	6.3%	7.6%	7.5%	9.3%	11.5%

SOURCE: *Sixteenth Census of the United States, Population*, I, Table 8.

there was a further decline in the level of American per capita earnings of foreign exchange. In the three decades beginning in 1815, United States merchants earned only between $10 and $15 million per year through the provision of shipping services. This decline was compounded by a sharp drop in world prices for American agricultural staples. In the crucial year of 1818, the price of cotton dropped from 33¢ per pound to 20¢, and the value of a barrel of flour decreased from $10 to $7. The results were quickly apparent: by the 1820's the per capita value of imports had dropped to a level below that of the 1770's (see Chart 6.1).

A similar decline in the per capita value of imported goods a half-century before, during the war for independence, had indicated a fall in the American standard of living and had increased the amount of social and political conflict among competing economic groups. Now, it did not. For by the 1820's the United States had begun to transcend the narrow economic framework of the eighteenth century and to escape from the tenuous prosperity based on wartime subsidies and fluctuating international commodity prices. Americans had begun to decrease their dependence on foreign goods by expanding their own manufacturing enterprises. They had also begun to increase the productivity of both the agricultural and nonagricultural sectors of the economy. This was a fact of crucial importance; for a rise in the level of per capita income depended, in the final analysis, on a corresponding increase in per capita productivity.

These changes would ultimately demand a fundamental alteration in the nature of American society, a transformation in the system of production that had barely begun. In 1815, as in 1700, the primary economic unit was still the family enterprise and the basic rhythm of life was still determined by the seasonal cycle of the agricultural year. Here the resemblance stopped;

over the course of the century the character of the northern agrarian landscape had changed significantly, within the bounds established by the earlier ways of life and work. In many of the longer-settled regions, such as Lancaster and Chester counties in Pennsylvania, 30% to 40% of the taxable rural residents were now laborers or artisans, living on the land and growing their own crops, but obtaining the bulk of their income from outside employment or through practicing a trade. The countryside surrounding the American cities, Alexander Hamilton reported in 1792, was "a vast scene of household manufacturing . . . in many instances to an extent not only sufficient for the supply of the families in which they are made, but for sale, and even, in some cases, for exportation." [2]

The appearance of these blacksmiths, shoemakers, weavers, and cabinetmakers had already decreased American dependence on imported manufactures by providing a domestic source of supply. Other household industries had provided work for thousands of men, women, and children in the processing of domestic primary products (such as wheat, pork, hides, and cheese) for export; butchers, tallow chandlers, soap boilers, and leather curriers were just a few of the occupations directly dependent on the agricultural sector.

Despite their relatively low productivity and limited potential for technological innovation, these household manufacturers turned out an impressive amount of goods. Six textile factories in Philadelphia produced 65,000 yards of material in 1809, while families living in the immediate vicinity of the city offered more than 230,000 yards for sale. In the end, however, the factory system would prove triumphant. Economies of scale and the possibilities of mechanization made it an inherently more productive method of manufacturing. Moreover, the maintenance of output at a steady rate over the entire year effected a dramatic increase in the productivity of a work force previously accustomed to the seasonal labor of the agricultural cycle.

Whatever the limitations on output, the system of household manufacture had a number of redeeming social characteristics. Men and women worked in their own homes or in those of their neighbors and clients, not in a large factory. If work was not always forthcoming and if the personal relationship between husband and wife was often adversely affected by the tensions of common labor, still these family units were relatively independent, working for themselves and subject only to the calculus of the market. Like the yeoman farmers who were their parents or neighbors, these artisans were small capitalists—now engaged in an industrial rather than in an agricultural enterprise. Both of these groups of small producers had similar interests and values: They did not want a society characterized by limitless economic expansion and accumulation, but a community composed of relatively prosperous and independent property owners.

The dreams of these "little" men and women were gradually dispelled by the coming of the factory system. Manufacturing was removed from its traditional home in the countryside and moved to the cities, thus increasing the differences between the urban and rural sectors of the economy. Previously cities had served commercial and administrative functions; now they emerged as the locus of industry as well. Also, the appearance of urban factories undermined the position of the working entrepreneurial family as the prime fabricator of processed goods; only the family farm and the small retail store remained as viable economic enterprises based on the traditional unit.

The dimensions of nineteenth-century life were slowly becoming apparent. A mass exodus of artisans and craftsmen from the countryside would swell the urban, industrial population; and these once-independent producers would become wage-earning proletarians, their children accompanying them to work in a factory at the age of 7 or 8 rather than being trained as apprentices in the homes of kinsmen or neighbors. The first operatives hired by the Englishman Samuel Slater (who came from a society in which this process of change was well advanced) when he set up his Steam Cotton Manufacturing Company in Rhode Island in 1790 were seven boys and two girls, all between the ages of 7 and 12. By 1812, Albert Gallatin reported, the 87 cotton mills in the United States employed 3,500 women and children and only 500 men.

Men, women, and children had always worked in order to live, but now they began, in ever increasing numbers, to labor in a different type of environment and within a different system of social relations. As early as 1771, 29% of the taxable residents of Boston were neither property owners nor dependents of a propertied member of the community. Selling their services for wages in a market economy, these proletarians lived outside the bounds of the traditional system of apprenticeship and indentured service. In Philadelphia, the older forms of work discipline continued to exist on a wide scale, but their substance was eroded by the fluidity of the new urban social order and by its commercial ethos. Over the course of the eighteenth century the obligations of the master to his indentured servant were gradually converted into monetary values (which were minutely specified in formal contracts). By their very nature, these market-oriented relationships were subject to change; in the years between 1795 and 1803 forty-nine different men served for brief

(The Rhode Island Historical Society)
The Slater Mill, Pawtucket, Rhode Island. English technology, southern cotton, and New England capital and labor joined together for the production of textiles, the first important manufacturing industry in the United States and the locus of a new form of work-discipline.

periods in the five journeyman positions in the Philadelphia cabinet shop operated by Samuel Aston.

Thus, the coming of the factory system did not create a new class of proletarians but merely accelerated a development that had begun in all of the major urban centers during the colonial period. Similarly, it had been the increasing commercialization of the American economy during the eighteenth century—and not the industrialization that occurred later—which initiated a decline in the economic and social position of many sections of the artisan class. The crucial factor in this deterioration was the increasing efficiency of the market mechanism and the trading network. When shoes or clothes or farm implements were imported from another village or town or from abroad for sale in a local market, the resident craftsman lost the monopolistic (or oligopolistic) control he had once exercised over the price bargain. He now had to sell at a competitive price, not for an amount that would reflect his actual cost of production. The position of the consumer had improved, but only at the cost of a decline in a certain class of producers.

To combat the impersonal calculus of the market, tradesmen attempted to exclude low-priced foreign imports and to maintain uniform rates among themselves. The mechanics associations were among the most vociferous supporters of the federal Constitution of 1787 because of the improved tariff protection it promised. And by 1805 Philadelphia shoemakers were demanding a schedule of prices which conformed with those established shortly before in New York. Subsequently, the printers of all of the major cities established uniform rates and standards in order to prevent the appearance of cut-throat competition. A final development was the creation by the subordinate journeymen of new organizations designed to prevent master craftsmen from cutting wages in order to maintain profits.

The problems of production for a market in which growth in supply constantly tended to exceed the increase in demand had long troubled American farmers and planters. Except in the case of the West Indian plantation owners, these agricultural producers had been unable to safeguard their financial position through purposeful action. There were too many independent producers to organize and, in any event, there was little hope of controlling the prices paid on the international market for their commodities. The response of the farmers and planters had therefore been to produce more and to accept a lower profit on each unit sold—a strategy that prompted westward expansion in search of fertile lands which would lower the cost of production.

By joining together to campaign for high tariffs and to establish price and wage schedules, the artisans and household manufacturers sought to avoid the harsh alternative of long hours of work for meager returns. But these tactics could be successful only if these producers could achieve a monopoly of the American market for their products. And this they could not do. Neither those who processed agricultural commodities for export nor the domestic producers of manufactured goods had sufficient political power to alter the economic system to their own advantage. They could not prevent the establishment of factories, whose machines and relatively unskilled wage laborers provided a much greater output than theirs, for the same cost.

All fundamental social changes have their share of benefit and of loss, of advantage to some groups and of disaster to others. And the mechanization of production offered no exception to this rule. Indeed it demonstrated the rule's cunning logic in a most graphic manner. The economic viability of many of the traditional artisan crafts was destroyed by the spread of the factory system; and thus a distinct social group, with a middle-class entrepreneurial attitude of its own, was gradually squeezed out of existence. This social cost was offset—if human suffering and deprivation can ever be reduced to a balance sheet—by the appearance of a new system of production, which increased the per capita output of the nonagricultural sector of the economy and made possible a dramatic rise in the gross national product of the society.

These inevitable social byproducts of economic change would have been easier for the men and the women of the time to accept if their financial benefits had been distributed in a fairly equitable fashion among all the members of the community. But because these alterations took place in a capitalist society in which the sanctity of private property and the pursuit of material gain were unquestioned, the bulk of the profits was appropriated by the entrepreneurs who had brought the factors of production together in a new form in the factory system. By 1860 the top 1% of the taxable population in Philadelphia owned between 40% and 50% of the entire wealth of the city, a significant increase from 1774 when the richest tenth of the inhabitants controlled only 54% of the net assets of the community.

The increased concentration of wealth only hinted at even more profound changes in the composition and structure of the urban social order and at a fundamental alteration in the character of life. Many lower-class groups increased their material standard of living under the new system of production, but only as a result of longer and harder hours of work—unceasing labor that went on from dawn to dusk for six days a week from one end of the year to the other. A new and more rigorous pattern of life and of work discipline had begun to replace the seasonal rhythm of the agricultural cycle. At first many men and women could (or would) not submit to the monotonous and severe discipline of the factory, preferring freedom and leisure to greater earnings. Past experience had taught them to view life as a continuous, coherent whole, as an indivisible combination of labor and play, of effort and enjoyment; not as a rigorous dichotomy of work and nonwork. In America, as in England, it was "neither poverty nor disease but work itself which casts the blackest shadow over the years of the Industrial Revolution." [3]

The passage of time and of generations would accustom men and women to the more demanding framework of urban and industrial existence, but it would not resolve the new social conflicts generated by its structure. In a detailed survey of Philadelphia in 1830, the Reverend Joseph Tuckerman reported:

[The] classes . . . who are wholly dependent upon wages are very numerous . . . and to a great extent are living, as a caste,—cut off from those in more favoured circumstances; and

doomed to find their pleasures, and sympathy in their suffering, alone among themselves.[4]

The sense of social distance between rich and poor had grown. And, with the disappearance of the large middle-class group of small artisan entrepreneurs, the continuity of the urban social ladder had been severed. Ordinary workers might aspire to rise up the ranks within a manufacturing concern, eventually winning a foreman's position through devotion and hard work; while foremen and clerical workers might plan for the day when they would use their own experience and savings to establish a small

Chart 6.2
Real Wages and Cost of Living in Philadelphia, 1790–1830
(1790 = 100)

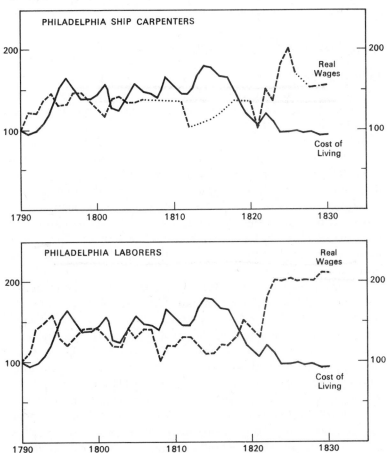

SOURCE: Based on data presented by Donald R. Adams, Jr., "Wage Rates in the Early National Period: Philadelphia, 1785–1830," *JEH* 28 (1968), Appendix, Tables VIII and IX.

enterprise of their own. But the fact that men and women continued to hope and to dream did not compensate for the new obstacles to occupational mobility imposed by the new mode of social relationships. Nor did it alter the fact that in the new system of economic organization there were proportionately fewer independent entrepreneurs with productive property of their own.

The rise in the material standard of living had been purchased at the cost of the quality of "independence" that had once been as prevalent among white Americans who were engaged in nonagricultural work as among members of the freeholding farming community. Alteration in the locus and character of manufacturing activity began a process by which a host of little societies, the *families,* would be replaced by a few massive groups, the *classes* of workers and employers, at the center of urban social and economic life.

Sequential Growth and American Economic Development

Industrial capitalism in America evolved slowly out of the commercial capitalism of the eighteenth century. This process, which took nearly fifty years to complete, occurred as various new factors—e.g., technology and capital imported from England, settlement of the western lands, increased immigration—were superimposed upon the relatively advanced economic and financial structure inherited from the past. Simply to list, in an additive fashion, the elements which combined to produce a sustained process of cumulative economic development is not, however, to explain the mechanism by which this breakthrough took place. This can be understood only in terms of the American success in circumventing the two traditional obstacles to economic development.

Throughout European history the agricultural sector of the economy had been subject to diminishing returns as the increase in population had gradually pressed upon the available land resources. The settlement of America represented but one in a long series of attempts to break out of this cycle. For a number of decades, it had worked. By 1775, however, diminishing returns had appeared in the British West Indies and in the American colonies. The American settlers could still produce agricultural commodities at a lower cost than their European competitors, but their comparative advantage was steadily decreasing despite the constantly falling costs of ocean shipping. Their land was not biologically exhausted; it was simply becoming more expensive to cultivate in terms of the yield obtained from a given input of capital and labor.

The possibility of geographic expansion into the interior of the North American continent provided a new opportunity to break out of the cycle of diminishing returns. In economic terms, the natural resources of this immense region were "free goods;" except for the military expense involved in subjugation of the Indian population, they represented a huge windfall profit for the society that came to exploit them.

The benefits of westward expansion first began to accrue to the citizens of the United States during the early decades of the nineteenth century. In 1806, when raw cotton was selling at 18¢ per pound, a Tennessee farmer could make a net profit of $200 per year by planting four acres of cotton on newly cleared land. These substantial profits, multiplied a thousand times over, financed the settlement of the southern uplands just as the international sale of tobacco in the previous century had subsidized the migration across Virginia. In 1790 there were 110,000 settlers in the territories that were to become the states of Kentucky and Tennessee; by 1820 the total had risen dramatically to 987,000.

Cotton had become a dynamic new force in the American economy. Between 1793 and 1815 the annual production of cotton rose from 3 million pounds to 93 million pounds. From 1815 until 1833 cotton exports amounted to one-third of the total value of all American exports, and from then until the outbreak of the Civil War they constituted one-half of the value of all commodities shipped abroad for sale. The institution of racial slavery, whose economic viability had been widely questioned at the end of the eighteenth century because of the declining profits in the tobacco industry, was given a new lease on life. In the upcountry of South Carolina and Georgia, the expansion of cotton cultivation raised the percentage of slaves in the total population from 18% in 1790 to 40% in 1820.

The appearance of the cotton economy, for all the wealth that it created, was not an unmixed blessing even for the white section of the community. The massive concentration of resources for its production delayed, for another century, the diversion of labor and capital into more productive forms of economic activity. In 1860, as in 1775, the South was still an economic "colony" with a low rate of domestic savings, a weak entrepreneurial spirit, few industries of its own, and a small urban population. It had remained a peripheral, quasi-aristocratic area within the world capitalist economy.

The North, in the meantime, was well on its way toward becoming one of the strongest bastions of industrial capitalism. Its highly developed commercial economy, substantial urban population, and widespread system of small-scale manufacturing had placed it in an ideal position to channel the high returns generated by the settlement of the interior into a process of capital accumulation and economic diversification. In so doing, it broke the other traditional obstacle to sustained economic growth—the absence of improvement in the productivity of the nonagricultural sector of the economy.

The first step in this process had been the creation of a financial and a political infrastructure conducive to a high rate of economic growth. By devising new forms of financial organization in the aftermath of independence, Americans had facilitated mobilization of the resources required to open up the interior regions for exploitation. Subsequently, the developmental policies pursued by the state governments attracted huge amounts of foreign capital. The aggregate American indebtedness grew from $80–90 million in the 1820's, to $200–250 million in the 1830's and 1840's, and to $350 million in the 1850's. It was this capital (not in the form of the private mercantile credit which had indirectly subsidized the expansion of the eighteenth century but rather in state-backed bonds and securities) that played a crucial role in speeding up the time-rate of the settlement of the western regions and in expanding the size-rate of the utilization of the natural resources of these rich areas.

As this process of sequential geographic growth got underway, it stimulated the entire economy of the northern half of the United States. More than 800,000 people (one-seventh of the population increase of the entire country) moved into the upstate counties of New York between 1790 and 1820, and many Americans began to settle in Ohio as well. As farm commodities, minerals, and forest products were shipped down the Erie Canal or along the Ohio River for sale along the American seaboard or in Europe, the income of these newly opened regions grew rapidly. At the same time the income of primary producers in the longer-settled eastern regions began to contract, since they were now being undersold by western farmers and lumbermen who had moved to (temporarily) more productive lands.

The slow decline in the level of profits in the older areas accelerated their rate of structural change. The market mechanism gradually diverted men and resources out of relatively unproductive occupations and into the fields of manufacturing, transportation, and commerce—where greater returns were to be obtained. In the end, the profits flowing into the more highly developed eastern regions through their sales of processed goods, their provision of marketing services, and their returns on invested capital more than offset the drop in income in their agricultural sectors. The total income of both eastern and western regions had now begun to rise at a faster rate than the

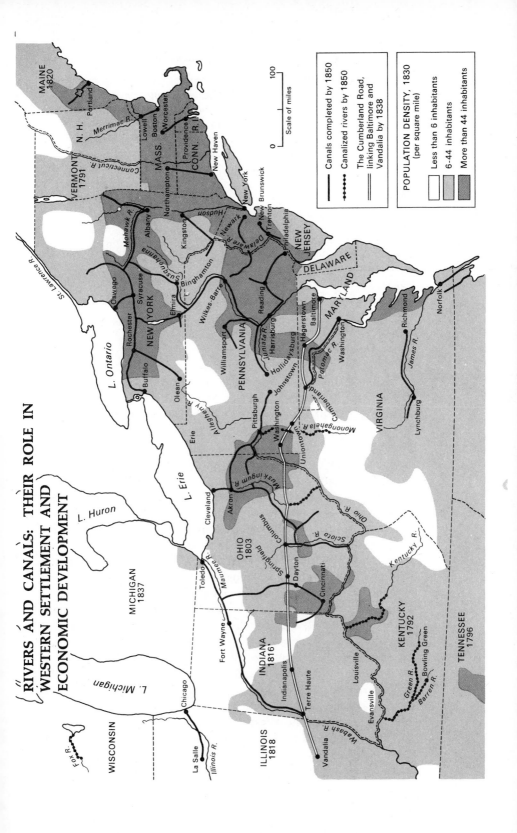

RIVERS AND CANALS: THEIR ROLE IN WESTERN SETTLEMENT AND ECONOMIC DEVELOPMENT

Canals completed by 1850
Canalized rivers by 1850
The Cumberland Road, linking Baltimore and Vandalia by 1838

POPULATION DENSITY, 1830 (per square mile)

Less than 6 inhabitants
6-44 inhabitants
More than 44 inhabitants

Scale of miles

0   100

WISCONSIN

Fox R.

La Salle

Illinois R.

L. Michigan

Chicago

ILLINOIS
1818

MICHIGAN
1837

L. Huron

L. Erie

Vandalia

Wabash R.

Terre Haute

Indianapolis

INDIANA
1816

Fort Wayne

Maumee R.

Toledo

Cleveland

Akron

Muskingum R.

OHIO
1803

Columbus

Springfield

Dayton

Scioto R.

Cincinnati

Ohio R.

Evansville

Louisville

Green R.

Bowling Green

Barren R.

KENTUCKY
1792

Kentucky R.

TENNESSEE
1796

Erie

Allegheny R.

Pittsburgh

Washington

Union

Monongahela R.

Cumberland

Johnstown

Holidaysburg

PENNSYLVANIA

Williamsport

Wilkes-Barre

Juniata R.

Harrisburg

Reading

Hagerstown

Baltimore

Washington

Potomac R.

MARYLAND

VIRGINIA

Richmond

James R.

Lynchburg

Norfolk

DELAWARE

Philadelphia

NEW
JERSEY

Trenton

Newark

Delaware R.

New Brunswick

New York

New Haven

CONN.

R.I.

Providence

Elmira

Binghamton

Susquehanna

Kingston

Hudson

NEW YORK

Rochester

Syracuse

Oswego

Buffalo

Olean

Genesee R.

L. Ontario

St. Lawrence R.

Albany

Mohawk R.

Northampton

MASS.

Worcester

Boston

Lowell

Merrimac R.

Connecticut R.

VERMONT
1791

N.H.

MAINE
1820

Portland

Table 6.3
Gross National Product Per Capita, 1800–1860

Year	Total Population (in Millions)	Percentage of Labor Force in Non-agricultural Sector	Per Capita Gross National Product (1840 = 100)
1800	5.3	17.4%	64.4
1810	7.2	16.3	61.9
1820	9.6	21.0	67.6
1830	12.9	29.3	81.8
1840	17.1	36.6	100.0
1850	23.2	45.2	110.4
1860	31.4	46.8	137.0

SOURCE: Paul A. David, "The Growth of Real Product in the United States Before 1840," *JEH* 27 (1967), Tables 4 and 8.

NOTE: The figures are national ones; regional variations were extensive and important.

growth of population. Between 1820 and 1830 the per capita gross national product rose from an index figure of 67.6 to 81.8 and during the following decade there was an even greater increase in the level of output per capita.

The growth of population and production in the interior of the continent had exerted much the same leverage on the economy of the northern seaboard regions as the colonization of America and the West Indies had done for the British economy during the eighteenth century. There were the same forward, backward, and final demand "linkages" between the economies of the primary producing areas and mercantile and manufacturing centers, only now this regional specialization and division of labor was taking place within the United States. One-third of the cotton produced in the southern states in 1815 was shipped to New England. There it was processed into textiles in plants financed by merchants who had shifted their interests from commerce to industry following the embargo of 1807. The production of this cloth provided work for thousands, absorbing the surplus agricultural population that had long been characteristic of this region. And, finally, when these textiles were sold in the West or the South, the income paid for the raw cotton and foodstuffs imported into New England from these primary producing regions, while leaving a handsome profit besides. The process of development in the Northeast had now become self-sustaining and cumulative: The high rates of return in the new markets of the West and South had resulted in expansion of old manufacturing industries, introduction of the factory system, and acquisition of capital equipment; all of which effected a significant increase in per capita output.

By 1850 the static productivity long characteristic of the nonagricultural sector of the economy had been clearly transcended. In the pig-iron industry the labor required for each unit of output was only half of what it had been in 1800, while in cotton textiles productivity was nearly four times as high. Moreover, the process of technological innovation that had been set off had resulted in the development of new forms of farm machinery (such as the horse-drawn, self-raking reaper introduced in the 1830's) which increased the productivity of the agricultural sector as well.

Table 6.4
Labor Requirements Per Unit of Output

Year	Cotton Textiles	Pig Iron	Ship Construc-tion	Wheat	Corn	Cotton
1800	100	100	100	100	100	100
1850	23*	50	68	55	70	60

SOURCE: Stanley Lebergott, *Manpower in Economic Growth: The American Record Since 1800* (McGraw-Hill, 1964), p. 156.
* 1860.

This "feedback" process was of vital importance. It meant that the costs of output in the agricultural sector could now be reduced by technology (rather than by western migration), thus permanently increasing the per capita output of the farming community. And this improvement in agriculture, in turn, permitted the continuous diversion of labor into the more productive urban manufacturing sector without a decrease in agricultural output. The proportion of the total population directly employed in agriculture fell from 83% in 1800 to 55% in 1850, but domestic consumption of foodstuffs remained high and exports of cotton and of processed foods continued to increase.

By the middle of the nineteenth century the northern areas of the United States had overcome the twin limitations on productivity by which the rate of growth had been constrained in the past. Between 1839 and 1899 (when sequential geographic development had, in a sense, come to an end) the American population increased at a rate of 21% per decade, but agricultural production grew by 28% per decade and industrial output by 42% per decade. The resulting rate of increase in the per capita gross national product of 17–21% per decade was impressive, although, interestingly enough, it was not as large as the growth rates of 21–29% sustained by seven other countries during their (subsequent) periods of industrialization. And yet the United States has emerged in the twentieth century as the wealthiest nation—in gross per capita terms—in the entire world. In part this achievement was the result of the early start of the American economy and its substantial potential for long-term development. But it indicated as well the successes of the agriculturally based, capitalistically oriented, commercial economy of the eighteenth and early nineteenth centuries. When the industrial revolution began to transform the American economy in the 1830's, the level of per capita output and wealth in the United States was far above that attained by most preindustrial societies.

The Context of Social Action

For men and women whose lives had been deeply rooted in the American soil, there had always been a natural hierarchy of allegiances: in political terms, to the village, to the colony or state, and finally—and much more distantly—to the empire or nation. For these rural folk there was a similar diffusion of interest and attention outward from the dense core of family existence—first to the members of the kinship group and then to the other inhabitants of the community. In this constricted social system the circumstances of daily life functioned, like the force of gravity itself, to pull men's minds and activities back to the individual and the concrete, to traditional religious beliefs and hereditary ties, and to the tiny scale of life of the local society.

In 1700, even in 1725, the lives of most Americans were constrained within the bounds of these "vertical" institutions of family, church, and community. Each of these social forms was a relatively self-contained and independent entity, and each embodied the same pattern of authoritarian relationships. The lines of force radiated downward from the father at the apex of the family unit to his legal dependents—wife, children, servants, and slaves; the minister spoke with the authority of God Himself; and there was a similar pyramid of power and status within the community.

In 1815 there was also a hierarchy of social and political power, but it was now based on different premises, functioned in rather new ways, and was somewhat less effective in controlling subordinate individuals and groups. For the people whom it sought to encompass within the bounds of its authority now functioned, in their daily lives, in a much wider range of social institutions. As the economy had become larger and more complex, the ties of kinship, religion, and community had receded in importance and a new set of social organizations had appeared, established along the "horizontal" lines of economic class and social status.

This process of social differentiation could be seen, for example, in the development of the legal profession. Before 1725 most men practiced law as a subsidiary occupation. Many planters in the South were familiar with the legal rules governing the ownership and transfer of property; and northern merchants had mastered, at least in a rudimentary form, the principles of the laws of contract. There was, therefore, little demand for a specialized group of legal brokers, especially since lawyers were regarded with great suspicion by an overwhelming majority of the population. Merchants feared them as potential rivals for political power; planters distrusted them as dangerous intriguers who could upset long-established land titles; while ordinary farmers shunned them as the agents of creditors or as prohibitively expensive and unnecessary intermediaries. As early as 1708, the Maryland Assembly established a schedule of legal fees to be charged for various court actions, and most other colonies imposed similar restrictions on the legal profession.

Social disapproval and economic circumstance thus combined to make the lawyer-entrepreneur the most characteristic member of the legal profession during the first half of the eighteenth century. During these years the main rewards of the practice of law came not from the fees extracted from clients, but from the opportunities offered by this occupation for the attainment of political office and the pursuit of lucrative economic activities (such as speculation in real estate).

The career of Daniel Dulany, who arrived in Maryland in 1704 at the age of 18, was archetypal. After serving an apprenticeship in the law office of George Plater, who was himself a planter and a provincial official, Dulany set out on his own, using his inside knowledge and his income from fees to speculate in land warrants. By 1715 he owned warrants on 13,500 acres of land, located mostly along the frontier of settlement. Dulany reaped an immediate return on this investment by leasing his property to tenants; then, as the growth of population brought a sharp appreciation in land values, he sold out at a substantial profit and reinvested his funds in other speculative property still further to the west. By the time of his death in 1753, Dulany was a rich man, with huge land holdings and an investment in an iron works. But neither this fortune nor his status in Maryland society proceeded, in the first instance, from his work or prestige as a lawyer.

The emergence of an American "bar," in the full sense of the term, was delayed until the volume of litigation was sufficient to supply full-time employment and adequate returns to men of considerable abilities. In Massachusetts the leading lawyers of the 1720's and 1730's were the Englishmen William Shirley and Robert Auchmuty, both of whom were practicing law while waiting for their English friends to win them appointments to high offices in the royal government. It was only in the 1740's that a capable group of native-born lawyers appeared in the province, and only in the next decade that the monetary returns attained an impressive level. John Tabor Kempe, the attorney general of New York in the years after 1759, derived an annual average income of £880 from his private law practice; while William Livingston, who began his career slightly earlier, averaged nearly £700 per annum during his twenty-four years at the bar. In country areas, where real estate transactions, probates, and commercial contracts were fewer in number and less complex, the rewards were more modest. Waightstill Avery, a lawyer in the backcountry of Virginia and North Carolina on the eve of the war for independence, had a gross income during one six-month period of £164, a sum that was still sufficient to make him one of the more affluent residents of this recently settled area.

As significant as the improved financial condition of the bar was its increasing self-consciousness and professionalism. In an attempt to eliminate untrained "pettifogging" practitioners, the New York bar successfully petitioned for the establishment of rigorous educational qualifications for those seeking to plead before the courts. After the 1750's a five-year apprenticeship was required for those without college training, while graduates were forced to serve as clerks in a law office for three years. The regulations outlined by the bar of Suffolk County, Massachusetts, in 1763 were even more stringent. Simply to practice as an "attorney" before the Inferior Court required a Bachelor of Arts degree and a three-year apprenticeship; while full status as a "barrister" admitted to plead before the Supreme Court necessitated two years of experience in the lower court and a formal recommendation from the bar itself.

The adoption of the distinction between attorneys (solicitors) and barristers revealed a conscious emulation of British practices and procedures by the status-conscious members of the American bar. In Massachusetts this effort to clothe the profession with dignity received literal fulfillment as lawyers eagerly adopted British gowns and periwigs. And in New York William Livingston led a successful attempt to found a law society to debate technical questions of legal procedure, modelling it directly on the Moot of Gray's Inns of Court in London. The American legal profession had now come to see itself as a distinct and self-defined group within the larger community; and it was taking deliberate steps to consolidate its privileged position.

The war for independence split the profession between Loyalists and Patriots and abruptly terminated the trend toward Anglicization, but it could not stem the growing size and influence of the American bar. By the 1830's Tocqueville would describe the legal profession as "the most powerful, if not the only counterpoise to the democratic element . . . the most powerful existing security against the excesses of democracy." [5] Many Americans, although agreeing with Tocqueville's analysis, refused to accept the "professional aristocracy" he had praised so highly. Beginning in the 1790's there was a widespread popular crusade to reform the legal system by replacing appointive with elective judgeships; by expanding the number of courts in which citizens could represent themselves; and by diminishing the educational requirements for the practice of law.

This attack on the expense of the legal system and its elitist character drew support from two distinct groups. Those Americans who wished to diminish the power of judges and lawyers supported legislation that would impose strict schedules of legal fees and give the sovereign people the power to dismiss judges as well as politicians from office. These democratic reformers were joined by those upwardly mobile, achievement-oriented individuals who wished to practice law themselves and who sought to remove the barriers posed by high educational standards and the apprenticeship system. Over the years the legal profession had become more and more of an exclusive and self-perpetuating caste. Only families in the wealthier classes could afford the "opportunity-cost" of sending their children to college in order to qualify them for admittance to the bar. The apprenticeship system also discriminated against those in the middle and lower ranks of society—for they lacked the personal or family contacts with the leading members of the bar which were necessary to gain entrance into this system of sponsored mobility.

The growing specialization of the American economy had encouraged the stratification of society along the lines of occupation and had generated an impulse toward "professionalism" in many spheres of life. As early as 1765, Dr. John

Morgan of Philadelphia had urged the establishment of a College of Physicians which would license doctors to practice in all of the colonies. This grandiose attempt to control entrance into the medical profession failed because of the decentralized character of American life, but local efforts were more successful. By 1772 the Medical Society of New Jersey had won legislative approval for its authority to license practitioners, but its effective power was limited by the absence of any medical institutions (such as hospitals) that could serve the regulating function of the courts of law in enforcing standards of practice and performance. In 1774 there were nearly 3,500 practitioners of the "medical Art" in the continental colonies, but less than 400 had any formal training and only 200 actually held degrees.

By the beginning of the nineteenth century, however, medical societies had appeared in all of the states. They had won the legal right to license practitioners in many localities and, especially in the larger urban areas, they sought to regulate standards and to establish common fees. This newly found organizational strength was paralleled by a rise in public confidence: when yellow fever epidemics struck most of the seaport cities in the 1790's, as many residents turned to medical men for inoculations as approached ministers for spiritual sustenance.

The social authority which had once been the acknowledged prerogative of the ministry had, in fact, now been partially appropriated by other high-status groups within the community. "Lawyers, physicians, professors, and merchants were classes," Henry Adams noted in his analysis of the American society of 1800, "and acted not as individuals but as though they were clergymen and each profession was a church."

This shift in the distribution of social power was the result, at least in part, of economic factors. The ministry had remained an office-holding profession offering security of tenure rather than great financial rewards, while law and medicine had gradually emerged during the eighteenth century as fee-for-service occupations which were much more lucrative. By 1800 the tenuous financial position of the clergy was being eroded still further by changes in population distribution and in societal values. In New Hampshire and elsewhere there appeared church contracts restricting the tenure of a minister to two to five years, with both the congregation and the incumbent preacher having the right to refuse renewal. For most ministers the single, lifelong pastorate of the past had now given way to a three-staged career which began and ended in a financially weak church; only during the prime of his ministry would a clergyman serve in a wealthy city-based congregation.

The values and practices of the market economy had finally

penetrated even the spiritual ethos of the house of God. In an effort to become more "competitive," some members of the clergy consciously cultivated the social graces and intellectual doctrines favored by urban congregations. Others moved to the West where they hoped their services might be more in demand in the wake of the great revivals which swept through the frontier in the 1790's. Like the men and women to whom they preached, ministers had found that their behavior was now more calculating than ever before and more suffused with economic considerations. In a society in which religious membership had come to be determined by voluntary consent, the clergy found that they could not rely simply on the force of tradition to guarantee them a secure and an established position of authority.

The failure of the clergy lay in the (largely unconscious) decisions by its members to confront the more fluid and more diverse social system of the early nineteenth century as individuals. Other professions and social groups had been more perspicacious, creating formal associations to protect their collective interests. A merchants club had been organized in Boston as early as 1763 and other businessmen's groups, such as chambers of commerce, appeared within a few decades. The lower orders of the urban population—mechanics, artisans, journeymen— were just as active in forming occupational organizations during these same years. Even in rural regions, where the forces of change were less apparent, there was a felt need for new types of institutions. Well-to-do farmers formed agricultural societies to collect and disseminate information on crops, soils, and techniques of cultivation. And the appearance of yearly county fairs in Massachusetts by 1810 permitted the entire community of farmers to compare methods and yields and to organize for political purposes.

By 1815 the scale of life had shifted, grown larger and more complex. The centrifugal forces of trade and war, of geographic migration and political participation had shattered the tiny self-contained cosmos of the agricultural village. Here, and especially in the more urbanized areas, men and women had gradually become more conscious of the larger social world in which they now lived. They realized, if only dimly, that they were dependent on state-wide or international markets for their economic prosperity; on the state or the federal government for remedial tariff or tax legislation; and on an abstract republican ideology for their sense of social identity. This perception was followed by the creation of new organizations—medical societies and mechanics associations, benevolent fraternities and charitable societies, Democratic-Republican clubs and Federalist Caucuses—all of which were intended to exert a measure of control over the larger and more diverse social space in which their members now worked and lived. The United States was the only country in the world, Tocqueville commented in the 1820's, "where the continual exercise of the right of association has been introduced into civil life." [6]

These attempts to overcome the effects of economic development and of unconscious social drift through the creation of new "horizontal" associations reflected the fact that the traditional "vertical" institutions of the family, the church, and the community were unable to comprehend the new complexity of social life and of individual experience. They indicated as well that a new pattern of social relationships had come to prevail in American society: Membership in these new organizations was not hereditary or compulsory, but voluntary; and the pattern of authority within these groups was one of equality, not mastery and subordination. Men or women with forceful personalities or with the experience of age might dominate the affairs of the meetings; but in these associations of equals, authority was far more tenuous than that embodied in the hierarchically organized institutions of the older society. Indeed, these voluntary associations were no less than the social analogues of the republican political institutions established between 1776 and 1787—groups composed of free and equal men and women who had joined together on a voluntary basis in the pursuit of the common good.

In these new associations, however, the point of reference was not the entire nation or even the whole community, but rather the interests of specific and well-defined groups within the society. When the Massachusetts Historical Society was incorporated in 1794, its membership was limited to thirty men, all of whom were drawn from the wealthiest and most influential inhabitants of the state. The hierarchy of status in the community, which had previously found an index only indirectly— in the tax lists, the offices of town government, or seating in church—had now assumed a tangible form in the exclusive membership of the various private voluntary associations. Mechanics, merchants, lawyers, and bricklayers lived in the same urban area (although now increasingly in their own residential districts) and were subject to the same laws; but they, like the members of the African Masonic Lodge, now inhabited separate mental communities, deriving sustenance and support from associations of their own occupation, class, or caste. The single-status hierarchy of the rural society of the early eighteenth century had been transformed into a more elaborate and more differentiated spectrum of power and authority. Unity had given way to multiplicity.

These changes were not universal. They were more obvious

and extensive in the North than in the South, in the urban areas of the United States than in the agricultural regions. Yet they pointed the way to the future. And wherever these alterations occurred, there were parallel changes in the character and structure of the family unit. The transfer of production out of the household in the nonagricultural sector of the economy and the breakdown of the apprenticeship system deprived the family of two of its most important functions. By the 1820's Mechanics Institutes appeared in all of the major cities to provide vocational training for the children of the working class. The offspring of the more privileged groups of the society were similarly accommodated in the system of public primary and secondary education which gradually emerged during the course of the nineteenth century. The school was on its way to becoming the most important instrument for formal education of the young.

As conditions of the urban environment deprived the family of its central institutional importance in economic and social life, the domestic, consumption-oriented conjugal unit of the twentieth century began to take shape. The transition was gradual and, in a sense, preordained. The nature of American agricultural life in the eighteenth century had been conducive to separation of the family from the wider society; it had also encouraged the creation of an elaborate and complex pattern of kinship. Although the nuclear household had stood alone in the middle of its property, it had been surrounded, within the community, by the conjugal units formed by brothers and sisters, aunts and uncles, parents and grandparents.

The ties of kinship now began to loosen in the urban environment, especially among the geographically mobile, achievement-oriented members of the middle classes. This group was at once the creator and the inheritor of the specialized nonfamilial institutions—schools, hospitals, business corporations, private social clubs—that now dominated the life of the urban regions. Members of the middle classes could re-orient their lives around these new agencies and enterprises. They were now able, if they so desired, to dispense almost entirely, during the course of their adult lives, with the ties created by the biological alignment of family and kinship. The conjugal unit stood alone, linked to society and family only by the bonds of self-interest and voluntary consent. The small, self-contained, and fragile group offered men, women, and children the psychological security denied them nearly everywhere else and, at the same time, intensified and aggravated the tensions that had always existed among the members of the nuclear household. The legacy was both contradictory and complex.

The world into which an American child was born in 1815

was more diverse than that confronting his ancestor of a century before. The cultural heterogeneity created by the immigration of the Scotch, Irish, and Germans during the first seven decades of the eighteenth century had been compounded by a vast increase in the number of religious sects, economic occupations, and social organizations. And in the process, the context of social action had shifted. As the numbers and the variety of their contacts with distant men, ideas, and institutions increased, individual Americans found that they were gradually pried out of the tight web of family and communal existence. The scale of life had changed, and so also had the structure of authority. Paternity had yielded to fraternity; orthodoxy to heterodoxy; social duties to individual rights.

Here, in embryo, was a social environment that would facilitate (even "cause") the appearance of modern individualism; for the effect of diversity was to present the individual ego with the possibility of choice among competing occupations, churches, associations, and values. These changes did not usher in a utopia, as the successful members of later generations were sometimes to claim, but they did create a new set of parameters —a new framework of life—within which much of human experience would be confined. The meanings of success and of failure, of happiness and despair, would be strangely altered by the hectic, materialistic, competitive world of nineteenth century America.

Within this broader and more crowded multidimensional social space, however, children were still born into families which were white or black, poor or rich, farmers or wage-earners. And the amount of control an individual could exercise over his environment—his effective amount of "choice"—was still determined largely by the class and status of the family into which he had been born. The daughters of merchants married lawyers; the sons of bricklayers became carpenters, laborers, farmers, or storekeepers. Only the very exceptional or the very fortunate man or woman could rise much above the social circumstances of birth. In this, as in any other society, a child was not born "free," but to parents who were members of a specific class or caste. And they, for the most part, could do little more than to teach their offspring what they themselves had learned, and enjoyed, and suffered.

The Structure of Politics

The growing scale of American life and the new ideological and social principles which bound the more diverse population together were most apparent in the political sphere. Neither political parties nor universal political institutions had existed before the war for independence. But by 1789 the citizens of the new American states had created a national republican government and endowed this central political authority with extensive powers in the areas of defense, commerce, land distribution, and finance. Within another decade political parties had appeared on the national level and had begun to encompass state and local political activities within the bounds of their organizations and ideologies. The tripartite politics of the colonial period—local, provincial, imperial—had now amalgamated into a single structure of power and authority.

The first tentative steps toward political integration had been taken, before the war, in response to external threats. An intercolonial Congress had met in Albany, New York, in 1754 to consider questions of administrative union and military defense in the face of French expansion into the interior of North America. And the subsequent imperial crisis prompted new efforts to concert policies on an intercolonial scale. The Stamp Act Congress in 1765 was followed, in 1768, by the creation of Committees of Correspondence which kept the various provincial assemblies informed of events in other colonies.

With the convening of the Continental Congress in the years between 1774 and 1776, the American political system entered a new phase in its development. Previously the lines of authority had radiated out from London, subordinating each colony to English control. Now this external system of control was replaced by an indigenous structure in which each of the newly independent and sovereign states was represented on an equal basis in a federal legislative assembly. This Congress of states declared war on Great Britain, raised and maintained the Continental Army through seven years of war, secured loans from foreign bankers and governments, and successfully negotiated a victorious peace in 1783.

The attempt to establish this central body on a permanent basis began in 1777, when the Congress asked the states to ratify Articles of Confederation which defined the powers of the federal government. Ratification was not forthcoming, however, until the pressures of the war itself forced the states to compromise their differences over claims to western lands. "Unless Congress are vested with powers, by the separate States, competent to the great purposes of war, or assume them as a matter of right . . . ," Washington warned his countrymen in 1780, "our cause is lost." [7] In 1781, under the threat of British invasion, the Maryland legislature became the final state to ratify the Articles, thus finally establishing the legitimacy of the de facto central government.

The Confederation government was thus a product of the war for independence. It was also an organization made necessary by the extant conditions of American life. For a century and a half the social and economic evolution of the continental colonies had taken place within an imperial framework; both goods and people had moved freely between one province and another —without tariffs, excise duties, naturalization papers, or entry permits. The assumption of complete sovereignty by the several states in 1776 was an historical aberration of major proportions. And it created a political vacuum that had to be filled if commerce and travel among these regions—now sovereign states— were to be resumed with the same freedom they had enjoyed in the past.

The inability of the Confederation government to fulfill this task to the satisfaction of all segments of the population stemmed from the fact that it had been a premature political and administrative expedient, devised under the pressures of war, rather than a governmental structure built in response to the social and economic forces present in American society. The Congress did not have a direct relationship with the various interest groups in the country. Nor was it designed to reflect their desires and needs, except insofar as these might be expressed by the representatives of an entire state. Equally important in generating pressure for its reform was the fact that the Confederation had much less authority than the imperial government which it had replaced. This paucity of central power loomed large in the minds of many Americans during the 1780's, when the postwar economic contraction and the increased amount of social conflict seemed to demand strong measures on a continental scale.

The first group to propose a strengthening of the powers of the Confederation government was composed of those men who had served under its aegis during the war for independence: military officers, foreign diplomats, congressional representatives, and federal financiers and bureaucrats. Their personal participation in the work of the central government had given this group a perspective on the affairs of the country which was far broader than that possessed by state and local officials, whose intellectual and emotional horizons were delimited by the boundaries of their own political units. For the members of this "nationalist" faction, there was a self-evident need to exert strong control over the disposition of western lands, the determination of tariff and commercial policies, and the diplomatic dealings with foreign states.

During the 1780's these nationalists struggled within the Confederation government to achieve implementation of their ideas. And they were partially successful. In 1785 the authority of the federal government over the western lands was confirmed and, in the Northwest Ordinance of 1787, the settlement of these fertile areas was begun on a rational and noncolonial basis. The new states were to be accepted into the Confederation on a basis of complete equality, and revenue from the sale of national domain was to be used to help finance the activities of the central government. Even as this program was going forward, the nationalists sought to win the approval of *all* of the states (as was required by the Articles of Confederation) for the imposition of a 5% impost on foreign imports. This measure was intended both to provide revenue to liquidate the war debt (which rose from $39 to $52 million between 1784 and 1790 because the income of the Confederation government was not sufficient even to defray the yearly interest charges) and also to replace the divergent tariff policies of the individual states by a uniform levy.

The sustained pressure exerted by the nationalist faction on the crucial question of the impost and the refusal of Rhode Island to approve this duty led to the calling of a Commercial Convention at Annapolis, Maryland, in 1786. Nearly all of the delegates who attended this conference—and the Constitutional Convention it arranged for Philadelphia the following year— were nationalists; and this bias was apparent in the document they composed in Philadelphia and sent to the states for ratification. The Constitution proposed the creation of a central political authority which was not a mere federation of sovereign states but a truly national government which, its architect James Madison explained, "instead of operating on the States should operate without their intervention on the individuals composing them."

The drift of circumstance and their own purposeful political action had enabled the nationalists to obtain considered discussion and a popular referendum on their new Constitution, but it was only the support provided by various social and sectional interest groups that secured its adoption. Urban artisans were attracted to the (so-called) Federalist cause by the apparent promise of protective tariffs on manufactured goods. Merchants and commercial farmers welcomed the movement for a stronger central authority as a means to eliminate the obstacles to interstate and foreign trade posed by local tariffs and taxes. Finally, there were many creditors and wealthy men—troubled by the inflationary monetary policies pursued by some of the state governments and frightened by Shays' Rebellion in Massachusetts— who supported the Constitution because of its conservative financial and political provisions.

The leaders of the Anti-Federalists (who opposed ratification) were drawn from all sections and all classes, but their arguments struck a responsive chord primarily among the small, self-sufficient farmers of the interior regions who stood to gain few immediate benefits from the creation of a more powerful central government. This noncommercial section of the population, however, was neither numerous enough nor powerful enough to defeat the coalition of creditors, merchants, and export-oriented farmers and planters whose interests the new Constitution had been designed to protect. With the victory of the Federalists in the state ratifying conventions in 1788 and 1789, the first major battle engendered by the existence of an independent political system in America was over. The weak and state-dominated government established by the Articles of Confederation had been superceded by a stronger central institution more directly responsive to interest groups within the society itself.

As long as states were the units of representation in the central government, individuals and factions who wished to secure new national legislation (or to prevent the enactment of measures which were prejudicial to their interests) had been forced to work through the factional politics of the state assemblies. By capturing control of the state's delegation to the Confederation Congress, an interest group could exert pressure on the national level. But when the lower house of the new federal Congress introduced direct representation by Congressional districts, these factional struggles were transferred from the state to the national level. In order to win a majority in the federal House of Representatives, it was necessary for each of the various factions throughout the nation to seek support in the society as a whole. And this affected the character of local politics, through the creation of more permanent forms of political organization and the enunciation of definite ideological programs and policies.

The structure of political authority established by the Constitution of 1787 thus encouraged the appearance of a national party system; but the rapid evolution of these institutions was the result of a number of disputes between Alexander Hamilton, the Secretary of the Treasury in the cabinet assembled by President Washington, and James Madison, the first Secretary of State. In order to guarantee national political stability, Hamilton proposed an interrelated series of financial measures designed to identify the interests of the members of the wealthy northern commercial classes with those of the new government. When Madison—the spokesman for the southern planter aristocracy and, more generally, for the agricultural interest—resisted the passage of this legislation, a sharp split occurred within the ranks of the Founding Fathers.

The first of Hamilton's proposals was to establish public credit on a firm basis by redeeming the depreciated Continental war securities from their present owners at their full face value. Madison opposed this plan, and suggested instead that the present holders—many of whom were speculators—should be paid the highest market value that their certificates had attained. This system, Madison argued, would insure both that the present holders of the securities would recoup their initial investment and that justice was done to the original purchaser who had supported the military effort during the dark days of the war (since it was he who would receive the difference between the face value and the highest market value). Despite its equitable features, Madison's proposal was defeated in the House of Representatives by a vote of 36 to 13. The complexity of the plan was one reason for its failure; a second was the fact that 29 of the 64 members of the House held securities themselves and thus stood to benefit personally from the adoption of Hamilton's scheme.

Madison and Hamilton clashed again (as the representatives of opposed economic interest groups) over the latter's suggestion that the national government assume all of the outstanding debts of the states. This plan, which was justified by the argument that most of these liabilities had been incurred during the national war for independence, was opposed by Virginia and by several other states—who had already retired most of their own debts by taxation and had no desire to help to pay the debts of others. Many southerners were also aware that northern speculators had bought up much of the remaining debts of Virginia, North Carolina, and South Carolina in the expectation that they might be redeemed at full value. Forty percent of the debt of $8 million still owed by these three states was held in 1790 by 47 nonresidents; and nearly one-quarter of this substantial sum was owed by only 13 individuals or firms, most of which were located in New York City. Here was a financial manipulation of monumental proportions: the southern states would pay a disproportionate amount of the war debt, and their citizens would be denied what they felt to be a fair share of the proceeds.

Only the transfer of the national capital from Philadelphia to a federal district on the Potomac River was sufficient to win southern support for assumption in the House of Representatives. This bitter financial dispute thoroughly alarmed the spokesmen for the planters who controlled the agricultural economy of the South. When Hamilton created the First Bank of the United States in yet another attempt to aid the mercantile and manufacturing interests, Madison and Jefferson moved into active opposition. By 1794, when Hamilton's excise tax of 25%

on whisky produced a revolt by western Pennsylvania farmers, who needed a light yet valuable product to transport to eastern markets, the cleavage within the Cabinet became irreconcilable.

The split within the Cabinet was soon duplicated in the country. Opposition to Hamilton's policies had been growing not only among the wealthy planters of the South, but also in sections of the northern farming population and in the lower ranks of urban society. These sentiments took on an active ideological tone as a result of the French Revolution. Democratic-Republican societies—modelled loosely on the Jacobin clubs —had appeared in all of the states by 1794 and had begun to condemn the "aristocratic" tendencies which they detected in Hamilton's economic policies and in his pro-British approach to foreign affairs.

The creation of the Republican party by Madison and Jefferson gave institutional expression to the divergent sectional, economic, and ideological interests that had suddenly become manifest within the nation. The struggle between the Republicans (the party of the established gentry of the South, young and socially ambitious capitalists in the Northeast, and the deprived farmers of the western regions) and the Federalists continued until Jefferson's victory in the election of 1800. Then, with the imposition of the embargo of 1807, which discriminated against the established northeastern merchant groups who constituted the backbone of the Federalist party, the conflict broke out again. Before the end of the war of 1812 restored a measure of stability to American political life, the Federalists of New England had spoken of secession if the interests of their class and section were not heeded—much as the Republican-inspired Virginia and Kentucky Resolutions of 1798 had threatened civil disobedience if the federal government enforced the repressive Alien and Sedition Acts.

As important as the specific matters at issue in each of these conflicts was the structural pattern of political activity they revealed. In each case one faction with definable sectional or economic interests had won control of the national government and had attempted to use its newly found political power to secure its ends. In the process it generated the formation of a counter-faction, composed of the representatives of those social groups whose interests its program threatened.

This dialectical process of factionalization had been an integral part of American provincial and state politics since the beginning of the eighteenth century, but it was only in the 1790's that these conflicts had found expression on the national level. And it was only now that they led to the creation of more or less permanent political organizations based on ideological principles. First Hamilton and then Madison and Jefferson attempted to create a national faction in the federal Congress to support their policies. Subsequently both Federalists and Republicans sought to broaden their political base on the state and local level in order to secure predominance in the national legislature. By 1796 there were "legislative caucuses" in each of the states. These caucuses, comprised of like-minded citizens, met to agree on a list of candidates for office and to offer potential nominees the institutional backing of a party organization.

Parties had appeared not because men wanted them—indeed, the Founding Fathers were almost unanimous in condemning their presence—but because there was no other way in which the people at large could be mobilized for effective political action. They were, in fact, the logical result of the doctrine of popular sovereignty enunciated during the American war for independence and of the ideological consciousness generated by the French Revolution. Political activity had not yet become the province of the masses (that would await the decline of deferential politics during the era of Jacksonian Democracy) but it was no longer the prerogative of the oligarchies of the late colonial period. Equally important, political issues had come to be formulated in abstract and ideological terms—not as mere conflicts between individuals and interests. Men were now elected to office because they stood for certain principles, because they propounded a certain vision of the American future.

With this transition to party organizations based on ideological doctrines, the structure of American politics had been extended to encompass the entire society within the framework of a single system of power and authority. Before 1774 there had been no purely political institutions in America (apart from the quasi-bureaucratic and politically neutral legal system) connecting one individual or one community to another. The political system had been basically cellular in nature, with each separate town or village or county running its own affairs and electing a local notable to represent its interests on the provincial level.

By the beginning of the nineteenth century, however, the autonomy of these individual cells of political life had been partially vitiated by the appearance, in each of them, of party struggles which reiterated in microcosm the conflicts being fought out on the state and national levels. The traditional cultural brokers—ministers, lawyers, merchants, planters, farmers of wealth and education—who had served as connecting links between the separate communities had now been joined by the politicians, men whose specific function it was to mediate disputes through the mechanism of the political process. This specialization of function was not yet complete, for most of the new political intermediaries were still "gentlemen of wealth and standing" and not professional politicians, but the direction of change was clear enough.

A new institutional system of power and prestige was being created. And it would eventually cut across both the traditional vertical hierarchies of family, church, and community and the new horizontal associations based on occupation, class, and ideology. A new principle of social unity had been found in the community of men declared free and equal and integrated into a sovereign nation. Here, in the conscious sense of membership in the national political order, was one of the principles of social and psychological identity that bound the increasingly diverse and stratified society of nineteenth-century America together.

The content of this new "nationalism" was as significant as its strength, and pointed directly at the inner essence of American society in 1815. In the decades following the Great Awakening the various Protestant denominations had gradually abandoned their narrow insistence on exclusive possession of the Word of God and had begun to view one another as equal members of a single family of belief, each with a separate personality, but all united by the common bonds of ancestry and interest. The result, in the end, was an American Protestant consensus, a general religious and missionary impulse which came to serve as one of the defining characteristics of the national identity during the nineteenth century.

To be an American was not simply to be a republican, but to be a Christian and a Protestant—if not as a church member then at least in conscience and morality. Church and state once again stood together as pillars of the social order, now joined by the business corporation and reinforced by the new ideals— equality of opportunity and material success—to which the majority of the white population now subscribed. Taken together, the trinity of republicanism, Protestantism, and capitalism formed an interlocking web of ideas which defined the limits of social action and established the ideological and institutional framework within which the next generations of Americans would struggle to work out their individual lives.

Notes to Chapter Six

1. Hannah Arendt, *On Revolution* (New York: Viking Press, 1963), pp. 61–62.
2. David Montgomery, "The Working Classes of the Pre-industrial American City, 1780–1830," *Labor History* 9 (1968): 13–14.

3. Edward P. Thompson, *The Making of the English Working Class* (New York: Pantheon Books, 1964), p. 446.
4. Montgomery, op. cit., p. 7.
5. Gary B. Nash, "The Philadelphia Bench and Bar, 1800–1860," *CSSH* 7 (1965): 204.
6. James Willard Hurst, *Law and Social Process in United States History*, 1960 (New York: DaCapo, 1971 reprint), p. 113.
7. Eric Robson, *The American Revolution in Its Political and Military Aspects, 1763–1783* (Hamden, Conn.: Shoe String Press, 1965), p. 163.

A FINAL PERSPECTIVE

When compared to the European society from which it sprang, the early history of the United States assumed a flat, almost one-dimensional character. It lacked richness, diversity, complexity—the peaks and contours of the cultural landscape formed by the slow accretion of institutions, artifacts, and traditions over long centuries. This disparity in social appearance stemmed from the origins of the American republic as a colonial venture, undertaken at a particular point in English history. Some classes, institutions, and ideas did not figure prominently in the migratory process, while many of those that did gradually withered in the new American environment. As in all colonial settlements, there was not a complete transplantation of the old society, but only a very partial and very selective re-creation of certain of its most prominent features.

Initially, this historical discontinuity served to reduce the diversity of the inherited civilization; to simplify its complex rules and customs; to exclude its variety and superfluity; and to narrow the range of wealth, status, and power. In seventeenth century America there was no traditional aristocracy, no subservient peasantry. This tendency toward uniformity and democracy—toward a society of republican simplicity and coherence—was later reinforced by certain aspects of the war for independence, which added a conscious element to the haphazard repudiation of the European past. Now even the intellectual residues and the cultural forms of the variegated society of the old world were swept away: In the American future there was to be no monarchy, no established church, no legally privileged class.

This process of erosion, of disintegration, was parallelled and, to a large degree, offset by the emergence of an indigenous American social and institutional structure. This was the result of an evolutionary process of economic and demographic change which imparted an increasing degree of complexity and structural differentiation to the relatively small, simple, and homogeneous settlements that had existed in 1700.

This indigenous development took two forms, each of which was a recognizable variation on the values and institutions present in the mother country. On the southern mainland (and on the islands of the West Indies), there was a bizarre and perverse re-creation of the English landed society of the sixteenth and seventeenth centuries, with a planter aristocracy presiding over a laboring force of black slaves. The importation of hundreds of thousands of Africans had enabled these white settlers to establish, in the new environment, a quasi-feudal society which no longer existed in England itself (but remained in backward areas of the British Isles, such as Ireland and the Scottish Highlands).

The social system developed by the northern American colonies looked more to the English future than to its past. The availability of land in America permitted (and encouraged) the emergence of a freeholding agricultural population on a much wider scale than was possible in the mother country. The character of agricultural production and trade discouraged the appearance of a landed aristocracy while facilitating the creation of a strong class of merchants and manufacturers. In the absence of traditional aristocratic values and institutions, the triumph of this capitalist class and system of production was complete. By the middle of the nineteenth century the ideology and the institutions that had come to prevail in the northern parts of the United States were the purest examples of capitalism in the entire world. Urban middle-class capitalism and a rural landed aristocracy—the two historical tendencies present in England at the time of the settlement of America in the seventeenth century—thus received their quintessential expression in the United States at the end of two centuries of social evolution in the new American environment.

The judgment of the performance of these two American social systems is at once a delicate and a complex task—if only because the individuals whose actual lives composed their histories viewed the reality about them from markedly different perspectives. Some of the inhabitants of English America in the years between 1700 and 1815 recorded their firm belief that their society constituted, in Thomas Paine's phrase, "the last best hope of mankind." But those who bequeathed such optimistic statements to posterity were, as a rule, neither red, nor black, nor poor, nor female. The true feelings of these historically mute groups have not found their way into the written record, although these men and women constituted, at any one time, a majority of all living Americans.

From the perspective of the present it is possible to say, with some confidence, that in their material circumstance and perhaps even in their spiritual condition, the white population of northern America was better off, as a group, than the inhabitants of most of the preindustrial agricultural societies that have existed during the long course of world history. But it is equally clear that the black population was the unwilling victim of a system of oppression as damaging and degrading as that found in any society which has called itself civilized. The legacy of this contradictory past extends even into the present, and the scales of historical justice have yet to record a final verdict. So that, in the end, there is no end at all.

ABBREVIATIONS

CSSH	*Comparative Studies in Society and History.*
EcHR	*Economic History Review*, Second Series.
EDCC	*Economic Development and Cultural Change.*
JAH	*Journal of American History.*
JEBH	*Journal of Economic and Business History.*
JEH	*Journal of Economic History.*
JSH	*Journal of Southern History.*
P&P	*Past and Present.*
PSQ	*Political Science Quarterly.*
Trends	*Trends in the American Economy in the Nineteenth Century*, National Bureau of Economic Research, vol. 24 in *Studies in Income and Wealth.* New York: Columbia University Press, 1966.
WMQ	*William and Mary Quarterly*, Third Series.

SUGGESTIONS FOR FURTHER READING

This bibliography is intended both as a guide to important secondary material for the interested student and as an acknowledgement of my intellectual debts to those scholars whose works I have used. The arrangement is by chapter (and by sections within each chapter). In many cases, a given article or book, although mentioned only once, has provided information and ideas used in a number of different contexts. A list of the abbreviations used for the most frequently cited publications is provided on p. 227. Paperbound editions are available for those titles followed by an asterisk.

Chapter One

In *A New England Town: The First Hundred Years, Dedham, Massachusetts, 1636–1736* (New York: Norton, 1970), Kenneth Lockridge postulates the existence of an American peasantry during the seventeenth century. My own interpretation is derived from the articles by George M. Foster, Eric Wolf, Clifford Geertz, and Lloyd Fallers in Jack Potter, et al., eds., *Peasant Society: A Reader* (Boston: Little, Brown, 1970); from Robert Redfield, *Peasant Society and Culture* (Chicago: University of Chicago Press, 1956); and from Conrad Arensberg and Solon T. Kimball, *Family and Community in Ireland*, 2nd. ed. (Cambridge: Harvard University Press, 1968). For a European comparison see Pierre Goubert, "The French Peasantry of the Seventeenth Century: A Regional Example," *P&P* 10 (1955).

Philip Greven's *Four Generations: Population, Land and Family in Colonial Andover, Massachusetts** (Ithaca: Cornell University Press, 1970) provides the most thorough demographic analysis of an American community yet undertaken. The statistical treatment by Jim Potter, "The Growth of Population in America, 1700–1860," in D. Glass and D. E. Eversley, eds., *Population in History: Essays in Historical Demography* (Chicago: Aldine, 1965) was helpful, as were the essays by Hajnal, Henry, McKeown and Brown, and Wrigley in the same volume. Important articles by Greven, Lockridge, and John Demos are conveniently collected in Stanley N. Katz, *Colonial*

America: Essays in Politics and Social Development (Boston: Little, Brown, 1971); while a helpful review of the literature is Greven, "Historical Demography and Colonial America," *WMQ* 24 (1967). The general European background is presented by Peter Laslett, *The World We Have Lost** (New York: Scribner, 1966) and by E. A. Wrigley, *Population and History** (New York: McGraw-Hill, 1969). Three important articles by Ernest Caufield, "Some Common Diseases of Colonial Children," in Colonial Society of Massachusetts *Publications* 35 (1942–1946); "A History of the Terrible Epidemic . . .," *Yale Jour. Biol. and Med.* 9 (1938–1939); and "The Pursuit of a Pestilence," in American Antiquarian Society, *Proceedings* 60 (1950), indicate the changing nature of the disease environment; as does Richard Shyrock, *Medicine and Society in America, 1660–1860** (New York: New York University Press, 1960); and John B. Blake, *Public Health in the Town of Boston, 1630–1822* (Cambridge: Harvard University Press, 1959).

Ester Boserup, *The Conditions of Agricultural Growth: The Economics of Agricultural Change under Population Pressure* (Chicago: Aldine, 1965) is a most stimulating treatment of an important problem, and provided the theoretical underpinnings for my discussion. Specific historical data was derived from John W. Oliver, *American Technology* (New York: Ronald, 1956); C. T. Smith, *The Historical Geography of Western Europe before 1800* (New York: Praeger, 1967); B. H. S. Van Bath, *The Agrarian History of Western Europe, A.D. 500–1850* (New York: St. Martin, 1963); and P. W. Bidwell and J. I. Falconer, *History of Agriculture in the Northern United States, 1620–1860* (East Orange, N.J.: Kelley, 1925, 1969). The general discussions in Edward Kirkland, *A History of American Economic Life*, 3rd ed. (New York: Appleton-Century-Crofts, 1951), and Paul Gates, *The Farmers' Age: Agriculture, 1815–1860* (New York: Harper & Row, Torch), were also of great assistance. See also Eric L. Jones, ed., *Agriculture and Economic Growth in England, 1650–1815** (New York: Barnes & Noble, 1967).

A general introduction to the study of the family is Dorothy R. Blitsten, *The World of the Family* (New York: Random House, 1963). Edmund S. Morgan, *The Puritan Family: Religion and Domestic Relations in Seventeenth Century New England** (Magnolia, Mass.: Peter Smith, n.d.), is a valuable account based largely on literary sources; John Demos, *A Little Commonwealth: Family Life in Plymouth Colony* (New York: Oxford University Press, 1971), attacks the same subject with the weapons of neo-Freudian psychology. A helpful treatment of the general controversy is David Rothman, "A Note on the Study of the Colonial Family," *WMQ* 23 (1966). A classic study of the changing pattern of family life in early modern Europe is Philippe Aries, *Centuries of Childhood: A Social History of Family Life** (New York: Knopf, 1962); while the eventual outcome is treated by Talcott Parsons, "Kinship Patterns of the Contemporary United States," in his *Essays in Sociological Theory,** rev. ed. (New York: Free Press, 1954). Four other articles of interest are: Joan Thirsk, "The Family," *P&P* 27 (1964); S. N. Greenfield,

"Industrialization and the Family," *Amer. Jour. Sociol.* 67 (1961–1962); H. J. Habakkuk, "Family Structure and Economic Change in Nineteenth Century Europe," *JEH* 15 (1955); and Kingsley Davis and Judith Blake, "Social Structure and Fertility: An Analytic Framework," *EDCC* 4 (1955).

Various models pertaining to the process of social change are to be found in two books by W. M. Williams, *A West Country Village: Ashworthy* (New York: Humanities Press, 1967); and *The Sociology of an English Village: Gosforth* (New York: Humanities Press, 1956). A more formal analysis is Everett E. Hagen, "Analytical Models in the Study of Social Systems," Appendix I in his *On the Theory of Social Change* (Homewood, Ill.: Dorsey Press, 1962). The cultural and historical relativity of the concept of time is considered by E. P. Thompson, "Time, Work Discipline, and Industrial Capitalism," *P&P* 38 (1967); and D. C. Coleman, "Labour in the English Economy of the Seventeenth Century," in Eleanora M. Carus-Wilson, ed., *Essays in Economic History** (New York: St. Martins, 1954–1962). For the idea of a multidimensional social space see Clifford Geertz, "Form and Variation in Balinese Village Structure," in Potter, *Peasant Society.* Other useful studies are Charles Grant, *Democracy in the Connecticut Frontier Town of Kent* (New York: Columbia University Press, 1961); K. Lockridge and Alan Krieder, "The Evolution of Massachusetts Town Government, 1640 to 1740," *WMQ* 23 (1966); Stanley Elkins and Eric McKitrick, "A Meaning for Turner's Frontier," *PSQ* 69 (1954); and Robert Walcott, "Husbandry in Colonial New England," *New England Quarterly* 9 (1936).

Chapter Two

In *Capitalism and Slavery** (New York: Russell and Russell, 1944) Eric Williams argues that the earnings from West Indian slave plantations and from the slave trade played a crucial role in the industrialization of England. A broader interpretation, which also stresses the importance of trans-Atlantic factors, is Eric Hobsbawm, *Industry and Empire: An Economic History of Britain since 1750* (New York: Pantheon, 1968). Other contributors to the debate are Ralph Davis, "English Foreign Trade, 1700–1774," *EcHR* 15 (1962); and D. E. C. Eversley, "The Home Market and Economic Growth in England, 1750–1780," in E. L. Jones and G. E. Mingay, eds., *Land, Labour, and Population in the Industrial Revolution* (New York: Barnes & Noble, 1967). A more theoretical statement is that of K. Berrill, "International Trade and the Rate of Economic Growth," *EcHR* 12 (1960). See also Phyllis Deane, *The First Industrial Revolution** (New York: Cambridge University Press, 1966); A. H. John, "Aspects of English Economic Growth in the First Half of the Eighteenth Century," in Carus-Wilson, *Essays;* M. L. Robertson, "Scottish Commerce and the American War for Independence," *EcHR* 9 (1956); and Robert Paul Thomas, "The Sugar Colonies of the Old Empire: Profit or Loss for Great Britain?" *EcHR* 21 (1968).

The actual workings of the sugar economy are described by Frank W. Pitman: *The Development of the British West Indies, 1700–1763** (Hamden, Conn.: Shoe String Press, 1967), and "The Settlement and Financing of the . . . Plantations . . ." in *Essays in Colonial History Presented to Charles McLean Andrews* (Freeport, N.Y.: Books for Libraries, 1931). Two articles by Richard B. Sheridan, "The Molasses Act and the Market Strategy of the British Sugar Planters," *JEH* 17 (1957), and "The Wealth of Jamaica in the Eighteenth Century," *EcHR* 18 (1965), are also important, as is Richard Pares, *Yankees and Creoles: The Trade between North America and the West Indies before the American Revolution* (Hamden, Conn.: Shoe String Press, 1968). The demography of the West Indies has been explored in brilliant fashion by Philip Curtin in *The Atlantic Slave Trade* (Madison: University of Wisconsin Press, 1969) and in "Epidemiology and the Slave Trade," *PSQ* 83 (1968). There is additional material in George W. Roberts, *The Population of Jamaica* (Cambridge: At the University Press, 1957), and in H. Orlando Patterson, *The Sociology of Slavery* (Cranbury, N.J.: Fairleigh Dickinson University Press, 1970).

Edmund Morgan, *Virginians at Home* (Charlottesville: University of Virginia Press, 1963), describes the relations between blacks and whites on the mainland; and there is some material on black family life in E. Franklin Frazier, *The Negro Family in the United States* (Chicago: University of Chicago Press, 1966, abridg. rev. ed.). Avery O. Craven's *Soil Exhaustion as a Factor in the Agricultural History of Virginia and Maryland, 1606–1860* (Magnolia, Mass.: Peter Smith, 1926) is still useful, but it must be supplemented by the more penetrating analysis of Eugene Genovese, *The Political Economy of Slavery** (New York: Pantheon, 1965). Two articles by Jacob M. Price, "The Rise of Glasgow in the Chesapeake Tobacco Trade, 1707–1775," *WMQ* 11 (1954), and "The Economic Growth of the Chesapeake and the European Market, 1697–1775," *JEH* 24 (1964), explore the growth of the international market for tobacco; while David Klingaman, "The Significance of Grain in the Development of the Tobacco Colonies," *JEH* 29 (1969), outlines the gradual transformation in the nature of the planter economy.

The distinction between growth and development is elaborated by Joseph Schumpeter, tr. by Opie Redvers, *The Theory of Economic Development** (Cambridge: Harvard University Press, 1934); the actual historical results are portrayed by Richard A. Easterlin, "Interregional Differences in Per Capita Income, Population, and Total Income, 1840–1950," in *Trends*. Anne Bezanson, et al., *Prices in Colonial Pennsylvania* (East Orange, N.J.: Kelley, 1935, 1971) contains a wealth of data. Two astute analyses based on price data are J. D. Gould, "Agricultural Fluctuations and the English Economy in the Eighteenth Century," *JEH* 22 (1962), and F. P. Braudel and F. Spooner, "Prices in Europe from 1450 to 1750," in *Cambridge Economic History of Europe*, vol. 4 (New York: Cambridge University Press, 1966). The work of Alice H. Jones will be of great use to historians; see her "Wealth Estimates for the American Middle Colonies,

1774," *EDCC* 18, no. 4, pt. II (1970). For the South see the fine article by Aubrey C. Land, "Economic Behavior in a Planting Society: The Eighteenth Century Chesapeake," *JSH* 33 (1967); Keach Johnson, "The Genesis of the Baltimore Ironworks," *JSH* 19 (1953); and the interpretations offered by Stuart Bruchey, *The Roots of American Economic Growth, 1607–1861** (New York: Harper & Row, 1965), and C. Vann Woodward, "The Southern Ethic in a Puritan World," *WMQ* 25 (1968). Three theoretical approaches to the study of the preindustrial city are E. A. Wrigley, "A Simple Model of London's Importance in Changing English Society and Economy, 1650–1750," *P&P* 37 (1967); Allen R. Pred, *The Spatial Dynamics of United States Urban and Industrial Growth, 1800–1914* (Cambridge: MIT Press, 1968); and James Lemon, "Urbanization and the Development of Eighteenth Century Southeastern Pennsylvania and Adjacent Delaware," *WMQ* 24 (1967). Gary Walton, "New Evidence on Colonial Commerce," *JEH* 28 (1968), describes the growth of the colonial shipping industry and Ralph Davis, "Earnings of Capital in the English Shipping Industry, 1670–1730," *JEH* 17 (1957), suggests its profitability. Some of the interactions between mercantile activity and urban development are analyzed by Bernard Bailyn, *The New England Merchants in the Seventeenth Century** (Cambridge: Harvard Univ. Press, 1955), and by J. A. Henretta, "Economic Development and Social Structure in Colonial Boston," *WMQ* 22 (1965).

Chapter Three

The general approach of this chapter owes a great deal to the insights developed in four works: Erik H. Erikson, *Childhood and Society,** rev. ed. (New York: Norton, 1968); David Potter, *People of Plenty: Economic Abundance and the American Character** (Chicago: University of Chicago Press, 1954); Lawrence Stone, "Social Mobility in England, 1500–1700," *P&P* 33 (1966); and Alex Inkeles and Daniel Levinson, "National Character: the Study of Modal Personality and Sociocultural Systems," in G. Lindzey and Elliot Aronson, eds., *The Handbook of Social Psychology,* vol. 4 (Reading, Mass.: Addison-Wesley, 1968).

Winthrop Jordan's *White Over Black: American Attitudes Toward the Negro, 1550–1812** (Chapel Hill: University of North Carolina Press, 1968) is a masterly analysis and the starting point for the study of colonial slavery. Stanley Elkins' seminal work, *Slavery: A Problem in American Institutional and Intellectual Life.** 2nd ed. (Chicago: University of Chicago Press, 1968) introduced the concept of a total institution. It should be supplemented by Erving Goffman, *Asylums; Essays on the Social Situation of Mental Patients and Other Inmates** (Chicago: Aldine, 1961), and the essays by Genovese and by Fredrickson and Lasch in *Civil War History* 13 (1967). Melville J. Herskovits, *The Myth of the Negro Past** (Magnolia, Mass.: Peter Smith, n.d.; Beacon Press, 1958), established the existence of African survivals in the new world. Additional material on this subject is presented by Philip Curtin, *Two Jamaicas: The Role of Ideas in a Tropical Colony, 1830–1865,* 1955 (New York: Greenwood Press, 1968), and H. Orlando Patterson, *The Sociology of Slavery* (Cranbury, N.J.: Fairleigh Dickinson University Press, 1970). Clyde Kluckhohn, *Mirror for Man: A Survey of Human Behavior and Social Attitudes** (New York: McGraw-Hill, 1949), discusses the use of language and the problems of environmental adaptation.

Bernard Bailyn's "Politics and Social Structure in Virginia," in James M. Smith, ed., *Seventeenth Century America* (Chapel Hill: University of North Carolina Press, 1959), provided the basic conceptual framework for the discussion of the southern aristocracy. Additional data and ideas were derived from Jackson T. Main, "The One Hundred," *WMQ* 11 (1954); Aubrey C. Land, "Economic Base and Social Structure: The Northern Chesapeake in the Eighteenth Century," *JEH* 25 (1965); and Jack Greene, "Foundations of Political Power in the Virginia House of Burgesses, 1720–1776," *WMQ* 16 (1959).

In *Poverty and Progress: Social Mobility in a Nineteenth Century City* (Cambridge: Harvard University Press, 1964) Stephan Thernstrom noted the existence of a proletarian population which floated between urban areas. Allen Kulikoff, "The Progress of Inequality in Revolutionary Boston," *WMQ* 28 (1971), finds a similar phenomenon in the previous century. On the servant population see John Demos, "Families in Colonial Bristol, Rhode Island . . . ," *WMQ* 25 (1968), and Lawrence W. Towner, " 'A Fondness for Freedom': Servant Protest in Puritan Society," *WMQ* 19 (1962). Edward Edelman, "Thomas Hancock, Colonial Merchant," *JEBH* 1 (1928), provides details of Hancock's life; while an impression of the mental and psychological world in which Hancock grew up may be derived from Michael Walzer, "Puritanism as a Revolutionary Ideology," *History and Theory* 3 (1961); Bernard Bailyn, "The Apologia of Robert Keayne," *WMQ* 7 (1950); Frederick B. Tolles, "Benjamin Franklin's Business Mentors: The Philadelphia Quaker Merchants," *WMQ* 4 (1947); and Elizabeth Bancroft Schlesinger, "Cotton Mather and His Children," *WMQ* 10 (1953). Two recent works of importance are Richard L. Bushman, *From Puritan to Yankee; Character and the Social Order in Connecticut, 1690–1765* (Cambridge: Harvard University Press, 1967), and John Demos, *A Little Commonwealth; Family Life in Plymouth Colony* (New York: Oxford University Press, 1971). The theoretical analysis by Robert Gutman and Dennis Wrong, "David Riesman's Typology of Character," in S. M. Lipset and Leo Lowenthal, eds., *Culture and Social Character* (New York: Free Press of Glencoe, 1966) clarified the nature of personality changes over time. M. W. Flinn, "Social Theory and the Industrial Revolution," in Tom Burns and S. B. Saul, eds., *Social Theory and Economic Change* (New York: Barnes & Noble, 1967) presented evidence as to the role played by religious sects in bringing about these alterations. See also Leonard Kasdan, "Family Structure, Migration, and the Entrepreneur," *CSSH* 7 (1965); and Geoffrey Gorer, *American People: A Study in National Character,** rev. ed. (New

York: Norton, 1964). Valuable quantitative data on the pattern of social and economic evolution is contained in Jackson T. Main, *The Social Structure of Revolutionary America* (Princeton: Princeton University Press, 1965), and James Lemon and Gary Nash, "The Distribution of Wealth in Eighteenth Century America . . . ," *Jour. Soc. Hist.* 2 (1968). A glimpse of the mental world of the lower-status groups is provided by James H. Hudson, "An Investigation of the Inarticulate: Philadelphia's White Oaks," *WMQ* 28 (1971).

Bernard Bailyn's *The Origins of American Politics** (New York: Knopf, 1968) delineates the contours of political life in the eighteenth century. My analysis of the changing structure of politics relies heavily on the work of Jack Greene; see his "The Role of the Lower Houses of Assembly in Eighteenth Century Politics," *JSH* 27 (1961), and "Changing Interpretations of Early American Politics," in Ray A. Billington, ed., *The Reinterpretation of Early American History** (San Marino, Calif.: Huntington Library, 1966). Four other articles of interest are Roger Champagne, "Family Politics Versus Constitutional Principles: The New York Assembly Elections of 1768 and 1769," *WMQ* 20 (1963); Mack E. Thompson, "The Ward-Hopkins Controversy and the American Revolution in Rhode Island: An Interpretation," *WMQ* 16 (1959); R. B. Sheridan, "The Rise of a Colonial Gentry: A Case Study of Antigua, 1730–1775," *EcHR* 13 (1961); and G. B. Warden, "The Proprietary Group in Pennsylvania, 1754–1764," *WMQ* 21 (1964).

My discussion of conflict and consensus models of social control relies heavily on the work of Michael G. Smith, *The Plural Society in the British West Indies* (Berkeley: University of California Press, 1965), and "Pre-Industrial Stratification Systems," in N. J. Smelser and S. M. Lipset, eds., *Social Structure and Mobility in Economic Development* (Chicago: Aldine, n.d.). The interpretation of New England society follows that of Michael Zuckerman, *Peaceable Kingdoms: Massachusetts Towns in the Eighteenth Century** (New York: Knopf, 1970), and "The Social Context of Democracy in Massachusetts," *WMQ* 25 (1968). Some of the effects of the cultural diversity of the middle colonies are explored by William H. Nelson, *The American Tory** (New York: Oxford University Press, 1962).

Chapter Four

In "Land, Population, and the Evolution of New England Society, 1630–1790," *P&P* 39 (1968), Kenneth Lockridge outlines some of the motive forces behind the movement to the West, but little has been written on the conflicts it engendered. Julian P. Boyd, "Connecticut's Experiment in Expansion: The Susquehannah Company, 1753–1803," *JEBH* 4 (1931), deals with the advance into Pennsylvania; while Brooke Hindle, "The March of the Paxton Boys," *WMQ* 3 (1946), traces the rise of Scotch-Irish agitation. Richard Maxwell Brown, *The*

South Carolina Regulators (Cambridge: Harvard University Press, 1963), provides an excellent survey of that movement and John Shy, *Toward Lexington: The Role of the British Army in the Coming of the American Revolution* (Princeton: Princeton University Press, 1965) deals at some length with the border wars along the New York frontier. See also, Julian P. Boyd, "The Sheriff in Colonial North Carolina," *N. C. Hist. Rev.* 5 (1928); E. R. R. Green, "The 'Strange Humors' That Drove the Scotch Irish to America, 1729," *WMQ* 12 (1955); and the general survey by Maldwyn A. Jones, *American Immigration** (Chicago: Chicago University Press, 1960).

My account of the Great Awakening relies heavily on the fine work of Richard L. Bushman, *From Puritan to Yankee.* A new and salutary theoretical approach to the evolution of colonial religion is presented by Robert G. Pope, "New England Versus the New England Mind: The Myth of Declension," *Jour. Soc. Hist.* 3 (1969–1970). The universal impact of the initial phase of the revival is argued by Edwin S. Gausted, "Society and the Great Awakening in New England," *WMQ* 11 (1954); while William G. McLoughlin, *Issac Backus and the American Pietistic Tradition** (Boston: Little, Brown, 1967), traces the subsequent divisions. The intellectual implications of the revival are outlined by Alice M. Baldwin, "Sowers of Sedition: The Political Theories of Some of the New Light Presbyterian Clergy of Virginia and North Carolina," *WMQ* 5 (1948). Arthur W. Calhoun, *A Social History of the American Family** (New York: Barnes & Noble, 1960), describes some of the changes taking place in family life; these should be compared with developments in England as analyzed by Levin L. Schucking, *The Puritan Family: A Social Study from the Literary Sources* (New York: Schocken Books, 1970). J. M. Bumsted, "Religion, Finance, and Democracy in Massachusetts; The Town of Norton as a Case Study," *JAH* 57 (1971) establishes the relationship between economic conditions and religious response.

Gordon S. Wood, "Rhetoric and Reality in the American Revolution," *WMQ* 23 (1966) takes issue with the recent "idealistic" interpretations of the movement for independence which neglect social and economic conditions. Another useful survey, written from the opposite point of view, is Page Smith, "David Ramsey and the Causes of the American Revolution," *WMQ* 17 (1960). My own analysis of the economic situation is based on an examination of the statistical data and the works of William S. Sacks, "Agricultural Conditions in the Northern Colonies Before the Revolution," *JEH* 13 (1953); Robert Paul Thomas, "A Quantitative Approach to the Study of the Effects of British Imperial Policy upon Colonial Welfare: Some Preliminary Findings," *JEH* 25 (1965); J. F. Shepard and G. M. Walton, "Estimates of Invisible Earnings in the Balance of Payments of the British North American Colonies, 1768–1772," *JEH* 29 (1969); and Richard B. Sheridan, "The British Credit Crisis of 1772 and the American Colonies," *JEH* 20 (1960). In tracing the relationship between the post-1755 period of prosperity (and recession) and social attitudes I have followed the interpretations of Edmund S. Morgan, "The Puritan

Ethic and the American Revolution," *WMQ* 24 (1967), and John Shy, *Toward Lexington*. Two works which question the direct economic causation of the Virginia decision for independence are Emory G. Evans, "Planter Indebtedness and the Coming of the Revolution in Virginia," *WMQ* 19 (1962), and Thad W. Tate, "The Coming of the Revolution in Virginia: Britain's Challenge to Virginia's Ruling Class, 1763–1776," *WMQ* 19 (1962).

The discussion of the disintegration of imperial authority is based on the conceptual model of Chalmers Johnson, *Revolutionary Change* (Boston: Little, Brown, 1966). A good general introduction to the problem is Charles M. Andrews, *The Colonial Background of the American Revolution,** rev. ed. (New Haven: Yale University Press, 1931), which also suggests the idea of British imperialism in the years following 1763. The effects of the new administrative measures are treated by Milton M. Klein, "Prelude to Revolution in New York: Jury Trials and Judicial Tenure," *WMQ* 17 (1960), and Thomas C. Barrow, *Trade and Empire: The British Customs Service in Colonial America: 1660–1775* (Cambridge: Harvard University Press, 1967). Richard Merritt has used a new methodological approach to trace the emergence of an American national feeling in "The Colonists Discover America: Attention Patterns in the Colonial Press, 1735–1775," *WMQ* 21 (1964). The most complete analysis of the events of 1765 is that of Edmund S. and Helen M. Morgan, *The Stamp Act Crisis: Prologue to Revolution** (Chapel Hill: University of North Carolina Press, 1953); but the articles by B. McAnear, "The Albany Stamp Act Riots," *WMQ* 4 (1947), and F. L. Engelman, "Cadwallader Colden and the New York Stamp Act Riots," *WMQ* 10 (1953), are also useful. The problem of the colonial mob is treated analytically by Gordon S. Wood, "A Note on Mobs in the American Revolution," *WMQ* 23 (1966), and at greater length by Pauline Maier, "Popular Uprisings and Civil Authority in Eighteenth Century America," *WMQ* 27 (1970). The best general treatment is by George F. Rudé, *The Crowd in History, 1730–1848** (New York: Wiley, 1964). Three attempts to determine the outlook and the motivations of lower-status groups are James Hudson, "An Investigation of the Inarticulate," *WMQ* 28 (1971); Jesse Lemisch, "Jack Tar in the Streets: Merchant Seamen in the Politics of Revolutionary America," *WMQ* 25 (1968); and Bernard Friedman, "The Shaping of the Radical Consciousness in Provincial New York," *JAH* 56 (1970). The intellectual frame of reference of the Patriot leaders is presented in brilliant fashion by Bernard Bailyn, *The Ideological Origins of the American Revolution* (Cambridge: Harvard University Press, 1967); while a very helpful discussion of the general problem of ideology is that of Peter Berger and Thomas Luckmann, *The Social Construction of Reality: A Treatise in the Sociology of Knowledge** (New York: Doubleday, 1966). Two other works which delineate the intellectual currents of the period are Richard Koebner, *Empire** (New York: Cambridge University Press, 1961) and John Bumsted and Charles Clark, "New England's Tom Paine: John Allen and the Spirit of Liberty," *WMQ* 21 (1964).

Chapter Five

Curtis Nettels, in *The Emergence of a National Economy, 1775–1815* (New York: Holt, Rinehart, & Winston, 1962), provides a good, detailed coverage of the entire period. Wartime difficulties are explored by Oscar and Mary Handlin, "Revolutionary Economic Policy in New England," *WMQ* 4 (1947); Richard B. Morris, "Labor and Mercantilism in the Revolutionary Era," in idem, ed., *The Era of the American Revolution** (Magnolia, Mass.: Peter Smith, n.d.); Sam Bass Warner, Jr., *The Private City: Philadelphia in Three Periods of Its Growth* (Philadelphia: University of Pennsylvania Press, 1968); Anne Bezanson, "Inflation and Controls, Pennsylvania, 1774–1779," *JEH* supp., 8 (1948); and Elizabeth Cometti, "Inflation in Revolutionary Maryland," *WMQ* 8 (1951). Gordon C. Bjork, "The Weaning of the American Economy: Independence, Market Changes, and Economic Development," *JEH* 24 (1964), presents an over-optimistic picture of American recovery. Postwar social conflicts are considered by J. T. Main, "Sections and Politics in Virginia, 1781–1787," *WMQ* 12 (1955); Philip A. Crowl, "Anti-Federalism in Maryland, 1787–1788," *WMQ* 4 (1947); and David Montgomery, "The Working Classes of the Pre-industrial American City, 1780–1830," *Labor History* 9 (1968). Two review articles by Richard Morris provide an incisive view of the literature: "Class Struggle and the American Revolution," *WMQ* 19 (1962) and "The Confederation Period and the American Historian," *WMQ* 13 (1956).

The best general treatment of the Loyalists is William H. Nelson, *The American Tory**; but see also Wallace Brown, *The King's Friends* (Providence, R.I.: Brown University Press, 1955); Paul H. Smith, "The American Loyalists: Notes on their Organization and Numerical Strength," *WMQ* 25 (1968); and Kenneth Scott, "Tory Associators of Portsmouth," *WMQ* 17 (1960). David H. Fisher, "The Myth of the Essex Junto," *WMQ* 21 (1964), and Richard D. Brown, "The Confiscation and Disposition of Loyalists' Estates in Suffolk County, Massachusetts," *WMQ* 21 (1964), trace the results of the Tory departure from Boston and also present important interpretations of the legal situation. Robert S. Lambert, "The Confiscation of Loyalist Property in Georgia, 1782–1786," *WMQ* 20 (1963), demonstrates the absence of wealth redistribution. The case for a shift in political power is argued by J. T. Main, "Government by the People: The American Revolution and the Democratization of the Legislatures," *WMQ* 23 (1966); but his view should be balanced by J. R. Pole, "Historians and the Problem of Early American Democracy," *Amer. Hist. Rev.* 67 (1962), who points up the continued "deference" in political life; and by Elisha P. Douglass, *Rebels and Democrats** (Chapel Hill: University of North Carolina Press, 1955). My discussion of women follows the fine theoretical analysis of Juliet Mitchell, "The Longest Revolution," *New Left Review* (1966). C. C. Ironside, *The Family in Colonial New York* (New York: Columbia University Press, 1942) was also helpful, as were the general treatments by Andrew Sinclair,

The Better Half: The Emancipation of the American Woman* (New York: Harper & Row, 1965), and Kate Millet, *Sexual Politics* (New York: Doubleday, 1970). The distinction between total and simple revolutions is derived from Chalmers Johnson, *Revolutionary Change* (Boston: Little, Brown, 1966). The transforming effects of the republican ideology are argued by Bernard Bailyn in his Introduction to *Pamphlets of the American Revolution, 1750–1776*, vol. I, ed. by Bernard Bailyn and J. N. Garrett (Cambridge: Harvard University Press, 1965); and by Cecelia M. Kenyon, "Republicanism and Radicalism in the American Revolution: An Old Fashioned Interpretation," *WMQ* 19 (1962). My own interpretation tends to follow the position taken by Thomas C. Barrow, "The American Revolution as a Colonial War for Independence," *WMQ* 25 (1968). Hannah Arendt, *On Revolution** (New York: Viking Press, 1963) offers an instructive comparison with the upheaval in France and points to the importance and the continuity of the colonial assemblies.

James Willard Hurst, *Law and Social Process in United States History* (New York: Da Capo, 1960, 1971) provides the point of departure for my discussion of legal matters. The evolution of land legislation is covered by B. W. Bond, Jr., *The Quit-Rent System in the American Colonies* (Magnolia, Mass.: Peter Smith, 1919); Roy M. Robbins, *Our Landed Heritage: The Public Domain, 1776–1936** (Magnolia, Mass.: Peter Smith, n.d.); and Clarence L. Ver Steeg, "The American Revolution Considered as an Economic Movement," *Huntington Lib. Quart.* 20 (1957). The coercion inherent in the market economy is elucidated by Karl DeSchweinitz, "Economic Growth, Coercion, and Freedom," *World Politics* 9 (1957); while its role in the process of economic development is clarified by Robert A. Lively, "The American System: A Review Article," *Business Hist. Rev.* 29 (1955). More detailed studies are Robert East, *Business Enterprise in the American Revolutionary Era*, 1938 (Magnolia, Mass.: Peter Smith, 1964); Oscar and Mary Handlin, *Commonwealth: A Study of the Role of Government in the American Economy, Massachusetts, 1774–1861* (Cambridge: Harvard University Press, 1969); Louis Hartz, *Economic Policy and Democratic Thought: Pennsylvania, 1776–1860** (Magnolia, Mass.: Peter Smith, n.d.); Milton S. Heath, *Constructive Liberalism: The Role of the State in Economic Development in Georgia to 1860* (Cambridge: Harvard University Press, 1954); and G. S. Callender, "The Early Transportation and Banking Enterprises of the States in Relation to the Growth of Corporations," *Quart. Jour. of Econ.* 17 (1902–1903). H. Jerome Cranmer, "Canal Investment, 1815-1860," in *Trends*, describes the heavy reliance on state funds; while F. W. Taussig, *The Tariff History of the United States*,* 8th ed. (East Orange, N.J.: Kelley, 1931), traces the rise of protectionist policies. The emergence of specialized financial institutions is traced by H. M. Larson, "S. and M. Allen—Lottery, Exchange, and Stock Brokerage," *JEBH* 3 (1931), and Arthur H. Cole, "The Evolution of the Foreign Exchange Market of the United States," *JEBH* 1 (1929). The crucial importance of the political state in the emergence of capitalism is argued by Eric J. Hobsbawm in *Labouring Men*,* ch. 2 (New York: Basic Books, 1965).

Chapter Six

An interesting discussion of the structural duration of social organizations is presented by Max Gluckman, "The Utility of the Equilibrium Model in the Study of Social Change," *Amer. Anthro.* 70 (1968). A useful classification of various models of social evolution is Richard P. Appelbaum, *Theories of Social Change** (Chicago: Markham, 1970).

Data on comparative standards of living was derived from Phyllis M. Deane, *The First Industrial Revolution** (New York: Cambridge University Press, 1966); A. H. Jones, "Wealth Estimates," *EDCC* 18 (1970); and Robert Gallman, "Gross National Product in the United States, 1834–1909," in National Bureau of Economic Research, *Studies in Income and Wealth*, vol. 30 (New York: Columbia University Press, 1966). Paul A. David, "The Growth of Real Product in the United States Before 1840: New Evidence, Controlled Conjectures," *JEH* 27 (1967), argues for an incremental process of early American economic development, taking issue with the important interpretations offered by George Rogers Taylor, "American Economic Growth Before 1840," *JEH* 24 (1964), and Douglass C. North, *The Economic Growth of the United States, 1790–1860** (Englewood Cliffs, N.J.: Prentice-Hall, 1961). Other works which bear on this question are Simon Kuznets, "National Income Estimates for the United States Prior to 1870," *JEH* 12 (1952), and Robert Gallman, "Commodity Output, 1839–1899," in *Trends*. The position of the urban laboring population during this period is explored by David Montgomery, "Working Classes," *Labor History* 9 (1968), and in two articles by Donald R. Adams, Jr., "Wage Rates in the Early National Period, Philadelphia, 1785–1830," *JEH* 28 (1968), and "Some Evidence on English and American Wage Rates, 1790–1830," *JEH* 30 (1970). See also H. Otuska, "The Market Structure of Rural Industry in the Early Stages of the Development of Modern Capitalism," in *Second International Conference of Economic History*, vol. 2 (Paris: 1965).

My analysis of American economic development and industrialization relies heavily on the work of Douglass C. North. In addition to *Economic Growth of the United States*, cited above, see his "The U.S. Balance of Payments, 1790–1860," in *Trends*; "International Capital Flows and the Development of the American West," *JEH* 16 (1956); and, most importantly (with Robert Paul Thomas), "A Theory of Economic Development," *JEH* 31 (1971). Other authors have developed somewhat similar types of explanations. The earliest, and the most technical, work is by James S. Duesenbury, "Some Aspects of the Theory of Economic Development," *Explor. Entrep. Hist.* 3 (1950), while later contributions include Douglas F. Dowd, "A Comparative Analysis of Economic Development in the American

West and South," *JEH* 16 (1956); George G. S. Murphy and Arnold Zellner, "Sequential Growth, the Labor–Safety–Valve Doctrine and the Development of American Unionism," *JEH* 19 (1959); and Alfred H. Conrad, "Income Growth and Structural Change," in Seymour E. Harris, ed., *American Economic History* (New York: McGraw-Hill, 1961). Much of the material in George Rogers Taylor, *The Transportation Revolution, 1815–1860* (New York: Harper & Row, Torch, 1968), bears on this question, as does the data presented by Stanley Lebergott, *Manpower in Economic Growth: the American Record Since 1800* (New York: McGraw-Hill, 1964), and by Jeffrey G. Williamson, *American Growth and the Balance of Payments, 1820–1913* (Chapel Hill: University of North Carolina Press, 1964). Finally, the general historical problem of economic growth and industrialization should be considered in the light of the hypothesis presented by Eric Hobsbawm, "The General Crisis of the European Economy in the Seventeenth Century," *P&P* 5 and 6 (1954).

Three works helped to crystallize my interpretation of the changing context of social action: Robert A. Nisbet, *The Quest for Community** (New York: Oxford University Press, 1953; paperbound as *Community and Power*); Elmon R. Service, "Kinship Terminology and Evolution," *Amer. Anthro.* 62 (1960); and Robert T. and Gallatin Anderson, "The Indirect Social Structure of European Village Communities," *Amer. Anthro.* 64 (1962). Material on the emergence of the legal profession is available in Aubrey C. Land, "Genesis of a Colonial Fortune: Daniel Dulany of Maryland," *WMQ* 7 (1950); Clement Eaton, "A Mirror of the Southern Colonial Lawyer . . . ," *WMQ* 8 (1951); Milton Klein, "The Rise of the New York Bar; The Legal Career of William Livingston," *WMQ* 15 (1958); Gary B. Nash, "The Philadelphia Bench and Bar, 1800–1860," *CSSH* 7 (1965); and John Murrin, "The Legal Transformation: The Bench and Bar of Eighteenth-Century Massachusetts," in Stanley N. Katz, *Colonial America* (Boston: Little, Brown, 1971). Richard Shyrock, *Medicine and Society in America 1660–1860** (New York: New York University Press, 1960), is a good study of the medical profession; while Daniel Calhoun, *Professional Lives in America: Structure and Aspiration, 1750–1850* (Cambridge: Harvard University Press, 1965), is an original analysis of both of these professions and of the ministry as well. L. B. Namier, "Nationality and Liberty," in his *Vanished Supremacies: Essays in European History, 1812–1918* (New York, Harper & Row, Torch) vividly portrays the emergence of a national identity and notes its relationship with republicanism. A brilliant theoretical treatment of the problem of "scale" is Godfrey and Monica Wilson, *The Analysis of Social Change,** ch. 2 (New York: Cambridge University Press, 1968). See also Robert Redfield, *The Little Community: Peasant Society and Culture** (Chicago: University of Chicago Press, 1955).

Seymour Martin Lipset, *The First New Nation: The United States in Historical and Comparative Perspective** (New York: Basic Books, 1963), is an imaginative analysis of the early political structure and culture of the American republic. The articles by Merrill Jensen, John Roche, and Stanley Elkins and Eric McKitrick in Leo Levy, ed., *The*

Forming of the Constitution (New York: Oxford University Press, 1970) describe the emergence of the nationalist faction and its political tactics. Lee Benson, *Turner and Beard: American Historical Writing Reconsidered** (New York: Free Press, 1960), cuts through much of the scholarly debate over the Constitution and provides a convenient conceptual approach to the problem. The suggestion that the struggle over the Constitution was the first of three major national political battles in the years before 1815 is made by Richard Hofstadter, *The Idea of a Party System* (Berkeley: University of California Press, 1969). The emergence of political parties is traced by Joseph Charles, *The Origins of the American Party System** (Magnolia, Mass.: Peter Smith, n.d.); William N. Chambers, *Political Parties in a New Nation: The American Experience, 1776–1809** (New York: Oxford University Press, 1963); and M. Ostrogorski, *Democracy and the Organization of Political Parties*, ed. by Seymour M. Lipset (Chicago: Quadrangle Books, 1964). See also the valuable article by Whitney K. Bates, "Northern Speculators and Southern State Debts, 1790," *WMQ* 19 (1962). Theoretical approaches to the study of political systems are Francis X. Sutton, "Representation and the Nature of Political Systems," *CSSH*, 2 (1959); Alex Weingrod, "Patrons, Patronage and Political Parties," *CSSH* 10 (1968); and S. E. Silverman, "The Community-Nation Mediator in Traditional Central Italy," in Potter et al. *Peasant Society* (Boston: Little, Brown, 1970). A fine description of the structure and practice of eighteenth century New England politics is Michael Zuckerman, *Peaceable Kingdoms** (New York: Knopf, 1970); while a broader analysis is Paul Goodman, "The First American Party System," in William N. Chambers and Walter D. Burnham, eds., *The American Party Systems: Stages of Political Development** (New York: Oxford University Press, 1967).

INDEX